# WAR
# MOVIES

Allied biplanes strafe German troops in one of the great silent war movies. *Wings*. It was the first film to win the coveted best picture Oscar (1928).

# WAR MOVIES

## Brock Garland

**Facts On File Publications**
New York, New York • Oxford, England

**WAR MOVIES**

**Library of Congress Cataloging-in-Publication Data**

Garland, Brock.
    War movies.

    Bibliography: p.
    Includes index.
    1. War films--History and criticism. I. Title.
PN1995.9.W3G37        1987              791.43′90′09358        87-9052

ISBN 0-8160-1206-7

Jacket Design: Richard Oriolo


Printed in the United States of America

10 9 8 7 6 5 4 3 2 1

# CONTENTS

To my family and the memory of those
who didn't make it back home

# INTRODUCTION

Imagine this scene:

A group of battle-scarred marines is holed up in the hospital of a small town. Yesterday they were a full platoon; today they're barely a squad. Hit by legions of unseen enemy, they've had to fall back and regroup. Their leader is Ripley—tough, no nonsense, but with a good heart. Their coward is Hudson—he's screaming that they're all going to die. Their traitor, they've all just found out, is Burke, who sold them out for profit. They are about to deal with him right then and there when the perimeter alarm sounds. The enemy has made it through the barricades. The marines raise their weapons, arm their grenades and prepare to blow whatever comes through the door to kingdom come.

Now, that's a fairly straightforward scene from the "lost patrol" subgenre of war movies. What makes it interesting is that the town the patrol is in is a mining outpost on an inhospitable, recently terraformed planet several light years from Earth; their rifles are thermopulse; Ripley is a woman, and the enemy about to come through the door is an insect-like species with metal teeth and sulfuric acid blood. The movie is *Aliens*, James Cameron's 1986 sequel to Ridley Scott's *Alien*.

Both Cameron's and Scott's films are about humans getting picked off, one by one, in the far reaches of deepest space by an exceptionally nasty creature(s); both fall into the science fiction category; both star Sigourney Weaver, and both made truckloads of money at the box office (although uncharacteristically, the sequel outgrossed the original), and yet they are very, very different. The original is basically a horror film, and the sequel is a war movie. It is a war movie because it is about futuristic marines that, sophisticated weaponry notwithstanding, are basically 20th-century grunts airlifted in to mop up a mess that just happens to be on another planet and not the sands of Iwo Jima.

A war movie, then, cannot be too strictly defined. At the risk of sounding too much like a legal brief, a movie is a war movie if it has, as its central action, subject, situation or background, people in armed, military conflict (although that conflict need not be

1

occurring at the time of the story, i.e., movies about vets, such as *The Best Years of Our Lives*). Most war movies are readily identifiable as such, falling directly into the heart of the genre—*Bataan*, *All Quiet on the Western Front*, *Apocalypse Now*. Others circle around the genre, scout at the fringes of what we generally think of as a war movie. Although *Gone with the Wind* is certainly a movie about the Civil War, we really see more fighting between Rhett and Scarlet than between North and South.

For that reason, this book may hold some surprises for you. The unmistakable war movies are here, but so are many of the interesting fringe dwellers, like *Alice's Restaurant* (because it was so critical of the Vietnam War), *Francis* (the first of the Donald O'Connor talking mule service comedies) and *Raiders of the Lost Ark* (Indiana Jones versus the Nazis could as easily have been Indiana Jones versus Thugee cult warriors).

These movies from the gray areas of the genre are important inclusions, for they add to the understanding of how films—good, bad and indifferent—have examined the many different aspects and ramifications of war. They show that while the war story is perhaps the oldest story known to man, there is always the possibility of some new angle, some new approach, perhaps even some new truth.

Because the genre is so broad, it can be difficult to get an overall mental picture of it. When one does take a bird's-eye view of the genre, the first thing one notices is that the history of the war movie parallels the history of war for the past century. Secondly, even more than in films as a whole, American movies have dominated this genre.

## HISTORY AND THE AMERICAN WAR MOVIE

The first bona fide war movie was *Tearing Down the Spanish Flag*, produced only hours after the United States declared war on Spain in April 1898. This first epic of combat ran no longer than 90 seconds and was filmed on a less-than-convincing studio set located in Manhattan's Morse Building. Nevertheless, the public, their pro-war sentiment fanned by the rabid press of the day, flocked to the penny arcades to see what then seemed an amazing, lifelike recreation of the actual event. So began a film genre.

Two years before America entered World War I, former President Theodore Roosevelt, a leader of the pro-war faction, persuaded the producer of *Tearing Down the Spanish Flag*, filmmaker J. Stuart Blackton, to produce a movie that would be a strong call to arms for America to join the French and British in their war against Germany. The result, *The Battle Cry of Peace*, depicted ruthless, slavering Huns intent on defiling American womanhood and bombing New York and Washington. Although decried by pacifists, the film did well at the box office and led to more of the same.

On April 6, 1917, America declared war against Germany. A week later, the Committee on Public Information was formed. Chaired by journalist George Creel, the "Creel Committee" sponsored books, lectures and, through its Division of Films, motion pictures to arouse the public against Germany.

Among the most notable of the films made after America entered the war were *The Kaiser-Beast of Berlin* (1918)—notable for its footage of President Wilson, General Pershing and King Albert of Belgium, included to make it look like a documentary; Cecil B. DeMille's *The Little American* (1918)—starring "America's Sweetheart," Mary Pickford; and *Shoulder Arms* (1918)—starring Charlie Chaplin.

Perhaps the best American war movie made during the actual conflict was D.W. Griffith's *Hearts of the World* (1919) (not entirely American as it was financed by the British War Office), filmed in France under actual combat conditions. In it, Erich Von Stroheim, a great director in his own right, first played his stereotyped cold-blooded German officer. The cast also included Lillian Gish, Robert Harron and fledgling actor Noel Coward.

Definitely the most novel of the wartime movies was *The Spirit of 76* (1917), which had Americans fighting alongside German allies against their old foe from revolutionary days, Great Britain. Producer Robert Goldstein was subsequently arrested and sentenced to 10 years in prison because the film was financed by hostile aliens.

After the war, interest in war movies waned. The first war picture to begin production after the Armistice, and the only one to turn a profit before 1925 was *The Four Horsemen of the Apocalypse* (1921), which is memorable both as the film that launched Metro as a major studio and as Rudolph Valentino's first star vehicle. In 1925, King Vidor's *The Big Parade* and Raoul Walsh's *What Price Glory* changed Hollywood's romanticized vision of warfare to something more realistic, showing the war through the eyes of ordinary enlisted men instead of glamourized officers.

Another great war film of the silent era was William Wellman's *Wings* (1928), which won the first Academy Award for Best Picture. Wellman, a veteran pilot himself, brought remarkable realism to his story of young pilots flying flimsy canvas and wood planes into the first battles to be fought in the air. With a cast including Richard Arlen, Buddy Rogers, Clara Bow (the "It" girl), and a bit part by a young Gary Cooper, the film was a tremendous hit. The breathtaking dogfights in *Wings* set the standard against which all succeeding aerial acrobatics are measured, and still seems as exciting as aerial battles staged in more recent films, such as *Top Gun* (1986). It's been said, in fact, that George Lucas closely modeled his space fighter battles in *Star Wars* (1977) after the dogfights in *Wings*. The public's love of air warfare movies continued into the coming of sound, with such efforts as Howard Hughes' *Hell's Angels* (1930) and Howard Hawks' *The Dawn Patrol* (1930).

The first great war film produced in sound was Lewis Milestone's *All Quiet on the Western Front* (1930), based on German writer Erich Maria Remarque's famous novel, which brought home the book's strong anti-war message by simply presenting, realistically, the true horror of the enterprise. Milestone won an Oscar as the Best Director and the film won the Best Picture Oscar.

By the late 1930s, when one didn't need a crystal ball to see trouble on the horizon in Europe and the Pacific, the film industry nevertheless shied away from controversial subjects such as the Spanish Civil War, the Japanese invasion of Manchuria, and Hitler's annexation of Czechoslovakia and Austria. Although *The Last Train from Madrid* (1937) used the Spanish Civil War as a backdrop, it never discussed the issues of the war or mentioned who was fighting it and why. Walter Wanger's *Blockade* (1938) at least took a stand for peace in Spain—on the side of the Loyalists, however, and so was banned in Germany and other fascist countries that supported Franco's rebels.

When war broke out in Europe in 1939, the first American movie to take a strong anti-Nazi stand was *Confessions of a Nazi Spy*. Other pro-British or anti-Nazi films of the day included *Four Sons* (1940), Chaplin's *The Great Dictator* (1940), and Alfred Hitchcock's *Foreign Correspondent* (1940), which depicted a German spy network operating in London. No less a critic than Reich Propaganda Minister Joseph Goebbels lauded Hitchcock's film as a "first class production, a criminological bang-up hit, which no doubt will make a certain impression upon the broad masses of the people in enemy countries."

The first movie to show an American in combat against the Germans was *A Yank in the RAF* (1941), made before America entered the war, in which a happy-go-lucky Tyrone Power survives two crash landings and Dunkirk with his British comrades. With President Franklin D. Roosevelt's restoration of the draft and, later, the Lend-Lease program to aid Britain's war effort, America was preparing for war—and so was Hollywood, with such movies-as-recruiting as *I Wanted Wings* (1941) and *Dive Bomber* (1941).

The popularity of these films, made during America's last year of peace, alarmed isolationists and America Firsters (an ultra-patriotic group led by flying hero Charles Lindbergh which believed the United States should stay out of the war as Hitler was sure to win) who complained to Congress, which called a hearing in September 1941 to investigate charges of warmongering by the studios. The hearings were heated, but the issue became moot on December 7 when the Japanese attacked Pearl Harbor.

Realizing the importance of film to propaganda efforts, President Roosevelt appointed Lowell Mellet to coordinate film production with the already existing, industry-backed Motion Picture Committee Cooperative for National Defense, less than two weeks after the bombing of Pearl Harbor. Using the MPCCND as a base, Mellet formed the War Activities Committee; its purpose was to channel government suggestions for film projects to the studios without having to take direct control of them. These suggestions would greatly shape the style and content of American war films for the duration. The Committee proposed six basic categories: the issues of war; the enemy; the allies; the production front; the home front; and, of course, the fighting men.

Hollywood was ready for war. While the normal gestation period for a film was nine months, *A Yank on the Burma Road* was out only seven weeks after Pearl Harbor. Notable films of that first war year were *Mrs. Miniver* (falling under the glorify-the-Allies category), which showed Greer Garson heading a heroically romanticized American idea of a British family as they survive under the German onslaught. Also released in 1942 was *Casablanca*, in which Humphrey Bogart's Rick personified all that was idealized as American—he's staunchly independent and reluctant to get involved, but ready to sacrifice everything for the cause when he does take a stand.

Few of the films of that first year of the war showed men in combat—people had to look at newsreels or read *Life* to see how the war was being fought—and one of the reasons was that America had yet to win a battle. Hollywood solved the problem, within the Government's guidelines, by glamourizing the Marines' brave stand against insurmountable odds during the war's first month, in *Wake Island*. The film helped create the "super-Marine" character, who could, given enough weaponry and ammunition, hold off an army indefinitely.

*Air Force* got around the problem of no-victories-yet by fabricating a complete fiction. It shows the crew of a B-17 bomber sinking Japanese ships, even though none had actually been sunk by land-based bombers at that point in the war. *Gung Ho* (1943) didn't need to falsify history as it depicted the real exploits of Marine Raiders carrying out a dangerous raid against Makin Island. As the war in the Pacific turned in favor of the United States, Hollywood came up with a succession of exciting action features, such as *Guadalcanal Diary* (1943) and *Thirty Seconds Over Tokyo* (1944), based on real operations.

Filmmakers also kept up with action on the European front with U-boat-versus-convoy movies (*Action in the North Atlantic* [1943]); movies that lauded a wartime ally, the Soviet Union (*North Star* [1943], written by Lillian Hellman); and a few that fell under the "know-your-enemy" propaganda category (*Hitler's Children* [1943] and *The Hitler Gang* [1944]).

As the war moved toward its conclusion, the moviemakers were left a few steps behind the string of victories, although several of the best of the genre were in production as the war ended—*Objective Burma* (1945), *The Story of G.I. Joe* (1945) and *They Were Expendable* (1945).

Not all American filmmakers stayed at home, however. Director George Stevens (*Giant, Shane, Gunga Din*) was stationed in Europe as head of a signal corps film unit. His color home movies contain some of the most riveting war footage ever shot. Director John Huston (*The Maltese Falcon, The Man Who Would Be King, Prizzi's Honor*) was also assigned to a photographic unit. His documentary of one part of the Italian campaign, *The Battle of San Pietro* (1945), was so shockingly realistic that it was not shown to the public until after the war was over. John Ford, another well-known director, became the highest ranking Hollywood film-maker, as a rear admiral. Ford's chronicle of the Pacific War is as exciting today as it was more than 40 years ago. Clark Gable and James Stewart were among those actors who flew combat missions in wartime service.

Unlike what happened just after World War I, there was no sudden disappearance of war movies after their peak in 1945. Nevertheless, fewer were made, and many of these explored a new category of the genre—the adjustment of veterans to civilian life. Perhaps the best of these, *The Best Years of Our Lives* (1946), swept the Academy Awards that year. The war continued to be fertile ground for Hollywood, and there was an upsurge of war movies in the late '40s. In June 1950, however, when North Korean forces invaded the newly created republic of South Korea, and the United Nations rushed to its defense, the filmmakers had a new setting.

The first Korean War movie was Sam Fuller's *The Steel Helmet* (1951), filmed in only 12 days in a Los Angeles park. Low budget and brief shooting schedule notwithstanding, it's still one of the best films to come out of that conflict, and, it's definitely superior to Ful-

ler's more elaborate Korean War movie, *Fixed Bayonets* (1952).

Other Korean War movies include *Retreat Hell!* (1952), which depicted the Marines' famous fighting retreat at the Chosin Reservoir; *Take the High Ground* (1954), the last film to be produced about the war while it was still being fought; and, perhaps the best of the bunch, *The Bridges at Toko-Ri* (1955), a thrilling air-action adventure. The most popular movie set during the Korean War, however, was Robert Altman's *M\*A\*S\*H*, released in 1969, 14 years after the end of the war. Despite its setting, it is in many ways more about the Vietnam war—and the vision of war that conflict generated—than about Korea. Amazingly, there hasn't been a Korean War film made since M\*A\*S\*H.

Although the next war available for American moviemakers was Vietnam, it was avoided for the most part in favor of a return to World War II subjects, with documentary-like recreations of military operations, such as *The Longest Day* (1963) and *A Bridge Too Far* (1977), and films that examined the ironies of war with a new sophistication, especially *Patton* (1970).

Vietnam had been the subject of a few films before America became mired in the political-military quagmire of that country. In 1948, Vietnam's civil war was the backdrop for an Alan Ladd melodrama, *Saigon*. Later, *China Gate* (1957) and *Jump Into Hell* (1955) depicted the failure of the French to maintain their control over Indochina. Audie Murphy was miscast as an American intelligence agent in a less-than-great version of Graham Greene's novel about the last days of French rule, *The Quiet American* (1958).

The only American film set in the war, and made while it was being fought, was John Wayne's *The Green Berets* (1966), which inappropriately superimposed a combination World War II/cowboys-and-Indians story onto Vietnam. Hollywood only began to make Vietnam movies several years after the war ended, and most of them were about the trials of returning vets, shown as lost souls (*Coming Home* [1977]), renegades (*First Blood* [1982]), or hair-trigger psychotics (*Taxi Driver* [1976]).

The first films after *The Green Berets* to show combat in Vietnam were *The Boys in Company C* (1978) and *Go Tell the Spartans* (1978). Two of the most notable Vietnam War films to date have been Michael Cimino's riveting look at the effect of war on three friends, *The Deer Hunter* (1978), and Francis Ford Coppola's trip into the heart of darkness, *Apocalypse Now* (1979).

In the early 1980s, fanned by the flames of a resurgent patriotism that accompanied Ronald Reagan to the Presidency, Hollywood came up with a new twist—while America may have lost the war in Vietnam, it could win on the movie screen. So came a string of movies exploiting the strong possibility that there are still American POWs alive in Indochina—Ted Kotcheff's *Uncommon Valor* (1983), the two Chuck Norris *Missing In Action* movies (released within six months of each other in 1984), and Sylvester Stallone's immensely popular star vehicle,

*Rambo: First Blood, Part II* (1985)—all of which had upbeat endings of American POWs being busted out of 'Nam. The trend in Vietnam war films seems to be shifting back to a more realistic appraisal of the conflict, with such features as Oliver Stone's award-winning *Platoon* (1986) and Stanley Kubrick's long-awaited treatment of the subject, *Full Metal Jacket* (1987).

While there has been a shortage of new conflicts to film in the 1980s, American filmmakers have proceeded undaunted. There have been a few films set in the war-torn countries of Central America. *Under Fire* (1983) and *Salvador* (1986) have probed the questions and ambiguities of the strife in that region. Clint Eastwood, in a search for a way to cap his movie about Marines being whipped into shape, *Heartbreak Ridge* (1986), wisely side-stepped the catastrophic Beirut involvement and picked instead the invasion of Grenada. Lacking a real aerial battle for their Navy fighter jocks to take part in, the makers of *Top Gun* (1986), in the tradition of many a Hollywood film, simply made up an encounter with Soviet pilots over the Indian Ocean.

## OTHER WARS

Of course, while war films have been around for only the past 90 years, there have been wars before that, and there will undoubtedly be more to come (unless there's one big preemptive one). These, too, have been the stuff of movies.

D.W. Griffith's monumental achievement, *Birth of a Nation*, was released at a time, 1915, when the last war Americans had been involved in on a large scale was our Civil War, 50 years before, and the next one was just a couple of years away. Griffith's film is an odd one. Today it's both difficult to believe and difficult not to admire.

He based his epic on the pro-Southern novel *The Clansman* by Rev. Thomas E. Dixon. The tainted motives of carpetbaggers, hostile, vengeful freed slaves and corrupt politicians were set against Southern chivalry, virginal heroines and the populist vigilantism of an idealized Ku Klux Klan. It's not as though the people of 1915 were ignorant of the implications of the story. Emotions ran high and the film was banned in several cities and states for fear of riots after several hundred protesting blacks stormed a theater where it was playing in Boston. Griffith, who considered himself a friend of blacks, was stunned by accusations of racism and attempted to defend himself in pamphlets and lectures.

But, if one can look beyond the suspect politics of the film, one sees that war movies have never been the same since, nor, in fact, have movies in general. *Birth of a Nation* set the standard for staging battles, depicting actual tactics and realistic weaponry. It also broke new ground financially as the first true blockbuster in the history of movies.

Other wars of history to be chronicled on film include everything from the American revolutionary war (Griffith's *America* [1924]) and the Napoleonic Wars (Kubrick's *Barry Lyndon* [1975] and the various versions of Tolstoy's *War and Peace),* to the slave revolt of Roman times (*Spartacus* [1960]) and British colonial wars (*Gunga Din* [1939]).

Instead of going back in time and picking an old war, there is also the option of looking ahead, with the freedom to make up a war. These are all, in different degrees, of the science fiction war subgenre. Among the best of these are William Cameron Menzies' *Things to Come* (1936), James Cameron's *Aliens* (1986) and, of course, George Lucas' epic rebels-versus-evil-empire *Star Wars* trilogy (which, although futuristic, was cleverly set in the past—"A long time ago, in a galaxy far, far away").

There is also a group of imagined-war movies which are set a little closer to Earth, although not necessarily any closer to reality. This group includes the wild, Communists-invade-America subgenre, so far composed of John Milius' rabidly hysterical *Red Dawn* (1984) and another Chuck Norris guns and karate outing, *Invasion U.S.A.* (1985).

There has also been a number of films about a war which, if perhaps unthinkable, is nonetheless imaginable—World War III. Some have used the outbreak of nuclear war as a setting for white-knuckle suspense (Sidney Lumet's *Fail Safe* [1964]), others have tackled it with the darkest of black humor to point up the inherent absurdity of the matter (Kubrick's *Dr. Strangelove* [1964]). Others have tried to examine what life would be like after such a holocaust (*On the Beach* [1959] and *Testament* [1983]).

## OTHER PERSPECTIVES

So far we have concentrated exclusively on American war films. However, while they do dominate the genre, other countries have made many excellent movies about war, and these provide different perspectives on the subject, giving us a larger, more complete picture of what war is all about.

After the United States, the other major producer of war films has been America's great ally in the two World Wars, Great Britain. During World War I, the British flocked to the music halls to see the latest documentary footage from the trenches. The competition to be the first with the pictures—alive today in the intense rivalry between local TV news teams—became fevered in World War I. One team managed to get *The Battle of the Somme* into the music halls within the then-amazing time of four weeks of the actual battle. Interestingly enough, the film was brutally honest about the horrors of that battle (more Britons died in the two days of the Somme than Americans in all the eight years of Vietnam), yet there was no adverse public reaction to

it. If anything, it bolstered pro-war sentiment.

The period after the first war was a hard time for British filmmaking, but during the second war they perfected the semi-documentary treatment of the genre. Two of the best of the many British war films made during the war were Carol Reed's exciting suspense thriller, *Night Train to Munich* (1940) and Noël Coward's compassionate men-at-sea saga, *In Which We Serve* (1942). Great Britain really didn't start making war movies again until after it had satisfied the post-war audience with more conventional subjects in the late 1940s and early 1950s.

In the 1950s there was an explosion of British war movies, including two very good ones, *The Cruel Sea* (1953) and *The Dam Busters* (1954), and one that ranks among the very best from any country: David Lean's *The Bridge on the River Kwai* (1957). To an extent, this surge of war movies in Britain reflected the low spirits of the country at that time. The war films harked back almost nostalgically to the war, to a time that, ironically, although racked by death and destruction, was nevertheless characterized by a sense of purpose and unity. In turn, film historians today look back fondly to British filmmaking in the 1950s when it was at its peak.

France has not produced a great many war films, but the few that it has are memorable. One of the great anti-war movies of all time is Abel Gance's *J'accuse* (1919), made before *Napoleon*, which included footage he shot on the front in 1918. Of equal stature is Jean

Renoir's seminal film, *Grand Illusion* (1937), about the absurdity of war (the "grand illusion" is that patriotism is something to die for), which won a special prize at Cannes in 1939, and was banned a year later when the Germans marched into Paris.

During World War II, French filmmakers were in an untenable position. Their country was occupied and Reich Propaganda Minister Goebbels tried to control the output of movies. With a few exceptions (most notably Carne's *Children of Paradise* [1943]), the films were quite awful, and because of the threat of censorship they generally stayed away from contemporary themes and dealt mostly in fantasy.

There have been several American films which have looked at World War II from the point of view of German soldiers (*The Eagle Has Landed* [1977] and Peckinpah's *Cross of Iron* [1977]), but before *Das Boot* (1981), there had never been a popular German film that portrayed German fighters in a sympathetic light. During World War II the Reich Film Chamber of Goebbels' Reich Ministry of Public Enlightenment and Propaganda was furiously active, churning out one documentary after another about the heroic fighting men (such as *Crew Dora* and *Fighter Squadron Lutzow*), but those were not seen outside of Germany. It wasn't until 1981 that the world saw how the Germans themselves felt about fighting the war. Political and emotional discussions aside, *Das Boot* is an exceptional war film. The film's greatest achievement is that it transcends good-guys-versus-bad-guys and shows how

brutal war is, regardless of which side one's on.

In the Soviet Union, every town has a statue to commemorate those brave men and women who died for Mother Russia in World War II. And yet, as important as that war is to the ethos of the country, we in the West rarely see war films from Russia. There have been historical epics, such as Sergei Eisenstein's *Alexander Nevsky* (1938) and *Battleship Potemkin* (1925), and Sergei Bondarchuk's version of Tolstoy's *War and Peace* (1966-67), but few contemporary war films. The best of those few are Mikhail Kalatozov's story about life on the homefront, *The Cranes Are Flying* (1957), which was named best picture at Cannes; Grigori Chikrai's *Ballad of a Soldier* (1960), which was the first Soviet film to win top prize at an American film festival (San Francisco); and Sergei Bondarchuk's *Destiny of a Man* (1959).

There have been several excellent war films from countries in the Eastern bloc. Czechoslovakian director Jiri Menzel's *Closely Watched Trains* (1966), set during the last years of Nazi occupation, was the second Czech film to win the best Foreign Picture Oscar (*The Shop on Main Street* won two years before). In Poland in the 1950s, Andrzej Wajda directed a masterful trilogy on the psychological effects of the war on a group of friends—*A Generation* (1954), *Kanal* (1956), and *Ashes and Diamonds* (1958).

There have been two war films of particular interest from Italy. One is Gillo Pontecorvo's *Battle of Algiers* (1965, co-produced with Algeria), a startling, neo-realist look at the French occupation of Algeria. Pontecorvo makes no pretense about objectivity, actively taking sides with the Marxist resistance. The other film of note is *Attack and Retreat* (1964), which Italy made in cooperation with the Soviet Union about the war on the Eastern front, which accurately portrays the suffering of the Italians who fought—and died—alongside the German Army in Russia.

In the late 1970s, when Australia made a sudden and dramatic impact on the film world, among the many good movies from "Down Under" were a few with war settings. Two of these explored the Australian view that they were treated as second-class by their British commanders when fighting Britain's wars, and that they were seen as expendable.

Bruce Beresford's *Breaker Morant* (1979) examined the hypocrisy of war in the true story of the courts-martial of three Australian men executed for murder, but really just sacrificed to achieve a political goal of the British during the Boer War. *Gallipoli* (1981) was director Peter Weir's look at the absurdity of one particular battle in World War I where wave upon wave of Australians were sent over the top as cannon fodder.

We don't have the space to look at the war films of every country in the world—there's probably one for every country, or at least one for every war—but it is important to acknowledge that they exist, and to seek them out. They may ask the same questions, but they give us different points of view—a young man in occupied Czechoslovakia, a captain of a U-boat, an Australian infantryman about to go over the top. If we're ever going to learn anything about war, these are things we have to know, and these war films can provide some of the answers.

## THE ART OF THE WAR FILM

Some war movies are undeniably better than others. Some have artistic merit, while others do not. If one were to broadly categorize the artistic aims of war films, three basic types would appear: propaganda, entertainment and those that aim for something more.

Propaganda has a rather negative connotation these days, but there's really nothing inherently wrong with it. As soon as you try to define it—Webster's calls it "any widespread promotion of particular ideas, doctrines, etc."—you realize that most any work of art has a hint of propaganda in it, that any artist with something to say is trying to convince others that what he says is true. But we usually use the word to describe anything that supports a view we don't subscribe to.

What is the difference between *A Yank in the RAF* and *All Quiet on the Western Front*, besides the fact that one is pro-war propaganda and the other is anti-war? Well, a key word in the Webster's definition above is "widespread." We might also add the words "concerted" and "coordinated." Propaganda works on a large scale, and is controlled, either consciously or unconsciously, by a movement, whether it be political, religious or whatever. Art, however, originates in an individual. Propaganda demonstrates, shows, illustrates—to prove a point. Art questions and examines.

The bulk of war films made just after a war breaks out and for the duration are generally propaganda. One question we have to ask of them: Does it work? Do these films, or any of the other thousands like them—including the scores put out by Goebbels' Reich Ministry—fulfill their purpose and change public opinion?

It doesn't seem likely. Most research on the effects of propaganda shows that, on its own, it won't change someone's mind on an issue, even if that person is undecided. However, it will reinforce existing shared opinions. This is what these war films were intended to do. In both World Wars, propaganda films were not supposed to change the minds of the minority in each country that might be against the war, but strengthen the resolve of those in favor of it.

This is why we don't see the same kind of war propaganda films anymore. In conflicts around the world, from Afghanistan to Nicaragua, the issues are more multi-faceted, less black and white. So, while propagandistic movies are still made, we see far fewer of them than in previous times. And when they are shown, they usually play only to the converted. Propaganda is now more likely to appear in TV movies made in support of such "war" efforts as the "war" on drugs or the "war" on child abuse, where the enemy is clear, defined and unambiguous.

Do propaganda movies have artistic merit? Absolutely. In fact, we can judge the artistic merit of war propaganda the way we judge the artistic merit of those short propaganda films we are inundated with daily—TV commercials. Here we look for good cinematography, fresh ideas, humor, excitement, an effect, and how well it sells its product. In the same way we can watch *Wake Island* and look at the performances, camera work, direction, humor, action and how well it sells its message: "marines are heroes." But the level of art is limited, encumbered by the propaganda's ulterior motive.

On a slightly higher level, we have the sheer, out-and-out entertainment war films. These often have some propaganda elements in them, but generally they are just about action and adventure. Most people didn't go to see *Rambo* because they wanted to hear a lecture on the plight of the Vietnam vet; they wanted to see Sylvester Stallone flex his oiled muscles and shoot explosive-tipped arrows. The makers of *Rambo* didn't make the movie primarily to change anyone's mind about the possibility of MIA-POWs in Southeast Asia; they made it to entertain.

The war films that reach for a little more than films like *Rambo* may also have an idea to sell and they may also be exciting. Most of all, though, they look deeper, for some truth about war, whatever that truth may be. Some try to take away the glamour of war and show the brutal reality of it (*All Quiet on the Western Front* and *Platoon*), or they revel in the excitement of war and try to find some way to the truth through that (witness the exhilarating helicopter attack scene in *Apocalypse Now*).

One thing these more ambitious war films have in common is a certain distance from the war—they are usually not made while "their" war is still being fought. There is usually a time lag of a few years, if not decades. *The Big Parade* and *All Quiet on the Western Front* were made seven and 12 years, respectively, after the end of World War I. Stanley Kubrick's brilliant *Paths of Glory*, also set during the Great War, was made four decades after it was over.

While the war is still on, or even shortly afterwards, emotions run too high to gain any objectivity. Propaganda needs no distance, indeed it thrives on closeness. But, ironically, if one wants to take a closer look at a war, one has to step farther away.

With films about the war in Vietnam, it wasn't until several years after the war was over that any sense could be made, on film, of that war. Even then, that first spurt of "good" Vietnam movies (*The Deer Hunter*, *Apocalypse Now*), which seemed to say all there was to say about the war, was followed a few years later by the "let's-win-it-this-time" revisionist spirit of *Uncommon Valor*, *Missing in Action* (parts I and II) and *Rambo*, which although all fine action movies are hardly landmark films. In fact, to many they are simply the patriotic propaganda movies that are usually made while a war is still on, a phase which the nature of the Vietnam war caused films to bypass, save for *The Green Berets*.

In 1979, Francis Ford Coppola claimed that his film, *Apocalypse Now*, was the "ultimate" Vietnam movie. Seven years later, Oliver Stone might make the same claim for his film, *Platoon*, based on his own experiences in the war. Who's right? Perhaps neither. Maybe some director, not even born yet, will make the "ultimate" Vietnam movie sometime in the next century; or perhaps critics of the future will look back and decide once and for all that the best Vietnam film really was *The Green Berets*.

Ultimately, in terms of artistic merit, a war film is no different than any other film. If it's obviously trying to sell something, then it can be good or not on that level, and if it's simply trying to entertain, then it can be somewhat better. But, if it's trying to find out something about war—what it's really like to be in one, what the effects are, what the issues are, why they occur in the first place—then it can be best of all.

There are many things, then, to consider about the war movie. We can look at a war movie historically, in terms of whatever war it's about; or we can look at it from the perspective of the country that produced it; or we can look at it in terms of its relative artistic merit. However one views the war film as a whole, it's clear that war has been an irresistible subject for filmmakers and audiences alike.

# THE MOVIES,
# A TO Z

For this guide, we have listed 450 movies alphabetically, A to Z, from classics to also-rans, with headings that include the release date, the studio that produced the film (or in the case of foreign movies, the country of origin), the director and the format (black & white or color). All titles that begin with "A," "An" or "The," or their foreign equivalents, are filed under the second word of the title, as in *The Bridge on the River Kwai*, which you will find under "B."

Our rating system is based on from one star to four stars, as follows:

    **** An exceptional war movie
    *** A good motion picture
    ** A fairly well-made film
    * A poor film

## ABOVE AND BEYOND (1952)

MGM   Melvin Frank and Norman Panama
  (Black & white)

With Robert Taylor, Eleanor Parker, Jim Backus, James Whitmore

This is the better of two Hollywood versions of the A-Bomb attack on Hiroshima. (The first is *The Beginning or the End*). Screen idol Robert Taylor does a credible job of portraying real-life B-29 bomber pilot Paul Tibbetts, who undergoes an emotional tug-of-war over the morality of his mission. He also has to placate his wife (Eleanor Parker), who is troubled and confused because of the secrecy surrounding the mission. The training sequences and the reenactments of the first nuclear strike are well done, and the scenes of Tibbetts' home life offer an insight into how military duties can disrupt the best of marriages.

Released at the peak of the Cold War, the film is an unabashed tribute to General Curtis LeMay (Jim Backus) and his controversial strategic bombing program. Today the story seems bombastic and overly pronuclear, but at the time it was considered a patriotic tribute. Politics aside, *Above and Beyond* is an exceptional movie and a worthwhile viewing experience.

Scriptwriter Beirne Lay, Jr., nominated for an Academy Award, was an ex-Air Force colonel who also wrote *I Wanted Wings* (1941), *Twelve O'Clock High* (1949) and *Strategic Air Command (1955)*.

***1/2

## ABOVE SUSPICION (1943)

MGM   Richard Thorpe (Black & white)

With Fred MacMurray, Joan Crawford, Conrad Veidt, Basil Rathbone, Reginald Owen, Felix Bressart

Not many Americans could afford a trip to prewar Europe, so few knew that MGM's wonderfully kitsch Austria existed only in Hollywood's imagination. Journeying there on a honeymoon, but really to trace a vanished scientist, Crawford and MacMurray—as the unlikeliest of Oxford dons—lock horns with former colleague Basil Rathbone, now a top Gestapo officer. The script, based on the novel by Helen MacInnes, has enough twists and turns to keep you interested, and the cast plays it for maximum propaganda value. When a Nazi soldier gives him a "Heil Hitler" salute, all-American MacMurray replies, "Nuts to you, dope!" Angered, the Nazi turns to another soldier and asks, *"Was heisst das* 'dope'?" Later, during a visit to a Salzburg museum, when Conrad Veidt shows the couple a medieval torture device for removing fingernails, Crawford comments, "A totalitarian manicure!"

This was the last film for professional Nazi Veidt, who died of a heart attack after filming was completed.

**1/2

## ABOVE US THE WAVES (1956)

Great Britain   Ralph Thomas (Black & white)

With John Mills, John Gregson, Donald Sinden, James Robertson Justice

The disabling of the German battleship *Tirpitz* in a Norwegian fjord by six midget British submarines was one of World War II's most heroic feats. As recalled here, the scenes in which the subs stalk the battleship provide a thrill

or two, but the stiff-upper-lip attitude of the upper-class officers is a bore. The movie sinks long before the action climax.
**

## ABROAD WITH TWO YANKS (1944)

United Artists   Alan Dwan (Black & white)
With Dennis O'Keefe, William Bendix, John Loder, Helen Walker

The comedy has dated somewhat, but there's still a laugh or two left in this wartime service farce. The punny title refers to two Yanks stationed in Australia who are after the same girl. William Bendix is hilarious as he turns "down under" inside out and wears a not very convincing drag outfit.
**

## ACROSS THE PACIFIC (1942)

Warner Bros.   John Huston (Black & white)
With Humphrey Bogart, Mary Astor, Sydney Greenstreet, Richard Loo

*The Maltese Falcon* was a big hit the year before, so Warners teamed director John Huston with three of his stars for this tame espionage thriller. Bogart, honing his cynical antihero image to a fine, hard edge, plays an officer cashiered from the prewar Army so he can spy on Japanese sympathizers. During a boat trip from Canada to Panama, fat man Sydney Greenstreet is on deck with plans to blow up the Canal, while Mary Astor provides a refreshingly sympathetic love interest. Chinese-Hawaiian passenger Richard Loo gave wartime audiences someone to boo. The bullet-riddled ending, according to Huston, was imposed by the studio.

After this one, Huston left Hollywood and accepted a commission in the Signal Corps as a lieutenant. For the next three years he produced a number of award-winning documentaries shot on various fronts, including *Report from the Aleutians* and *The Battle of San Pietro.*
***

## ACTION IN THE NORTH ATLANTIC (1943)

Warner Bros.   Lloyd Bacon (Black & white)
With Humphrey Bogart, Raymond Massey, Alan Hale, Julie Bishop, Ruth Gordon, Sam Levene, Dane Clark

Bogart, in uniform in Hollywood only, teams up with Raymond Massey as the mate and captain, respectively, of a flag-waving American Liberty ship carrying war materiel to Russia. In a clever ploy Massey rams a U-boat after luring it away from the convoy. He evades the other U-boats by various acts of bravery before reaching safety in Murmansk. Although not Bogart's best effort, the film draws the viewer into the excitement of the U-boat war and underscores the very real bravery of the merchant marine. The battle scenes, not always convincing, were shot in so-called miniature, in the sea off Santa Barbara. The model ships were so large, in fact, that only two of them fit on the 50-foot railroad flatcar that transported them to the California location.
**1/2

## THE AFRICAN QUEEN (1951)

Great Britain   John Huston (Color)
With Humphrey Bogart, Katharine Hepburn, Robert Morley, Peter Bull, Theodore Bikel

A perennial favorite, this grand comedy-adventure never fails to gain new fans whenever it is shown on television. Bogart and Hepburn are in peak form as the cinema's most winning odd couple: he, the grizzled skipper of a`broken-down riverboat; she, a missionary spinster who is his passenger. The time is 1915 and the place is East Africa, where World War I is being fought by the British and German colonists. True blue Britons, Bogey and Katie risk life and limb chugging upriver with a lovestruck plan to sink an immense German warship with a homemade torpedo.

Surprisingly, the production was going nowhere until director John Huston suggested that Hepburn play the role as if she were Eleanor Roosevelt, thus bringing a comic dimension to the story not in James Agee's script (or the novel by C. S. Forester). The special effects are first-rate, and few realize that *The African Queen* shooting over the rapids is a miniature model with tiny likenesses of the stars. The mosquito attack, viewers will be happy to learn, was accomplished by shooting through tea leaves stirred in a glass aquarium after specially bred insects refused to perform.
****

## AGAINST THE WIND (1948)

Great Britain    Charles Crichton (Black & white)
With Simone Signoret, Jack Warner, Robert Beatty, Gordon Jackson, James Robertson Justice

Another stiff-upper-lip wartime espionage caper, this one about Belgian saboteurs being trained in England and parachuted back home. The suspense, which derives from the fact that one of them is a traitor, doesn't pay off until a rip-roaring chase at the end. Notable primarily for Signoret's first appearance in an English-language film.
**

## AIR CADET (1951)

Universal-International    Joseph Pevney (Black & white)
With Stephen McNally, Gail Russell, Rock Hudson

Fledgling air aces train for jet combat in the Korean War. Rock Hudson, in training as an actor, is one of them. Don't stay up for this turkey.
*1/2

## AIR FORCE (1943)

Warner Bros.    Howard Hawks (Black & white)
With John Garfield, Gig Young, John Ridgely, Arthur Kennedy, Charles Drake, George Tobias, Harry Carey, James Brown, Ann Doran

Forget the heavy-handed propaganda and don't hesitate to get on board for this thrilling saga of the air war in the Pacific. Made at the request of and with the full cooperation of the U.S. Army Air Corps (at the time flapping its wings to gain equal status with the Army and Navy), the film follows the crew of a B-17 Flying Fortress, the *Mary Ann*, on a course that places them at every Pacific battle site during the war's first six months. From San Francisco they arrive in Pearl Harbor on December 7, 1941, just in time for the Japanese sneak attack. Next stop is the ravaged Clark Field in the Philippines, under constant assault from the invading Nipponese Army. After fighting it out with "Jap" infiltrators, they escape to Australia and the Battle of the Coral Sea.

No single crew could serve in so many missions, of course (and there is no record of a B-17 sinking a Japanese vessel during the war's first year). But because of the low-key performances and the accretion of accurate detail, the story rings true. Typically, the underlying theme of director Hawks is team effort, as exemplified by John Garfield as the rear-gunner Winocki, who learns the importance of loyalty and commitment the hard way. "Maybe the story is high-flown," wrote *New York Times* critic Bosley Crowther, "maybe it overdraws recorded fact a bit. We'd hate to think it couldn't happen—or didn't—because it certainly leaves you feeling awfully good."

A real B-17, later lost in combat, was used for exteriors, while a $40,000 full-scale interior doubled for the craft on a Hollywood sound stage. The convincing battle theaters were actually locations in the Tampa Bay, Florida, area.

***1/2

## THE ALAMO (1960)
United Artists   John Wayne (Color)
With John Wayne, Richard Widmark, Laurence Harvey, Richard Boone, Frankie Avalon, Patrick Wayne, Linda Cristal, Chill Wills, Joseph Calleia

John Wayne cemented his legend with this splashy historical epic, which he conceived, directed (with a little help from John Ford), produced and starred in. The historically accurate screenplay by James Edward Grant chronicles the heroic events of 1836, when Mexico's General Santa Anna swept north through Texas and wiped out 180 revolutionaries valiantly defending themselves in the ruins of a mission chapel called the Alamo. The tables were turned six weeks later, when other seekers of Texas independence rallied to the cry of "Remember the Alamo!" and defeated Santa Anna at San Jacinto.

The brilliantly staged siege is a long time coming, and at 192 minutes the film occasionally becomes boring, but Wayne is fascinating to watch as he steps confidently—and permanently—into the role of Mr. America. Cast as Davy Crockett, he makes a delayed star entrance dressed in buckskin, representing as no other actor could the confident, two-fisted, supremely capable and patriotic fantasy that became the ideal American male. "Some words give your heart a warm feeling," he later drawls. "'Republic' is one of those words."

***

## ALICE'S RESTAURANT (1969)
United Artists   Arthur Penn (Color)
With Arlo Guthrie, Pat Quinn, James Broderick, Michael McClanathan

Not a war movie per se but included here because of its strong pacifist attitude toward the Vietnam War. Immensely popular in its time, the film follows the adventures of musician Arlo Guthrie and his hippie friends, who hang out at a local restaurant owned by the wise and generous Alice. Guthrie, playing himself, goes to great lengths to avoid being drafted and turns his induction physical upside down with a great deal of anxiety and jocular wit. Hollywood was turning out these counterculture, "flower-power" comedies by the droves during the late 1960s, and most have dated badly. With the exception of some lyrical photography and a scene of Arlo visiting the deathbed of his famous father, Woody Guthrie, *Alice's Restaurant* is of interest primarily as nostalgia for the "Big Chill" generation.

**

## ALIENS (1986)

20th Century-Fox James Cameron (Color)
With Sigourney Weaver, Carrie Henn, Michael Biehn, Paul Reiser, Lance Henrikson, Bill Paxton, William Hope, Jeanette Goldstein, Al Matthews

While the first *Alien* (1979), directed by Ridley Scott, was a horror film set in space, this one is without question a war movie set in space. Sigourney Weaver reprises her role as Ripley, the sole survivor of the first encounter with the nasty seven-foot-tall insect with two sets of metal teeth and acid for blood. As the movie opens, Ripley is discovered adrift in her space ship, still in suspended animation after 57 years. At first no one believes her about the alien, but when the mining colony that has since been built on the planet where the aliens were first discovered ceases contact, a company of 23rd-century Marines are sent to find out what's going on. Ripley and mining company executive Burke (Paul Rieser) go along for the ride. Soon after the marines arrive, the aliens start decimating the no-longer cocky warriors. It's up to Ripley and Newt, a little girl and the only colony survivor, to show them how to survive. Director Cameron, who flexed his action muscles in his first film, *The Terminator* (1983), knows how to make the tension mount, continually raising the ante and cranking up the suspense, as this lost patrol of Marines (the basic mixed-bag, with a coward, a traitor, a tough Hispanic [in this case, a woman], a stoic leader, and a trusty android [it's the 23rd century after all]) struggles to stay alive. Weaver and the others are wonderful, the writing good, the special effects excellent and the final battle between Ripley and the Queen-Bee of the aliens astounding.

****

## ALL QUIET ON THE WESTERN FRONT (1930)

Universal Lewis Milestone (Black & white)
With Lew Ayres, Louis Wolheim, Slim Summerville, John Wray, Russell Gleason, Richard Griffith, Beryl Mercer

Obvious at times and distanced by a primitive sound track, this antiwar classic nevertheless packs an emotional wallop. Its source is Erich Maria Remarque's German novel of World War I—and of the best and most controversial books to come of the creative renaissance that occurred during the postwar Weimar Republic. Remarque, a former journalist who had been wounded on the Western Front, based the story on his own combat experiences and recalled the horror of war in minute detail. Audiences around the world shared his dismay at the war's tremendous waste of young lives, but many German veterans found the book—and the film — disgraceful. When Adolf Hitler, another wounded veteran, came to power, he promptly banned both.

The plot is simple and straightforward: A German high-school class enlists in the infantry at the urging of their bellicose teacher during the wave of patriotic fervor that swept through the country when war was declared in August 1914. Director Lewis Milestone focuses his camera on the debilitating effects of trench warfare, week-long artillery bombardments, and machine-gun sweeps during suicidal frontal assaults. He follows the young soldiers from the Great War's glorious beginnings to its dismal finish in 1918.

An early talkie, the film added a new urgency to the war movie by exploiting the clamorous noise of battle: the thunderous rolling barrages, the death rattle of slow-firing Maxim machine guns, the whine of ricocheting bullets, and the animal grunting of hand-to-hand combat. Moreover, Milestone's casting of inexperienced actors give the characters a sense of adolescent innocence and a believable quality of "What am I doing here?" anxiety. They

ALL QUIET ON THE WESTERN FRONT: The second sound production to win an Academy Award for best picture.

contrast well with Louis Wolheim's gruff but comic old soldier who condemns generals on both sides for their stupidity. Lew Ayres, in *the* role of his long career, gives one of the most poignant performances ever seen on the screen. The famous last scene (a soldier's hand reaches for a butterfly on Armistice Day) is sure to bring moisture to the most battle-scarred eyes.

Remarque's classic novel was filmed again to great effect as a 1979 TV movie starring Richard Thomas, Ernest Borgnine, Ian Holm and Patricia Neal. Delbert Mann directed.

****

ALL QUIET ON THE WESTERN FRONT: Lew Ayres (right) and Louis Wolheim (left) battle the enemy and the elements.

## ALL THE YOUNG MEN (1960)

Columbia   Hal Bartlett (Black & white)

With Alan Ladd, Sidney Poitier, Glenn Corbett, Ingemar Johansson, James Darren, Mort Sahl

Sidney Poitier was still paying his dues when he made this Korean War potboiler. Alan Ladd is his squad commander, a racist whose hatred of Poitier soon takes precedence over the battlefield. The script exploits rather than illuminates race relations, and no one survives its insincere moralizing. On hand are comedian Mort Sahl trading quips with everyone and former heavyweight boxing champion Ingemar Johansson trying to fake a movie career.

**

## ALL THROUGH THE NIGHT (1942)

Warner Bros.   Vincent Sherman (Black & white)

With Humphrey Bogart, Peter Lorre, Judith Anderson, Jane Darwell, Conrad Veidt, Kaaren Verne, Phil Silvers, Jackie Gleason

Bogart followed *The Maltese Falcon* with this nutty comedy/espionage drama, which works in spite of itself thanks to an accomplished supporting cast. Here, German fifth columnists are played for laughs, as Bogart enlists a gang of Brooklyn hoods to round up a den of Nazi spies operating in New York. Future TV stars Phil Silvers and Jackie Gleason contribute to the mayhem.

**

## AMBUSH BAY (1966)

United Artists   Ron Winston (Color)

With Hugh O'Brian, Mickey Rooney, James Mitchum, Harry Lauter, Tisa Chang

Good action scenes highlight this rout-ine Marine melodrama, shot on loca-tion in the Philippines. O'Brian and Rooney are effective as a pair of two-fisted leathernecks who lead their men on a dangerous mission on an island occupied by the Japanese. They know every dirty trick in the book and never fail to use them. Best scene: Mitchum (Robert's son) makes a Molotov cock-tail, only to find out he doesn't have a match to light it. Fortunately, there's a cigarette butt nearby, discarded by a Japanese sentry.

**1/2

## AN AMERICAN GUERRILLA IN THE PHILIPPINES (1950)
**Also titled** *I Shall Return*

20th Century-Fox   Fritz Lang (Color)

With Tyrone Power, Tom Ewell, Micheline Presle, Bob Pattern, Tommy Cook, Robert Barrat

Praising the deadly game of guerrilla warfare used to be a popular Hollywood pastime—until the Vietnam War changed all that and guerrillas went to work for the other side. Accordingly, Tyrone Power plays the guerrilla as a hero figure. A naval officer left behind in the Philippines after MacArthur's hasty departure, he joins a group of native freedom fighters to keep the war alive until the general can fulfill his famous vow "I shall return." There are some fascinating behind-the-scenes glimpses of guerrilla life, and the climactic battle between the Japanese and the in-surgents, surrounded in a church, is a good one. Unfortunately, the rest of the movie rarely reaches this level of excitement.

**1/2

## THE AMERICANIZATION OF EMILY (1964)

MGM   Arthur Hiller (Black & white)

With Julie Andrews, James Garner, Melvyn Douglas, James Coburn, Joyce Grenfell, Keenan Wynn

Slick, cynical and highly amusing, this black comedy never attained the popu-larity it richly deserves. James Garner is in fine form as a junior naval officer stationed in pre-D-Day England, where his main function is to supply the brass with girls and to provide Admiral Melvyn Douglas with every creature comfort. Julie Andrews, matching Garner line for line, plays his lover, an English war widow. She in-itially rebuffs him because she doesn't want to experience another loss, but relents when she learns he is a coward and has a cushy staff job. When the Navy decides that the first man to die on the Normandy beaches should be one of their own, Garner finds himself being shanghaied to fulfill the role.

The comedy, especially when Garner hits the beach and is chased by commanding officer James Coburn, wielding a Colt .45, is a bit farfetched, but the love story is mature, believable, and understandable. Paddy Chayefsky's incisive script is based on William Bradford Huie's novel.

***1/2

## AMIN: THE RISE AND FALL (1981)

Great Britain   Sharad Patel (Color)

With Joseph Olita, Geoffrey Keen, Denis Hills, Leonard Trolley

Like Hitler, Napoleon, Genghis Khan, and other demented rulers, Idi Amin continues to exert a strange fascination on the public. A physically immense and boastful Ugandan, Amin loved to issue outrageous statements to the press, which initially took him to be a harmless buffoon. It soon became apparent, however, that his Groucho Marxist rule wasn't funny at all: It is estimated that he put to death from 100,000 to 300,000 of his countrymen.

This exploitive movie biography compresses eight years of the dictator's reign into two hours and concentrates on Amin's atrocities. Lead Joseph Olita bears a remarkable resemblance to the obese Amin, and his historically accurate lines are as chilling as they are comic. ("See what happens to bad mommies," he tells his children, while displaying to them the dismembered body of his unfaithful wife.) Also in the cast is Denis Hills, a former Amin prisoner, playing himself. The Israeli rescue of hostages skyjacked by terrorists to Entebbe was previously dramatized in the theatrical film *Operation Thunderbolt* and the TV movies *Raid on Entebbe* and *Victory at Entebbe*.

Not for the squeamish.

**1/2

AMIN: THE RISE AND FALL: Kenyan actor Joseph Olita (center) plays the sadistic Ugandan dictator.

## ANCHORS AWEIGH (1945)

MGM   George Sidney (Color)

With Frank Sinatra, Gene Kelly, Kathryn Grayson, José Iturbi, Dean Stockwell, Pamela Britton

One of the best of the "service musicals"—a Hollywood hybrid devised during World War II—*Anchors Aweigh* stars young Frank Sinatra and Gene Kelly in tailor-made roles as two gobs on leave in Los Angeles. While there they fall in love, visit the Hollywood Bowl for a fantasy number and meet pianist José Iturbi. Sinatra, then the heartthrob of millions of bobby-soxers, is top-billed, but Kelly steals the show in a dance with Jerry, the put-upon mouse of the cartoon series *Tom and Jerry*. The number seamlessly combines live action with animation. Frank and Gene repeated their roles in the far superior musical *On the Town* (1949).

Other wartime service musicals include *Star-Spangled Rhythm* (1942), *This Is the Army* (1943) and *Thousands Cheer* (1943). The plots were kept far away from war fronts; their purpose was to entertain only.

**1/2

## ANGELS ONE FIVE (1952)

Great Britain   George More O'Ferrall (Black & white)

With Jack Hawkins, Andrew Osborn, Michael Denison, John Gregson, Cyril Raymond, Dulcie Gray

Good ensemble performances brighten this low-budget, behind-the-scenes look at the Battle of Britain. There are no bombastic American egos attempting to outdo each other here, only some upper-class RAF types cooperating to the full to save Britain from Nazi bombardment. A big success in England, the movie launched Jack Hawkins on a long career of military roles. Modest but crisply detailed, and more satisfying than England's later big-budget epic *Battle of Britain* (1969).

***

## THE ANGRY HILLS (1959)

MGM   Robert Aldrich (Black & white)

With Robert Mitchum, Stanley Baker, Gia Scala, Donald Wolfit, Theodore Bikel, Elisabeth Mueller

Characterization is conspicuously missing from this well-cast version of a litte-known novel by Leon Uris. Robert Mitchum stars as a war correspondent who takes up with Greek partisans circa 1940. Although director Robert Aldrich can't quite manage so many speaking parts, he delivers a goodly bit of creative violence and some impressive Greek scenery.

**1/2

## ANZIO (1968)

**Also titled** *The Battle for Anzio*

Italy/U.S.   Edward Dmytryk (Color)

With Robert Mitchum, Peter Falk, Arthur Kennedy, Anthony Steele, Robert Ryan, Patrick Magee, Earl Holliman

Not even its top-flight cast can save this Trojan horse from cinematic disaster. Produced by epic-*meister* Dino de Laurentiis, the film centers on a small group of U.S. Army Rangers who are part of the 1944 Allied landing in Italy. Along for the ride is war correspondent Robert Mitchum, who is given to antiwar moralizing. Inevitably, Mitchum, miscast, picks up a Thompson submachine gun to defend himself and kills a German sniper.

The film reconstructs the Anzio beachhead, where the Allies landed behind enemy lines to challenge the strong German defensive position, called the Gustav Line. However, General George Lucas, a cautious warrior, hesitated before deploying his more than 50,000 troops, and as a result they were caught in a German defensive action. The stalemate lasted from January, when the initial landings were made, to late May of the same year. When it focuses on the problems of high command, the film briefly comes to life; otherwise it's a confusion of cliché battle scenes.

*1/2

## APOCALYPSE NOW (1979)

United Artists   Francis Ford Coppola (Color)
With Marlon Brando, Martin Sheen, Robert Duvall, Frederic Forrest, Dennis Hopper, Sam Bottoms, Harrison Ford, Larry Fishburne, Albert Hall

Experiencing *Apocalypse Now* is something like stepping through Alice's mirror and, instead of discovering Wonderland, you find yourself deep in the hellish nightmare that was the Vietnam War. Based loosely on Joseph Conrad's *Heart of Darkness*, a turn-of-the-century novel about corruption in colonial Africa, the script (by Coppola and John Milius) follows the alcoholic Captain Willard on a dangerous boat trip deep into the

APOCALYPSE NOW: Marlon Brando (left) listens intently to producer-director Francis Ford Coppola on the set.

APOCALYPSE NOW: Captain Willard (Martin Sheen, center) warily enters Kurtz's compound as a burned-out photojournalist (Dennis Hopper, left) expounds on the mad colonel's mystical approach to war. Chef (Frederic Forrest, right) reluctantly escorts the Special Forces assassin.

Cambodian jungle. His assignment is to assassinate a renegade Green Beret colonel named Kurtz (Marlon Brando), who is fighting his own private war.

The journey upriver in a "brown water" Navy patrol boat might well be a trip on the River Styx. Willard (Martin Sheen), already convinced that everyone is crazy—perhaps even himself—is bombarded by vignettes of war at its worst and most senseless: A mad hatter of an airmobile commander (Robert Duvall) attacks a Vietcong vil-

lage with Wagner's "Ride of the Valkyries" blaring from his helicopter's loudspeakers (he also loves the smell of napalm in the morning); a USO show featuring *Playboy* Bunnies turns into a riot; a sampan filled with innocent civilians is destroyed by the nervous, drugged-out boat crew; a wild tiger attacks a mango-gathering expedition; and firefight after firefight culminate with the explosive Battle of Do Lung Bridge. Viewers may feel shortchanged by Coppola's inconclusive ending, but the final scenes can be construed as a reflection of America's inchoate understanding of the conflict.

"The most important thing I wanted to do in the making of the film," Coppola explained, "was to create a movie experience that would give its audience a sense of the horror, the madness, the sensuousness and the moral dilemma of the Vietnam War." At once philosophical, mystical and mesmerizingly violent, Coppola's war collage packs too many conflicting thoughts into 153 minutes to attain the status of a masterpiece, but it remains Hollywood's most powerful antiwar statement to date.

A financial and creative gamble, the film barely broke even at the box office, mostly because Coppola's perfectionism kept driving up the budget. (The rigors of shooting scenes over and over in the Philippine jungles reportedly brought about Sheen's heart attack, which delayed filming.) Final cost of the movie was a whopping $31 million. Unfortunately, when seen on the home screen, the stunning battle scenes lose some of their impact. ****

APOCALYPSE NOW: As assault helicopters fly overhead, U. S. troops celebrate a Catholic Mass.

## APPOINTMENT IN LONDON (1953)

Great Britain   Philip Leacock (Black & white)

With Dirk Bogarde, Ian Hunter, Bryan Forbes, Bill Kerr, Dinah Sheridan

Former documentary filmmaker Philip Leacock manages a certain verisimilitude in this day in the life of a Bomber Command squadron circa 1943. What's missing is an adequate budget and decent production values, an affliction common to British war movies of the period. Leacock, it might be noted, once made a top-secret documentary about the British contribution to the war for Churchill to show to Roosevelt at the Quebec Conference in 1943.

**

## ARISE MY LOVE (1940)

Paramount   Mitchell Leisen (Black & white)

With Ray Milland, Claudette Colbert, Walter Abel, George Zucco, Dennis O'Keefe

The well-oiled script by Charles Brackett and Billy Wilder keeps this star vehicle purring nicely, even if it doesn't complete the journey. Milland and Colbert play American reporters in Europe who fall in love during the Spanish Civil War and experience many of the headline-making events preceding World War II. Expatriate Wilder's subtle anti-isolationist warning is underscored by a replay of the sinking of the *Athenia*, a British steamer torpedoed without warning by U-boats in 1939 with 28 Americans aboard.

**1/2

## ARMORED ATTACK

**See** *North Star*

## ARMORED COMMAND (1961)

Allied Artists   Byron Haskin (Black & white)

With Howard Keel, Tina Louise, Earl Holliman, Burt Reynolds, Marty Ingels

The Nazis once sent a beautiful Mata Hari to infiltrate a U.S. Army outpost during the Battle of the Bulge . . . didn't they? Burt Reynolds doesn't believe it, and you won't, either. Smitten Howard Keel gets to expose Miss Louise, who has already exposed as much as the censor would allow.

*

## ATTACK! (1956)

United Artists   Robert Aldrich (Black & white)

With Jack Palance, Eddie Albert, Lee Marvin, Buddy Ebsen, Robert Strauss, Richard Jaeckel

War isn't heroic, in maverick director Robert Aldrich's eyes; rather, it's gloomy, savage and idiotic. *Attack!* drives home his point with the force of a sledgehammer. Jack Palance, at his smoldering best, is an infantry platoon leader whose men have been killed because of the ineptitude of company commander Eddie Albert. A sniveling coward, Albert is kept in command by his superior officer, who is afraid for his future political career if Albert's true nature is discovered. Trapped in an overrun Belgian village, Albert finally goes to pieces and gets what he deserves.

"I wanted to show the terribly corrupting influence that war can have on the most normal, average human beings," Aldrich explained, "and what terrible things it makes them capable of—things they wouldn't be capable of otherwise." Because the film depicted an American officer responsible for the deaths of his own men, it was denied the cooperation of the outraged Defense Department. Later, when *Attack!* was shown at the Venice Film Festival, the U.S. ambassador walked out.

***1/2

### ATTACK AND RETREAT (1964)

U.S.S.R./Italy   Guiseppe De Santis (Color)
With Peter Falk, Arthur Kennedy, Tatiana Samilova

Good battle scenes and evocative photography are the only reasons for watching this sprawling epic, coproduced by the Soviet Union and Italy, who were on opposite sides during World War II. Fighting alongside invading Germans on the Eastern Front, the Italian Army is quite accurately devastated by the Russians. The horror of war apparently is the film's subject, but it's the combat scenes that hold one's interest. The bloody battles are filmed with a sweeping grandeur in the Russian countryside and are graphic enough to occasionally send shivers up the spine.

**1/2

### ATTACK FORCE Z (1979)

Australia   Tim Burstall (Color)
With Mel Gibson, John Philip Law, Sam Neill, Chris Haywood, Koo Chuan-hsiung

Hollywood may not care, but Australia also fought in World War II. Keeping the record straight, the Aussies supply their own war movies, few of which ever get to the States. An exception is *Attack Force Z*, a tidy, authentic and brutal thriller about a small commando unit operating on the Japanese-controlled Malay Peninsula. Production credits are Hollywood-caliber, and military equipment and tactics are presented accurately (the men use silenced M-3 "grease guns" and handle them properly). The graphic violence may be too strong for some.

**1/2

### ATTACK ON THE IRON COAST (1968)

Great Britain   Paul Wendkos (Color)
With Lloyd Bridges, Andrew Keir, Susan Lloyd, Mark Eden

German defenders get a fair shake in this low-budget suspenser about a daring raid by Canadian commandos on an installation guarding the French coast. Any similarity between *The Guns of Navarone*—the blockbuster war movie of the early 1960s—is purely intentional. Worth a look if you've nothing better to do.

**1/2

### AT WAR WITH THE ARMY (1950)

Paramount   Hal Walker (Black & white)
With Dean Martin and Jerry Lewis, Polly Bergen, Mike Kellin

Somehow, Dean Martin and Jerry Lewis became major comedy stars as the result of this unfunny service farce, based on a Broadway play. Martin, crooning as always, plays a sergeant who drafts dumb Pfc. Lewis to bail him out of a romantic tight spot. You've got to *love* Martin and Lewis to like this one.

*

### AWAY ALL BOATS! (1956)

Universal-International   Joseph Pevney
   (Color)

With Jeff Chandler, George Nader, Lex Barker, Richard Boone, Julie Adams

Life aboard a Navy transport ship is well-delineated in this above-average World War II sea tale. But Jeff Chandler is unbelievably heroic as a hard-as-nails commanding officer pulling an inexperienced crew into shape for amphibious assaults on a Pacific island. Best scene: the crew scrambling to maintain damage control after the ship is hit by a kamikaze. The excellent color photography is augmented with little-seen U.S. Navy combat footage.
**1/2

## BABY BLUE MARINE (1976)
Columbia   John Hancock (Color)
With Jan-Michael Vincent, Glynnis O'Connor, Katherine Helmond, Richard Gere

Washed out of boot camp and put on a bus for home, ex-gyrene Jan-Michael Vincent wanders into a bar and strikes up a conversation with a gray-haired Marine Raider. He has obviously seen a bit of action because of the ribbons on his chest. Although he looks 40, the Marine tells Vincent he's only 20. (The makeup is so good that even a dedicated fan will have trouble recognizing Richard Gere in his film debut.) The burned-out vet doesn't want to go back to combat, so he gets Vincent drunk, knocks him out and exchanges his real Marine uniform for Vincent's faded blue utility fatigues.

Vincent finds the rest of the journey much easier as a war hero who has been to Guadalcanal. Along the way he meets the challenge of a "Who's the best?" duel from an Army paratrooper, takes part in a manhunt for Nisei Japanese who have escaped from an internment camp and becomes the recipient of a good woman's love. Although Vincent's encounters ring true and there's an authentic period feel, the film is poorly structured and never quite jells. The idea was better served as comedy in *Hail the Conquering Hero* (1944).
**1/2

## BACKGROUND TO DANGER (1943)
Warner Bros.   Raoul Walsh (Black & white)
With George Raft, Brenda Marshall, Sydney Greenstreet, Peter Lorre, Turhan Bey, Osa Massen

American spy George Raft is on the trail of Nazi agents in a back-lot version of Turkey. But except for banging a few heads together, Raft doesn't seem to care much. Fortunately, there's the great Raoul Walsh to keep the kettle boiling and Lorre and Greenstreet — Hollywood's weirdest duo — to supply the intrigue. Tune in early, or you'll miss a terrific automobile chase.
**1/2

## BACK TO BATAAN (1945)
RKO   Edward Dmytryk (Black & white)
With John Wayne, Anthony Quinn, Beulah Bondi, Richard Loo, Leonard Strong, Lawrence Tierney, Fely Franquelli, Philip Ahn, Paul Fix

With the Duke in command, can victory be far behind? Wayne, the quintessential strong man triumphing over nearly impossible odds, is Madden, an Army colonel ordered to mobilize guerrilla resistance just before the fall of Bataan. Saved from the infamous death march is Anthony Quinn, as the grandson of a noted Filipino patriot, who listens to Wayne's lessons in free-

BACK TO BATAAN: John Wayne leads the way as a guerrilla leader. Courtesy of RKO Pictures, Inc. Copyright © 1945 RKO Pictures, Inc. All Rights Reserved.

dom before the Japanese take it away. All the stock guns-and-glory ingredients are here in abundance—and they work extremely well: Freedom fighters rake the Nipponese with Thompson submachine guns that scarcely need reloading; a young Filipino martyr is killed but takes a truckload of Japanese soldiers with him; the guerrillas kill a Japanese officer who executed the school principal (who refused to lower the American flag). To cap it all off, there's a roll call of Bataan victims at the finale and a dozen extras who were POWs at Cabanatuan Prison outside Manila; the prison's liberation is repeated in the film.

A grand, entertaining flag-waver—if you can ignore the potent racist references to "slant-eyed devils."

\*\*\*

BACK TO BATAAN: John Wayne (left) and Anthony Quinn plan guerrilla operations. Courtesy of RKO Pictures, Inc. Copyright © 1945 RKO Pictures, Inc. All Rights Reserved.

## BALLAD OF A SOLDIER (1960)

U.S.S.R.   Grigori Chukrai (Black & white)
With Vladimir Ivashev, Sharma Prokhorenko, Antonina Maximova

There isn't a speck of propaganda in this moving Soviet-made romance, which was the first Russian movie to win top prize at an American film festival (San Francisco). It also got an award at Cannes in the same year. A deceptively simple film, it follows a young Russian soldier on four days' leave from the front to visit his mother. Traveling by train and by hitchhiking, he finally makes it home on foot with barely enough time left to get back to his unit. Along the way he meets a crippled soldier, a faithless wife, a buffoon of a sentry, and others whose lives have been changed by the war. He also falls in love with a girl, Shura, then returns, only to be killed at the front. Superbly acted and photographed, the film offers a rare look at Russian domestic life during World War II.
****

## BATAAN (1943)

MGM   Tay Garnett (Black & white)
With Robert Taylor, George Murphy, Thomas Mitchell, Lloyd Nolan, Robert Walker, Lee Bowman, Desi Arnaz, Barry Nelson, Philip Terry

Inspired performances, taut direction and great battle footage turned this harrowing drama into one of the big hits of 1943. Robert Taylor, shedding his glamour-boy image, plays a sergeant in command of a small unit left behind to delay the Japanese advance during the American retreat to the Bataan Peninsula. Facing certain death or mutilation are future California Senator George Murphy as a selfless pilot, Robert Walker as a naïve sailor caught up in the land war, and Lloyd Nolan as a cynical professional soldier who comes through when the going gets tough. At the finale, Taylor, the lone survivor, digs his own grave, inserts a makeshift cross, and delivers his own patriotic funeral oration while machine-gunning a horde of attacking Japanese.

An uncredited reprise of *The Lost Patrol*, the film is dated somewhat by its artificial back-lot look. but it's still one hell of a war movie.
***

BATAAN: Lloyd Nolan wields a heavy Thompson submachine gun with one hand as he disarms a Japanese soldier with the other in a staged studio publicity shot.

BATAAN: Robert Taylor confronts Lloyd Nolan. Personality conflicts among unit members occur often in war movies.

## BATTLE CIRCUS (1953)

MGM   Richard Brooks (Black & white)

With Humphrey Bogart, June Allyson, Keenan Wynn, Robert Keith, William Campbell

When is a B-movie quickie considered an A-line production? When it has big stars like Humphrey Bogart and June Allyson in the cast. The stars are paired as a doctor and nurse who fall in love while assigned to an Army mobile surgical hospital in Korea. There's a perfunctory war story lingering in the background, touching on new medvac techniques brought about by the helicopter, but the film barely scratches the surface of the conflict, then still being fought. Tough guy Bogart has won many a scrap in his day, but he's defeated here by Brooks's script and direction and an ill-starred match with the lachrymose Miss Allyson. The result is a mis-M\*A\*S\*H and a waste of Bogey's talent.

\*1/2

## BATTLE CRY (1954)

Warner Bros.   Raoul Walsh (Color)

With Van Heflin, Aldo Ray, Tab Hunter, Dorothy Malone, Mona Freeman, Anne Francis, James Whitmore, Raymond Massey, Nancy Olson

"Tell it to the Marines!" is the battle cry, but it's doubtful that real-life gyrenes would respond to the mawkish way it's uttered here. Replete with pulpy subplots, the film chronicles the rugged basic training of a group of World War II recruits who become involved with a number of beautiful women before being shipped off to combat in Saipan. The usually reliable Raoul Walsh operates at half speed here and fails to do justice to Leon Uris's exciting—and truthful—novel. The male cast is good, but Dorothy Malone comes off best, as a desperate over-30 woman attracted to a younger man (Tab Hunter). Walsh, cleverly sidestepping the Production Code's ban on nudity, has Malone disrobe completely while sitting sideways in a conveniently placed armchair.

\*\*1/2

## BATTLEGROUND (1949)

MGM   William Wellman (Black & white)

With Van Johnson, George Murphy, James Whitmore, John Hodiak, Richard Jaeckel, Ricardo Montalban, Denise Darcel

No one wanted another war movie in 1949, according to studio head Louis B. Mayer. But producer Dore Schary persisted (the project had already been vetoed by Howard Hughes at RKO), and the result was a smash hit, with Academy Awards for scriptwriter Robert Pirosh and cameraman Paul Vogel, as well as a nomination for a best picture oscar.

Under the no-nonsense direction of William Wellman, the film's matinee idol cast actually look like real GI's suffering through the Battle of the Bulge. Cut off from air support, supplies and reinforcements, the paratroopers fight off wave after wave of elite German assault troops and battle the elements during a lonely and snowy Christmas and New Year. They are eventually relieved by Patton's Third Army. Like Wellman's previous war movie *The Story of G.I. Joe* (1945), this one combines sentimentality with hard-hitting action and leavens both with flashes of insightful humor.

***1/2

## BATTLE HYMN (1957)

Universal-International   Douglas Sirk (Color)
With Rock Hudson, Dan Duryea, Anna Kashfi, Don Defore, Martha Hyer, Jock Mahoney, James Edwards

Real-life flying parson Colonel Dean Hess is given the Hollywood treatment in this glossy panegyric set in the Korean War. Rock Hudson strives for improbable perfection as the colonel who, troubled by innocent war casualties, rescues South Korean orphans. While Hess's good works are beyond reproach, director Sirk introduces a sly note of irony that seems to be mocking the idea of religion in the service of war (implicit in the title). He nevertheless gives his audience the usual reassuring pieties.

**

## BATTLE OF ALGIERS (1965)

Algeria/Italy   Gillo Pontecorvo (Black & white)
With Brahim Haggiag, Jean Martin, Yacel Haggiag, Rommaso Neri, Samia Kerbash

BATTLEGROUND: Van Johnson (second from left) starred in this reenactment of the 101st Airborne Division's brave stand at Bastogne during the Battle of the Bulge in World War II.

Made by an Italian director with private funding, this pro-Algerian reprise of Algeria's fight for independence was banned in France for years, and when it finally opened in Paris, anonymous callers threatened to bomb the movie theater. The film became nearly as controversial in the United States, where government officials and law enforcers regarded it as a movie textbook of urban guerrilla warfare, with techniques that could easily be adopted by radicals, war protesters and black-power groups.

Filmed in the Italian neorealist style pioneered in such films as *Open City* and *The Bicycle Thief*, it follows the struggle between the FLN (Algeria's freedom fighters) and the country's French rulers. Right-wing French vigilantes step in, and soon the bombings and shootings escalate until it's no longer safe to be in Algiers. Paratroopers arrive from France, and the insurgents are further provoked and brutally tortured. At times the French seem to be winning, but revolutionary fervor ultimately wins out, bringing a note of delirious triumph to an otherwise painful ordeal. Shot like a newsreel—with hand-held cameras loaded with high-contrast, high-grain film—*Battle for Algiers* is so overpowering in its true-to-life details that it's difficult to remember you are watching a fictional film.

***1/2

## BATTLE OF BRITAIN (1969)

Great Britain   Guy Hamilton (Color)
With Michael Caine, Trevor Howard, Michael Redgrave, Laurence Olivier, Christopher Plummer, Robert Shaw, Ralph Richardson, Kenneth More, Edward Fox, Harry Andrews, Ian McShane, Curt Jurgens, Susanna York

Too many characters and a muddled script spell defeat for this big-budget version of the Battle of Britain. One of World War II's most exciting stories has been made ponderously confusing, and it's difficult to follow the plot unless you are familiar with the battle. The heroic stand of the British and the brave Luftwaffe bombers are given equal attention, with the only villains being Hitler and Hermann Göring, head of the German Air Force. Every aspect of the 1940 battle is shown in detail: the importance of radar, aerial tactics, strategic blunders by the Germans, and bickering among the general staffs of both countries.

The film comes to life only in the dogfight sequences against azure blue skies. The Spitfires, Hurricanes, Heinkels, Messerschmitts and Stukas are all the real thing and stunning to see in action. Unfortunately, the oxygen masks worn by pilots of both sides make it impossible to figure out who the characters are. But these scenes will jolt you back to attention.
**1/2

## BATTLE OF THE BULGE (1965)

Warner Bros.   Ken Annakin (Color)
With Henry Fonda, Robert Shaw, Robert Tyan, Dana Andrews, Charles Bronson, George Montgomery, Telly Savalas, Ty Hardin, James MacArthur

History, plot and acting are beside the point in this clangorous battle spectacle based on a small incident in the Battle of the Bulge. A throwback to national clichés, it's the old Hollywood story with the same stock characters, dressed up with lots of vivid stage blood and shot in stereophonic Ultra-Panavision. The message, if there is one, seems to be that in war human life counts for nothing. Only Robert Shaw manages to build a character out of his steely SS *Gruppenführer*, whose crack Panzer division seriously threatens the Allies in the Ardennes Forest. Director Ken Annakin did better with the British scenes of *The Longest Day* (1962).

*1/2

## THE BATTLE OF THE CORAL SEA (1959)

Columbia   Paul Wendkos (Color)
With Cliff Robertson, Gia Scala

You were expecting the eponymous battle, maybe? (It was the first in which naval air fleets fought each other, and in which all the fighting was done by pilots. Neither the American nor the Japanese fleet saw each other.) Don't look here for the facts. This clinker is about submarine commander Cliff Robertson, with all the info needed to win the battle, escaping capture by the Japanese. Movies like this make you wonder whose side filmmakers are on.

*

## BEACHHEAD (1954)

United Artists   Stuart Heisler (Color)
With Tony Curtis, Frank Lovejoy, Mary Murphy

Curtis and Lovejoy help win the war as two Recon Marines scouting a Japanese minefield on one of the Solomon Islands. Slowing down the action is a routine love affair (considered steamy in its day) between Curtis and Murphy,

as the daughter of a lovable French planter. The combat scenes leave much to be desired.

**

## BEACH RED (1967)

United Artists   Cornel Wilde (Color)
With Cornel Wilde, Rip Torn, Burr de Benning, Jean Wallace

Made on a limited budget with a small cast, *Beach Red* represents a tour de force for star Cornel Wilde, who also produced and directed the film. The story, based on a novel by Peter Bowman, concerns a group of Marines who attempt to recapture a Japanese-held Pacific island in 1943. Its strong antiwar message is directed toward a later generation, however—protesters against the Vietnam War, then at its peak. Graphically realistic and brutally bloody, the film drives home its point memorably, and neither side of the battle comes off as morally superior. You probably won't see this one on commercial television with its more violent scenes intact.

***

## BEAU GESTE (1939)

Paramount   William Wellman (Black & white)
With Gary Cooper, Ray Milland, Brian Donlevy, Robert Preston, Susan Hayward, J. Carrol Naish, Broderick Crawford, Albert Dekker

There have been scores of Foreign Legion films since, but this one's the winner and still champion. Cooper, Milland and Preston are in their manly prime as three brothers who join the Legion and, except for Milland, die noble deaths in hand-to-hand combat with the Arabs. Brian Donlevy almost steals the show as a sadistic sergeant, and the opener, with corpses defending the desert fort, is a stunner.

P. C. Wren's novel about valor, brotherly love and self-sacrifice was previously filmed as a silent by Herbert Brenon in 1926. One of the most popular films of the 1920s, it starred Ronald Colman, Ralph Forbes and Neil Hamilton. The 1966 color version of the story was less successful.

For boys of all ages.

***

### BEAU GESTE (1966)

Universal   Douglas Heyes (Color)

With Dean Stockwell, Doug McClure, Telly Savalas, Leslie Nielsen, Leon Gordon

Mediocre in every way, this wide-screen Technicolor remake of the timeless classic (see the previous listing) dispenses with the story's dashing romance and concentrates on the desert battle between the Arabs and the Legionnaires. Gone is the crucial moral question of whether to rebel or not, replaced with a routine adventure. The cast lacks the charisma of the previous films' stars, and Savalas, as nasty as he can be, can't fill Brian Donlevy's boots.

*1/2

### THE BEDFORD INCIDENT (1965)

Great Britain   James B. Harris (Color)

With Richard Widmark, Sidney Poitier, Eric Portman, Martin Balsam, James MacArthur, Donald Sutherland

Richard Widmark is at his most obstinate as the skipper of a U.S. Navy destroyer who hunts down a Soviet submarine as if he were Captain Ahab. Interfering with Widmark's best-laid plans is magazine reporter Sidney Poitier, playing the first role in which his race isn't mentioned. Director Harris and company do all the right things and create a convincing milieu of suspicion and claustrophobia.

**1/2

THE BEDFORD INCIDENT: Richard Widmark (standing right) briefs the ship's officers.

## BEDKNOBS AND BROOMSTICKS (1971)

Walt Disney   Robert Stevenson (Color)
With Angela Lansbury, David Tomlinson, Sam Jaffe, Roddy McDowall

*Mary Poppins'* piquant charm is conspicuously missing from this colorful follow-up, which also mixes live action with animation. Angela Lansbury plays a good witch who joins forces with two British children circa 1940 and uses her magic to foil the German invasion. The special effects are up to Disney's high standards, however, and won Academy Awards for Alan Maley, Eustace Lycett and Danny Lee.
**1/2

## THE BEGINNING OR THE END (1947)

MGM   Norman Taurog (Black & white)
With Brian Donlevy, Robert Walker, Tom Drake, Hume Cronyn, Audrey Totter, Godfrey Tearle

"The long awaited dramatic story of the Atomic Bomb," read the poster advertising this "behind the scenes" look at the development of the deadliest weapon known to man. Actual events and historical personages—such as Godfrey Tearle as Franklin D. Roosevelt—mingle with fictional characters and situations, creating a believable if inaccurate scenario. "The bombing and the Alamogordo test are effectively staged," wrote critic James Agee, "though hardly adequate to one's information, let alone one's imagination of how to handle the information creatively."

Still worthy of note are the special-effects explosions, handled by A. Arnold Gillespie. Since no film of an atomic blast was yet available (the project was still classified by the U.S. government), Gillespie burst open a small dye-filled sac under water. As the dye floated to the surface, it formed a realistic mushroom-shaped cloud. Superimposed over shots of a real explosion, the footage was realistic enough to attract the attention of the U.S. Air Force, which used it later in instructional films.
**1/2

## A BELL FOR ADANO (1945)

20th Century-Fox   Henry King (Black & white)
With John Hodiak, William Bendix, Gene Tierney, Glenn Langan, Richard Conte, Marcel Dalio

A touching, often humorous tale of American occupation forces in Sicily during World War II. Hodiak, as the military administrator, and Bendix, as his sergeant, make friends with locals and see to it that Adano's beloved bell, destroyed in the war, is replaced. It's one of Hollywood's first movies to deal with the end-of-the-war effects of the American military presence in Europe. Based on the award-winning novel by John Hersey.
**1/2

## BERLIN EXPRESS (1948)

RKO   Jacques Tourneur (Black & white)
With Merle Oberon, Robert Ryan, Paul Lukas, Robert Coote, Roman Toporow, Charles Korvin

Postwar Berlin is the setting for this satisfying thriller, which takes place on a crack express train bound for Berlin. The heroes are a trio of American, British and Russian officers who, along with a few "good" Germans, want to reunify Germany. The villains are a group of underground Nazis who will stop at nothing to murder a German statesman, the only man capable of uniting the country. Standing together to maintain a European common cause is what the film is about, but it's most intriguing aspect is its vivid sense of place: Cinematographer Lucien Ballard shot many of the scenes in Frankfurt and Berlin, leaving us with a permanent reminder of the war's devastation.

**1/2

## THE BEST YEARS OF OUR LIVES (1946)

RKO   William Wyler (Black & white)

With Fredric March, Dana Andrews, Harold Russell, Myrna Loy, Teresa Wright, Virginia Mayo, Cathy O'Donnell, Hoagy Carmichael, Steve Cochran, Gladys George

With the war over, Hollywood turned to the problems faced by ex-servicemen returning home. Even before the war's

end, Americans were wondering if boom times brought about by the war effort would continue into the postwar age. There had been a severe but short-lived depression after the previous war, and economists wondered if there would be enough jobs for all the men coming back to claim their birthrights.

No other film reflects these concerns as well as *The Best Years of Our Lives*, a prestige film that spawned a score of sociopolitical melodramas during the late 1940s. The idea reportedly came to producer Samuel Goldwyn after reading an article in *Time* magazine on the problems of readjustment to civilian life. Goldwyn commissioned novelist MacKinley Kantor to write a screen treatment, which Kantor instead turned into the novel *Glory for Me*. Playwright Robert Sherwood adapted it to the screen. Hired to direct was William Wyler, who had served in the U.S.

THE BEST YEARS OF OUR LIVES: Dana Andrews (left) is assigned a plane ride home.

Army Air Force since directing *Mrs. Miniver* (1942) and was familiar with the problems of returning veterans.

Set in a fictional midwestern town, the story focuses on three ex-G.I.s who come home and try to resume their prewar lives. Ex-banker Fredric March readjusts to his job and loving wife after a few initial doubts, while former soda jerk Dana Andrews finds himself unappreciated by his faithless wife and boss, who stayed comfortably at home during the war. The most poignant moments come from remarkable newcomer Harold Russell — who actually lost both hands during the war — as an emotionally wounded vet who suspects his fiancee of wanting to marry him out of pity.

Seen today, the film is a bit smug and self-satisfied, and Wyler's direction lacks his usual visual flair. But the performances are outstanding, and there are many sequences that linger in the memory: Andrews poignantly sitting in the Plexiglas nose of a B-17 consigned to a bomber graveyard; the taxi ride to their homes as they share a comradely sense of anticipation; Russell smashing his steel hand through a garage window in angry frustration. The winner of Academy Awards for best picture in both the United States and Great Britain, it also won Oscars for best actor (March), best supporting actor (Russell, whose only film this was), screenplay (Sherwood), editing (Daniel Mandell), musical score (Hugo Friedhofer) and best director (Wyler). Russell won an additional, special Oscar for "bringing hope and courage to his fellow veterans."

The film was remade in 1975 as a soggy television movie by Daniel Petrie, with Tom Selleck, Dabney Coleman and James R. Miller.

****

## BETWEEN HEAVEN AND HELL (1956)

20th Century-Fox   Richard O. Fleischer (Color)
With Robert Wagner, Broderick Crawford, Terry Moore, Buddy Ebsen, Brad Dexter, Robert Keith, Mark Damon, Skip Homeier

Robert Wagner stars as a spoiled southern sergeant at war with the toughened military unit he finds himself with after Pearl Harbor. Nasty neurotic Broderick Crawford is on hand as a CO who teaches Wagner the score—the hard way. Somehow, between the antiwar and brotherhood messages, the group earns the title "Hell Fighters of the Pacific." The battle scenes are good if somewhat predictable.

**1/2

## THE BIG LIFT (1950)

20th Century-Fox   George Seaton (Black & white)
With Montgomery Clift, Paul Douglas, Cornell Borchers, Bruni Lobel, O. E. Hasse

World War III seemed to be waiting in the wings during the summer of 1948, when Soviet occupation forces suddenly cut off all surface links to Berlin from the West. Then, as it does now, Berlin lay well within the boundaries of Communist East Germany, even though the city had been divided into zones occupied by the victorious Allies: the United States, Great Britain, France, and Russia. The Soviets finally relented nearly a year later, after Allied pilots succeeded in doing the impossible—airlifting enough food, fuel and raw materials to keep alive more than 250,000 Berliners.

A tribute to the men who made this feat possible, *The Big Lift* casts Montgomery Clift and Paul Douglas as U.S. Air Force partners with opposing ideologies: Clift likes Germans, Douglas doesn't. The well-intentioned story seems dated now, and it leaves a lot out, but the as-it-happened scenes (filmed on the spot) are exciting and will show you what the experience was like.

**1/2

## THE BIG RED ONE (1980)

United Artists   Samuel Fuller (Color)
With Lee Marvin, Mark Hamill, Robert Carradine, Bobby DiCicco, Kelly Ward

One of the best of Sam Fuller's war movies (*The Steel Helmet, Fixed Bayonets, China Gate, Merrill's Marauders*), this mini-epic is almost autobiographical. The title refers to the 1st Infantry Division, and its large red No. 1 shoulder patch; Fuller served in the unit during World War II. Lee Marvin stars as a grizzled veteran sergeant of World War I who finds himself leading a squad of youngsters through Sicily, the Normandy invasion, France, Belgium and finally Czechoslovakia. Professionalism and common sense are on Fuller's mind, and both qualities help Marvin and his three buddies come out of the war in one piece.

Fuller expertly mixes humor with heavy combat scenes and tosses in comments on the irony of war. After a tense scene in which Mark Hamill drags a 50-foot length of piping loaded with TNT (a Bangalore Relay) across a minefield at Omaha Beach on D-Day, the sergeant delivers a French woman's baby in a German tank. Fresh out of rubber gloves, he covers his fingers with condoms.

"Making the picture was a labor of love," said Fuller. "If all you GI's out there like it, I'll know I was on the right track."

***

## BITTER VICTORY (1958)

U.S./France   Nicholas Ray (Color)
With Richard Burton, Curt Jurgens, Ruth Roman, Raymond Pellegrin, Anthony Bushell, Christopher Lee

Director Nick Ray, who usually does a fine job, forgot to put the zing in this one. Curt Jurgens, outshining top-billed Richard Burton, plays the latter's CO, who is troubled by an undeserved medal for a raid on Rommel and by Burton's affair with his wife (Ruth Roman). The conflicts create an intriguing situation that ultimately comes to naught. The film was shot in French and dubbed in English, which may explain its awkward remoteness.

**

## BLOCKADE (1938)

United Artists   William Dieterle (Black & white)
With Henry Fonda, Madeleine Carroll, Leo Carrillo, John Halliday, Vladimir Sokoloff, Reginald Denny

As with the Spanish Civil War itself, *Blockade* represents Hollywood's dress rehearsal for the mass carnage that was World War II. Set in a blockaded port in

Spain during the Civil War, the film is essentially an espionage drama. Henry Fonda, playing a progressive peasant farmer, becomes involved with lady of fortune Madeleine Carroll and is persuaded to take up arms and join the cause. A flop with the critics and at the box office, the film apparently confused audiences because it neglected to explain clearly Spain's political dilemma. Audiences were baffled as to which side Fonda was on, although his Loyalist bias is apparent to the knowing viewer. Moreover, American Communists supported *Blockade*, while the Roman Catholic press denounced it. It was banned in fascist Spain, Italy and Germany.

**1/2

## BLOOD ALLEY (1955)

Warner Bros.   William Wellman (Color)
With John Wayne, Lauren Bacall, Paul Fix, Joy Kim, Mike Mazurki, Anita Ekberg

John Wayne, an amateur boater in real life, expresses his hatred of communism in this tall tale of a two-fisted American sailor imprisoned in a Chinese jail. When friends help him escape, he loads the entire village aboard his boat for an occasionally thrilling dash through a Red Chinese blockade. Along for the ride are a miscast Lauren Bacall, as a missionary's daughter, and buxom Anita Ekberg, who has to be seen to be believed as a stowaway clad in a burlap bag.

*1/2

## BLOOD ON THE SUN (1945)

United Artists   Frank Lloyd (Black & white)
With James Cagney, Sylvia Sidney, Wallace Ford, Robert Armstrong, John Emery, Rosemary de Camp, Jack Halloran

Cagney plays Cagney in this fast-paced espionage thriller—and who could ask for more? Set in 1929 Japan, the story has Cagney outwitting the Japanese on their home turf by stealing the Tanaka Plan, the country's blueprint for its future conquest of the Far East and Pacific islands. Cagney's efforts to get the information to the American embassy make for a thrilling, if farfetched, hour and a half.

Made just before the end of the war, the film takes a revisionist attitude toward the Japanese, in that not all are depicted as villains. Those who are, however, raise their wartime standard to a new level of treachery. Among the Occidentals cast as Orientals is Jack Halloran as a hulking secret policeman. His hand-to-hand battle with Cagney is one of the latter's best fight sequences. Art directors A. Roland Fields and Wiard Ihnen won an Oscar for their evocative re-creation of prewar Japan.

***

## THE BLUE MAX (1966)

20th Century-Fox   John Guillermin (Color)
With George Peppard, James Mason, Ursula Andress, Jeremy Kemp, Anton Diffring, Michael Vogler

Here's your chance to see World War I from the cockpit of a German fighter. Air ace George Peppard is one of the pilots ruthlessly vying for 20 kills and the title medal. Of less interest is what's happening on the ground, where Peppard seduces Ursula Andress, the wife of his commanding officer, James Mason, who plots a fit-

ting revenge. With the exception of Mason, the performers woodenly attempt to portray Teutonic dispassion. The dogfights are spectacular, and are beautifully staged in real biplanes, some left over from the Great War and others constructed from old schematics especially for the film.
**

## BOMBERS B-52 (1957)

Warner Bros.   Gordon M. Douglas (Color)
With Natalie Wood, Efrem Zimbalist, Jr., Karl Malden, Marsha Hunt, Don Kelly

Unless you enjoy watching B-52s take off, fly around and land, this Cold War paean to the Strategic Air Command may disappoint you. The burden of the story has to do with a USAF sergeant (Malden) who's thinking about leaving the service to earn more money. His commanding officer (Zimbalist) is having a romance with his daughter, Natalie Wood. It all ends happily, as so many fifties movie romances do.
*

## THE BOYS IN COMPANY C (1978)

U.S./Hong Kong   Sidney J. Furie (Color)
With Stan Shaw, Craig Wasson, Andrew Stevens, Michael Lembeck, James Canning, James Whitmore, Jr.

Filmed in the Philippines, this Vietnam War movie was intended as pure entertainment, but it's impossible to look past its more serious, cynical portrait of the war. Slimly budgeted, the film looks as if, in the words of one critic, "it was shot on a three-day pass." The barracks-room laughs are abundant, however, although the scenes that provoke them have a familiar look. The setups are straight out of Hollywood's old boys-will-be-boys Marine Corps recruit movies.

The one important difference, however, is the film's overlay of pessimism. No sooner have the recruits arrived in Vietnam than they realize the war is a sham, that both sides are committing atrocities, and that there will be no true victors. "They're all gonna come back in body bags," wisecracks a heart-of-gold sergeant when replacements arrive. Well-filmed action scenes and scathing dialogue make it an entertaining if low-budgeted war movie.
**1/2

## BRASS TARGET (1978)

MGM   John Hough (Color)
With George Kennedy, John Cassavetes, Sophia Loren, Robert Vaughn, Max Von Sydow, Patrick McGoohan

Few military leaders have been as controversial as U.S. Army General George S. Patton. And controversy continues to stalk old "Blood and Guts" long after his death, the result of an automobile accident in December 1945. According to this account of his last days, Patton was assassinated by a group of American officers who stole German's gold reserves. Well photographed in scenic Switzerland and Germany, *Brass Target* is confusingly plotted and indifferently acted, but it exerts a certain fascination because of its conspiratorial combination of fact and fiction.

The film is based on *The Algonquin Project*, a taut novel by Frederick Nolan, who got the idea from a rumor he heard whispered at a diplomatic recep-

tion: "He was removed because he was an embarrassment." Nolan also noted that $25 million worth of gold had disappeared from the Reichsbank (the gold has never been recovered) and that Patton's death occurred during a national security gap—in the 18-month period between the dissolution of the OSS and the formation of the CIA.
*1/2

## BREAKER MORANT (1979)

Australia   Bruce Beresford (Color)
With Edward Woodward, Jack Thompson, John Waters, Charles Tingwell

The injustice of military justice is the subject of this much-honored Australian film, which won an Academy Award nomination for best screenplay. Edward Woodward is the square-jawed Morant (the title refers to his life as a horse-breaker in Australia), commander of a counterinsurgency unit of Australian colonials recruited to put down South African *Kommandos* during the Boer War. When several South African prisoners are killed, the deaths become an international incident, prompting the British Army to look for a scapegoat. The commander and two of his men are promptly court-martialed—even though they were acting under orders—and executed. Based on a true incident, *Breaker Morant* offers a thought-provoking look at how political pressures affect military decisions (as well as an uncomfortable reminder of American problems in Vietnam). It falls short of the outraged fury of Kubrick's *Paths of Glory*, however, and never quite reaches its intended heights.
***

## THE BRIDGE AT REMAGEN (1969)

United Artists   John Guillermin (Color)
With George Segal, Ben Gazzara, Robert Vaughn, Bradford Dillman, Peter Van Eyck, E. G. Marshall

By March 1945, the Allied juggernaut had pushed through Germany to the Rhine, against fierce but collapsing German defenses. Most of the Rhine's bridges had been destroyed, but to its amazement, the American First Army found an intact railway bridge at Remagen, 12 miles south of Bonn. The bridge had been wired with dynamite that had not been detonated. Delighted, Army engineers cut the wires, and the Allies crossed the Rhine dry-shod. (When Hitler found out, the major who had failed to blow up the bridge was shot.)

This fictionalized version of the incident concentrates on the internal squabbling among officers and men on both sides, which underlines the film's *Catch-22* message about the futility of war. Americans Segal, Gazzara and Dillman clench their teeth and snarl a lot, while Vaughn, as the inept German officer, seems to be in over his head. The combat scenes are well photographed, however, and the German scenes convincingly take place in dark cellars, tunnels and bomb shelters, conveying the Wehrmacht's claustrophobic back-against-the-wall position. Be warned: The battle scenes are earsplitting.
**1/2

## THE BRIDGE ON THE RIVER KWAI (1957)

Great Britain/U.S.   David Lean (Color)
With William Holden, Alec Guinness, Jack Hawkins,

Sessue Hayakawa, James Donald, Percy Herbert, Geoffrey Horne, André Morell

Conceived as one of the cinema's answers to television, then siphoning off viewers with its small black-and-white screens, this expensive prestige production was the template for scores of wide-screen Technicolor battle epics that followed. It also set a standard by which all others are measured and has since been enshrined in the war movie pantheon.

The setting is a Japanese prison camp near the Kwai River in Burma, where a brutal tug-of-war is taking place between the harsh commandant of the camp (Sessue Hayakawa) and Colonel Nicholson (Alec Guinness), the equally obstinate leader of the British POWs. After withstanding torture to make his point that, under the Geneva Convention, officers do not undertake physical labor, Nicholson makes an abrupt about-face: He agrees

THE BRIDGE ON THE RIVER KWAI: Alec Guinness (left) looks on in amazement as William Holden removes a sentry before sabotaging the bridge. Guinness won a best actor Oscar for his performance.

THE BRIDGE ON THE RIVER KWAI: William Holden (left) takes a break with a beautiful guide before continuing on a commando raid.

to help the Japanese to build a bridge, losing sight of the fact that this bridge, which he insists must be "a proper bridge," will further Japan's war effort. A proud martinet, Nicholson rationalizes that work will maintain the morale of his men, who then will be given proper rations and medical care. If he can pull it off, his men—and Britain itself—will achieve a victory in their defeat.

When the bridge is nearly finished, a commando unit led by a British major (Jack Hawkins) and a cynical American escapee (William Holden, playing a variation on his Oscar-winning role in *Stalag 17*) converges on the camp. At the spectacular climax, the commandos wire the bridge with dynamite as a

Japanese train prepares to cross it. Nicholson spots the commandos and tries to stop them, but at that moment a bullet rips through his body and he falls on the plunger that sets off the explosives. The ambiguous ending has been criticized by some, but according to Guinness, "the fall is fifty-fifty accidental, and as the character dies he is meant to be regretting his actions."

The film is adapted from Pierre Boulle's novel, which is itself loosely based on the building of the Burma Railway by British POWs during World War II. Almost beyond criticism as a movie, *The Bridge on the River Kwai* reshuffles the facts quite a bit. Since the countryside around the real River Kwai was flat and monotonous, the picture was shot in picturesque Ceylon. That the Japanese were incompetent engineers is an exaggeration, and Nicholson bears little resemblance to a real Colonel Toosey, who fought for the rights of British POWs in a camp in Burma. The destruction of the bridge was pure invention. (In fact, a real bridge and a real train were destroyed for the movie—at a cost of $250,000.)

The Motion Picture Academy lavished seven Oscars on the film, including best picture, best director (David Lean, making his first war film since codirecting 1942's *In Which We Serve*), best actor (Guinness), best cinematography (Jack Hildyard), best editing (Peter Taylor), best music (Malcolm Arnold) and best screenplay. The latter was awarded to novelist Boulle, who, although he spoke and wrote only in French, was given screen credit. The script, in fact, had been written by Carl Foreman and Michael Wilson, both of whom had been blacklisted by the HUAC in the early 1950s and had to work under pseudonyms. Hollywood corrected this injustice in 1985 by giving Oscars to their widows.

\*\*\*\*

## A BRIDGE TOO FAR (1977)

U.S./Great Britain　Richard Attenborough (Color)

With Dirk Bogarde, James Caan, Michael Caine, Sean Connery, Elliott Gould, Gene Hackman, Anthony Hopkins, Ryan O'Neal, Laurence Olivier, Robert Redford, Liv Ullmann, Edward Fox, Wolfgang Preiss, Hardy Kruger, Maximilian Schell

According to one critic, at a running time of nearly three hours, this *Bridge* is "much, much too long." But military buffs probably will appreciate the film's detailed re-creation of Operation Market Garden, an Allied offensive launched in the Netherlands in September 1944. At the time, the Rhine was still the main barrier between the Allied forces and the heart and homeland of the Germans. The bridge at Arnheim was considered a good place to cross it, so 35,000 American, British and Polish paratroopers were dropped into Holland in history's largest air assault. Unknown to the Allied Command, however, was the fact that two Panzer divisions had been assigned to the invasion area for refitting. As a result of poor intelligence and grave strategic and tactical errors, most of the British and Polish paratroopers were either killed or captured in one of the Allies' worst defeats.

Budgeted at $26 million, the film restages the battle awesomely, especially when seen in its original widescreen format with a stereo sound track. For the air drop, scores of vintage C-47s were used, along with dozens of gliders and hundreds of paratroopers, accompanied by a booming musical score. Among the imposing combat sequences are the heroic attempt by Anthony Hopkins and the British 2nd Parachute Battalion to hold Arnheim against superior German forces, and the 82nd Airborne's assault across the Waal River. There are too many star cameos, however, which clutter and confuse the story with perfunctorily played characters. And Gould and O'Neal are dreadfully miscast as senior American officers who behave more

like Boy Scout den fathers. For a clearer vision of the battle read Cornelius Ryan's *A Bridge Too Far*, the nonfiction book on which this film is based.
**1/2

## THE BRIDGES AT TOKO-RI (1954)

Paramount   Mark Robson (Color)
With William Holden, Mickey Rooney, Fredric March, Grace Kelly, Robert Strauss, Earl Holliman

Based on the best seller by James Michener, this Korean War drama was the big movie hit of 1954. A polished, big-budget production with top stars and spectacular special effects, it's still a winner. The story concerns Navy carrier-based jet pilots and helicopter rescue teams, with the focus on William Holden, who managed to jockey a Panther jet and grapple with domestic problems (Grace Kelly plays his wife). Outclassing Kelly and Holden is Mickey Rooney, turning in a surprise performance as a mad hatter of a helicopter pilot.

Especially effective are the bridge attacks, which last only a few minutes. The Navy jets realistically dodging heavy antiaircraft fire as they launch rockets to their targets are actually

THE BRIDGES AT TOKO-RI: William Holden (seated, center) and other carrier pilots are briefed before the attack.

miniatures created by John Fulton, who won an Academy Award for his contribution. (His aircraft choreography was later coped by George Lucas for the science-fiction film *Star Wars*.) Politicos might note that this is the movie from which President Ronald Reagan borrowed the line "Where do we find such men?," which he used at the 40th anniversary of the D-Day invasion. The question is asked by fatherly admiral Fredric March after several of his men are killed in action.

***1/2

## BRIGHT VICTORY (1951)
**Also titled** *Lights Out*

Universal-International  Mark Robson (Black & white)

With Arthur Kennedy, James Edwards, Peggy Dow, Julia Adams, James Edwards, Minor Watson, Will Geer

Arthur Kennedy was named best actor by a New York critics' poll and won an Oscar nomination for this sensitive portrayal of a GI blinded in combat. Director Mark Robson sidesteps the maudlin traps laid by his subject, and the result is a genuinely moving film. Initially a racial bigot, Kennedy changes his mind when he is befriended by another sightless ex-GI (James Edwards), who happens to be black. With the patient help of girlfriend Peggy Dow, also excellent, and Edwards, Kennedy learns to live with his handicap and return to civilian life.

***

## BUCK PRIVATES (1941)

Universal  Arthur Lublin (Black & white)

With Bud Abbott and Lou Costello, the Andrews Sisters, Alan Curtis, Jane Frazee, Nat Pendleton, Shemp Howard

One of the big hits of 1941, *Buck Privates* brought together Abbott and Costello and the Andrews Sisters, the hottest comedy team and singing act of their day. As two bumbling draftees, Abbott and Costello run through their classic burlesque routines while getting in and out of scrapes during basic training. Many of the routines still are hilarious, and the nostalgic swing music is the best of its kind. Two of the songs, in fact, are almost synonymous with the wartime era: "Boogie Woogie Bugle Boy from Company B" and "Apple Blossom Time."

Made after the U.S. government reinstated the draft in April 1941, the film connected with a generation of civilians who had to undergo a similar experience to become fighting soldiers. Military buffs will enjoy seeing the vintage Army uniforms and weapons in action. In the disposable sequel, *Buck Privates Come Home* (1947), the comedy duo adopts a displaced French orphan.

***

## BUONA SERA, MRS. CAMPBELL (1968)

United Artists  Melvin Frank (Color)

With Gina Lollobrigida, Telly Savalas, Phil Silvers, Peter Lawford, Shelley Winters, Lee Grant, Marian Moses

Twenty years after the war, a group of Air Force veterans returns to a small Italian town with their wives for a reunion with the folks they liberated. Now middle-aged and paunchy, they attempt to relive the past with an allnight party that includes too much *vino* and jitterbugging, which their backs are no longer up to. Lawford, Savalas and Silvers add to the sophisticated fun as three illegitimate papas who have been sending checks to ageless beauty Lollobrigida all this time. Each believes he is the father of her child.

**1/2

## THE CAINE MUTINY (1954)

Columbia   Edward Dmytryk (Color)

With Humphrey Bogart, José Ferrer, Van Johnson, Fred MacMurray, Robert Francis, E. G. Marshall, Tom Tully, Lee Marvin, May Wynn

Loyalty, both personal and professional, is called into question in this engrossing, finely wrought adaptation of Herman Wouk's best sel-ler, which won a Pulitzer Prize for fiction. Bogart is at his subtle peak as the paranoid Captain Queeg, commander of the *Caine*, a World War II Navy destroyer escort. Van Johnson also is impressive as the officer charged with mutiny after assuming command of the ship in a typhoon, after Queeg apparently lost his nerve. Fred MacMurray, in an atypical role, is properly unctuous as Queeg's nemesis, who uses Johnson as a cat's paw. The courtroom scenes are the crux of the drama, with Queeg again crumbling under stress while nervously palming steel ball bearings as defense attorney José Ferrer, who dislikes his clients, turns the court-martial into the captain's trial.

THE CAINE MUTINY: Humphrey Bogart starred as the neurotic Captain Queeg.

THE CAINE MUTINY: Van Johnson (right) relieves Humphrey Bogart of his command.

Wouk's novel also was made into an award-winning Broadway play titled *The Caine Mutiny Court-Martial*.

***1/2

### THE CAMP ON BLOOD ISLAND

Great Britain   Val Guest (Black & white)

With André Morell, Edward Underdown, Carl Mohner, Michael Goodliffe, Barbara Shelley, Ronald Radd

Old wartime hostilities still were being maintained 13 years after the war's end, when this low-budgeter was made. The setting is a Japanese prisoner-of-war camp under the command of a merciless samurai, who despises his British inmates because they had allowed themselves to be captured. When they attempt to break out, he punishes them brutally and sadistically. There are a number of scenes guaranteed to get your hate glands pumping.

*1/2

### CAPTAIN CAREY, U.S.A. (1950)
**Also titled** *After Midnight*

Paramount   Mitchell Leisen (Black & white)

With Alan Ladd, Wanda Hendrix, Francis Lederer, Joseph Calleia, Jane Nigh, Celia Lovsky

Former O.S.S. agent Alan Ladd returns to Italy after the war to track down the traitors who exposed him to the Gestapo. It's one of Ladd's lesser detective vehicles, but there's "Mona Lisa" to listen to—a song that won an Oscar for Ray Evans and Jay Livingstone.

**

## CAPTAIN EDDIE (1945)

20th Century-Fox   Lloyd Bacon (Black & white)
With Fred MacMurray, Charles Bickford, Lynn Bari, Thomas Mitchell, Lloyd Nolan

After Captain Eddie Rickenbacker made headlines throughout America for surviving 22 days adrift in the Pacific during World War II, Fox rushed out this tribute to his tenacious bravery. MacMurray stars as Rickenbacker, adrift in a life raft and recalling in flashbacks his adventures as an aviation pioneer. (Rickenbacker won the Congressional Medal of Honor and the Croix de Guerre in World War I.) The minuscule plot is slickly sentimental and hardly the true story.

**

## CAPTAIN NEWMAN, M.D. (1963)

Universal   David Miller (Color)
With Gregory Peck, Tony Curtis, Angie Dickinson, Bobby Darin, Eddie Albert, Jane Withers, Robert Duvall, James Gregory

A nice change of pace, this behind-the-battlefront drama stars Gregory Peck as an Air Force psychiatrist treating shell-shocked patients. First on Captain Newman's agenda is combat veteran Bobby Darin, getting an Academy Award nomination for his performance as a young enlisted man with a bad case of nerves. Newman constantly locks horns with military brass for considering the welfare of his patients above all, but he's given strong support by nurse Angie Dickinson and con-artist/orderly Tony Curtis.

**1/2

## CAPTAINS OF THE CLOUDS (1942)

Warner Bros.   Michael Curtiz (Color)

With James Cagney, Dennis Morgan, Brenda Marshall, George Tobias, Reginald Gardiner, Alan Hale

Then one of the most war-minded of studios, Warner Brothers produced this action quickie at the behest of the government, which was urging Hollywood to create war "vitamins." Cagney, whose next film would be *Yankee Doodle Dandy*, plays a Royal Canadian Air Force pilot who changes from heel to hero under fire. The story resembles a recruiting poster, but there are some good flight scenes—and it's always a pleasure to watch Cagney at work.

**1/2

## CARBINE WILLIAMS (1952)

MGM Richard Thorpe   (Black & white)
With James Stewart, Jean Hagen, Wendell Corey, Paul Stewart, Carl Benton Reid, James Arness

The success of *The Stratton Story* brought James Stewart another screen biography, this one as the man who invented and perfected the M1 Carbine for the armed forces. Jailed for shooting a revenue man, Williams spends his time in prison developing the new weapon, under the nose of sympathetic warden Wendell Corey. Although Stewart's characterization softens the real-life Williams quite a bit, the story is engrossing, especially if you're interested in weapons research and development.

**1/2

## CARVE HER NAME WITH PRIDE (1958)

Great Britain   Lewis Gilbert (Black & white)
With Virginia McKenna, Paul Scofield, Jack Warner, Denise Grey, Sidney Tafler, Alain Saury

Virginia McKenna is fairly convincing as Violette Szabo, the real-life British widow of a French officer; she is recruited as a spy and parachuted into Nazi-occupied France. Captured while working for the French Resistance, she dies a heroine's death at the hands of the Gestapo. Although respectful of its subject, this film lacks commitment, despite the rare presence of Paul Scofield, considered the second greatest actor in the English-speaking world (after Laurence Olivier).

**

## CASABLANCA (1942)

Warner Bros.   Michael Curtiz (Black & white)
With Humphrey Bogart, Ingrid Bergman, Claude Rains, Paul Henreid, Conrad Veidt, Sydney Greenstreet, Peter Lorre, S. Z. Sakall, Dooley Wilson, Marcel, Leonid Kinsky

As comfortable and as reassuring as an old pair of shoes, *Casablanca* is one of those rare movies that people never seem to tire of seeing. The most entertaining of the World War II romances, it offers a winning synthesis of cynical toughness and patriotic sentimentality, marvelously served up by director Michael Curtiz and a cast of now-legendary players. Bogart plays Rick Blaine, 36, battered by life but with his ideals somehow untouched, now the owner of Rick's Cafe Américain, a tacky gambling club in Vichy Casablanca. Into the club comes old flame Ilsa Lund (Ingrid Bergman), now trying to get her fugitive patriot husband (Paul Henreid) to safety in Lisbon. Bogart, realizing the impossibility of recapturing the past, shows that he's a softie after all by

allowing Henreid to fly to safety with Bergman, aided by the lecherous chief of police, Captain Renault (Claude Rains).

There are a number of marvelous scenes and lines, that movie buffs can quote by heart: A group of German soldiers bellows "Deutschland über Alles" in the cafe as French patriots stand and drown them out with *La Marseillaise*, the French national anthem; Peter Lorre as the slimy little Ugarté, asking, "You despise me, Rick, don't you?" "If I gave you any thought I probably would"; Rick's comment when he first spots Ilsa, "Of all the gin joints in all the towns in all the world, she walks into mine." Bergman's much-quoted line "Play it again, Sam," which was used as the title of Woody Allen's homage to Bogart, is actually, "Play it, Sam," the song in question being *As Time Goes By*, sung by Dooley Wilson.

As a war movie, *Casablanca* had little military action, which isn't surprising, since few films released in 1942 confronted the question of how the war actually was being fought. Few knew where Casablanca was at the time, but the film received a shot in the arm a week after its release when Roosevelt and Churchill met at the famous Casablanca Conference. Another lucky break was the casting. Originally set to play Rick, Ronald Reagan dropped out to serve in the U.S. Air Force, and Ann Sheridan (replacing Hedy Lamarr) was busy on another picture. Only Bogart, who was too old to be drafted, was available. The film won three Oscars, including best picture, best screenplay

(Howard Koch, Philip G. Epstein, and Julius J. Epstein) and best director (Michael Curtiz). Its source is a flop Broadway play titled *Everybody Comes to Rick's* by Murray Burnett and Joan Alison.

Warner later produced a forgotten TV series based on the movie. Aired on ABC during the 1955-56 season, *Casablanca* starred Charles McGraw as Rick Jason, the cafe's new proprietor, and Marcel Dalio—who had appeared in the film—as Captain Renaud. The series presented stories of romance, adventure and intrigue.

****

## CAST A GIANT SHADOW (1966)

United Artists  Melville Shavelson (Color)

With Kirk Douglas, Angie Dickinson, Yul Brynner, Senta Berger, Frank Sinatra, Topol, John Wayne, Gary Merrill, Jeremy Kemp, Luther Adler, Stathis Gialleis, James Donald

That bigger doesn't always mean better is an object lesson illustrated by this unwieldy dramatization of the Israeli-Arab conflict circa 1948. Kirk Douglas is top-billed as Colonel Marcus, the American military lawyer who served in World War II and then shaped up the Israeli Army. There are plenty of combat scenes for the action buff and too many big stars vying for attention in tiny roles as they pay reverence to the new Jewish state. Director/producer/screenwriter Shavelson wrote a mordantly funny book about the location shooting, titled *How to Make a Jewish Movie.*

*1/2

## CASTLE KEEP (1969)

Columbia  Sydney Pollack (Color)

With Burt Lancaster, Patrick O'Neal, Peter Falk, Jean-Pierre Aumont, Al Freeman, Jr., Bruce Dern, Astrid Heeren, Tony Bill

An adaptation of William Eastlake's allegorical novel about war, civilization and individual conscience. Battle-scarred Major Burt Lancaster, sporting an eyepatch, and seven of his men are trapped in a historic Belgian castle filled with art treasures during the Battle of the Bulge. Should Lancaster listen to his conscience and make a last stand against the Germans, or should he listen to the pleas of castle owner Jean-Pierre Aumont and spare the priceless treasures? Scriptwriters Daniel Taradash and David Rayfiel only intermittently capture the subtleties of Eastlake's novel (and its parallels to the then-current Vietnam War). The performances are uneven and the action finale is absurd by any standard.

*

## CATCH-22 (1970)

Paramount  Mike Nichols (Color)

With Alan Arkin, Richard Benjamin, Martin Balsam, Art Garfunkel, Buck Henry, Jack Gilford, Jon Voight, Anthony Perkins, Bob Newhart, Paula Prentiss, Martin Sheen, Orson Welles

Scriptwriter Buck Henry couldn't fit the entire story in, but he's selected some fine moments from Joseph Heller's modern war classic of the absurd. Director Nichols found a perfect Yossarian in Alan Arkin and a fine cast to bring to life Heller's gallery of loonies. Especially memorable are Jon Voight as Milo Minderbender, a war-profiteering supply officer, and Bob Newhart as the reclusive Major Major, not to mention rotund Orson Welles as the fun-loving General Dreedle.

The story takes place at a U.S. Air Force base in the Mediterranean during World War II. Heller's antiwar message pivots on bombardier Yossarian, who pleads insanity so he doesn't have to fly more combat missions. According to the unit's doctor (Jack Gilford), this makes him sane and hence able to return to combat. ("No sane man would wish to fly, therefore anyone wishing to stop cannot be insane.") This is the impossible Catch-22 of the title. The men at the base are killed one by one, and the only survivor starts swimming to sanity—toward neutral Sweden. Henry's condensation is episodic, and Nichols never really brings it together, but the anecdotes are brilliantly staged.

In addition to deflating thoroughly the idea of heroism in the cause of war, *Catch-22* carried combat gore to new heights. In the film a man is cut in half by a low-flying plane, and another hangs on to his intestines as they tumble out of his abdomen.

***1/2

## CAUGHT IN THE DRAFT (1941)

Paramount   David Butler (Black & white)
With Bob Hope, Dorothy Lamour, Lynne Overman, Eddie Bracken, Clarence Kolb, Paul Hurst

Selective Service was something new when Paramount cast Bob Hope as a reluctant draftee who manages to foul up everything and everyone he gets involved with. Old standby Dorothy Lamour, the love interest of the Hope/Crosby "Road" pictures, plays the girl Pfc. Hope falls for the colonel's daughter. It's still very funny over 45 years later. The other hit service comedy that

year was Universal's *Buck Privates*, with Abbott and Costello.

**1/2

## CEASE FIRE! (1953)

Paramount   Owen Crump (Black & white)
no cast listing

Independent movie maker Owen Crump shot this semidocumentary in Korea with a cast of amateurs. Made just before the peace talks brought the war to an end in July 1953, it records the day-to-day activities of an Army infantry unit on the 38th Parallel. There's an authentic feel to the proceedings, especially when the film is seen in its original 3-D format. War buffs and historians will appreciate it.

**

## CHAIN LIGHTNING (1950)

Warner Bros.   Stuart Heisler (Black & white)
With Humphrey Bogart, Eleanor Parker, Raymond Massey, Richard Whorf, Roy Roberts, James Brown

Not even Bogey can save this airborne dud, which casts him as a World War II bomber pilot now testing jets. There are a few good action scenes and an intriguing array of early jet aircraft—but then there's all the rest.

*1/2

## THE CHARGE OF THE LIGHT BRIGADE (1936)

Warner Bros.   Michael Curtiz (Black & white)
With Errol Flynn, Olivia de Havilland, Patric Knowles, C. Aubrey Smith, David Niven, Donald Crisp, Nigel Bruce, Spring Byington, J. Carrol Naish

Errol Flynn cemented his stardom with this grand old warhorse, the fourth time it was filmed. Flynn, paired with Olivia de Havilland, his most compatible leading lady, leads the famous suicidal cavalry charge to settle a score with villain Surat Khan. Nominally based on Tennyson's poem about the bravery of a British light-cavalry brigade during the Crimean War, the film plays fast and loose with history (most of the action has been shifted to India), but it's a satisfying, well-aged slice of Hollywood baloney.

Forget the 1968 color remake from Great Britain. Stars Trevor Howard and John Gielgud add a note of quality to what is an otherwise embarrassing production directed by Tony Richardson in much the same style as his earlier film, *Tom Jones* (1963).

\*\*\*

## CHE! (1969)

20th Century-Fox   Richard Fleischer (Color)
With Omar Sharif, Jack Palance, Robert Loggia, Cesare Danova, Barbara Luna, Woody Strode

A "radical-chic" hero of the 1960s, Ernesto "Che" Guevara gained international fame when he forsook the practice of medicine in Argentina to become a full-time revolutionary. His great moment came, of course, when he helped Fidel Castro install a Communist regime in Cuba. In late 1967 he was captured and executed by a Green-Beret-organized unit of the Bolivian Army while fomenting revolution in Bolivia. Fox, sensing a box-office winner in the headlines, stitched together this ideology-laundered caricature, with limpid Omar Sharif playing Che in starched fatigues and clench-jawed Palance as a cigar-chomping Castro. This film may be one

of the reasons why Castro is so angry at the United States.

\*

## CHINA DOLL (1958)

United Artists   Frank Borzage (Black & white)
With Victor Mature, Li Li Hua, Ward Bond, Bob Mathias, Stuart Whitman

Director Frank Borzage pours on the suds in this World War II romance between a Flying Tiger and a beautiful Chinese housekeeper. The couple is killed in action, and their daughter later visits his old air crew in America for a tearful finale. Find something better to do.

\*

## CHINA GATE (1957)

20th Century-Fox   Samuel Fuller (Black & white)
With Gene Barry, Angie Dickinson, Nat King Cole, Lee Van Cleef, Paul Dubov, George Givot

Made after the French lost in Vietnam in 1954, *China Gate* sees the Foreign Legion as a group of heroes attempting to hang on to Indochina. After a prologue about France's mission to contain communism (and to close Red China's "gate" to Vietnam), squad leader Gene Barry sabotages a Commie supply dump with the help of his former Eurasian lover, the mother of the child he previously abandoned. As usual, writer/director Fuller lets his characters heft the burden of his political beliefs, and the cast is about as authentic as his film's sense of history. He knows how to make film *move*, however, and the action scenes always are exciting.

\*\*1/2

## CHINA VENTURE (1953)

Columbia    Don Siegel (Black & white)
With Edmond O'Brien, Barry Sullivan, Jocelyn Brando

Two Navy officers and a nurse attempt to rescue an admiral held captive by Red Chinese guerrillas. Director Siegel, still in training, recycles threadbare wartime conventions, holding them up like flash cards for programmed audience response. Confucius say turn off set and get a good night's sleep.

*1/2

## THE CLAY PIGEON (1949)

RKO    Richard Fleischer (Black & white)
With Bill Williams, Barbara Hale, Richard Quine, Richard Loo, Martha Hyer, Frank Fenton

Inspired by an incident in which a former POW spotted his former Japanese prison guard in Los Angeles, this tingly little thriller has seaman Bill Williams awakening from a coma in a naval hospital, then learning he is to be court-martialed for treason. Shocked, he sets out to find a friend who can clear him, only to discover that the friend had been killed in a Japanese prison camp and that he himself is accused of the murder. Williams's wife, Barbara Hale (better known as Della in the TV series *Perry Mason*), is properly suspicious as the dead buddy's wife.

**1/2

## CLOAK AND DAGGER (1946)

Warner Bros.    Fritz Lang (Black & white)
With Gary Cooper, Lilli Palmer, Robert Alda, J. Edward Bromberg, Vladimir Sokolov, Helene Thimig

The cloak-and-dagger intrigues described here are the work of the U.S. Office of Strategic Services (OSS), the forerunner of the Central Intelligence Agency (CIA). A highly efficient weapon of war, the OSS was organized in 1941-42 by Roosevelt's special envoy General William J. Donovan (at the time, critics said the initials stood for Oh, So Secret). Gary Cooper, miscast as a university nuclear physicist turned spy, parachutes into Germany because he's the only man capable of communicating with a fellow scientist kidnapped by the Nazis. Director Fritz Lang, working at half speed, saves his best scene for last, when captive physicist Helene Thimig is casually shot by her Nazi nurse just as Allied agents arrive to rescue her.

Lang, an expatriate German who left the country when Hitler came to power, originally had Cooper telling the audience that the A-Bomb secret wasn't the sole property of the United States. This ominous warning against nuclear proliferation was dropped by Warner, and the film ends with the rescue of the elderly scientist.

**1/2

## CLOSELY WATCHED TRAINS (1966)

Czechoslovakia    Jiri Menzel (Black & white)
With Vaclav Neckar, Jitka Bendova, Vladimir Valenta, Josef Somr, Vlastimil Brodsky, Jiri Menzel

Writer/director Jiri Menzel's engaging sex comedy was awarded an Oscar, only the second to be won by a Czech film. (The first was *The Shop on Main Street* two years before.) Set in the last years of the Nazi occupation, the story concerns a shy adolescent boy in training as a railway station guard who attempts to lose his virginity. The results are often hilarious and often touching, as his search for love leads him to become a resourceful saboteur. Based on Bohumil Hrabal's novel, the film was made during a period of liberalization in Czechoslovakia, before Soviet troops marched into the country in 1968 and restored "order." Best scene: a joyful moment in which an obliging secretary has her bare bottom authorized with the official railway stamp.

****

## COCKLESHELL HEROES (1956)

Great Britain    José Ferrer (Color)

With José Ferrer, Trevor Howard, Anthony Newley, Victor Maddern, Dora Bryan, Peter Arne, David Lodge

Director José Ferrer puts himself through the paces as a Royal Marine officer who forms a sabotage unit from military malcontents for a top-secret mission. After too many training scenes, the 10-man group embarks on Operation Cockleshell, a canoe trip 75 miles upriver into Vichy France to blow up five blockade runners anchored in the heavily guarded port of Bordeaux. Ferrer, sporting a pretty good British accent, handles his tandem chores well, and the operation is a heart-thumping success. Scriptwriters Bryan Forbes and Richard Maibaum based the story on a mission carried out by the Royal Marine Boom Patrol, forerunners of the Royal Marine Commandos Special Boat Squadron, one of the most elite military units in the world.

**1/2

## THE COLDITZ STORY (1955)

Great Britain    Guy Hamilton (Black & white)

With John Wills, Eric Portman, Lionel Jeffries, Bryan Forbes, Christopher Rhodes, Anton Diffring, Theodore Bikel

A high-spirited tale of British POWs plotting their escape from a top-security Nazi fortress in Saxony's Colditz Castle. It seems a bit "stiff upper lip" today, but the eccentric cast works up some moments of hilarity, and director Hamilton convincingly depicts prison camp life as it probably was—dull and maddeningly repetitive.

This is one of the first war movies to play POW life for comedy, a trend sparked by *Stalag 17*, made two years earlier. In 1971 British television retooled *The Colditz Story* for a less successful sitcom.

**1/2

## COMING HOME (1978)

United Artists    Hal Ashby (Color)

With Jane Fonda, Bruce Dern, Jon Voight, Robert Carradine, Penelope Milford

A popular and critical success, *Coming Home* presents the Vietnam War as an unseen villain causing heartaches and insurmountable problems on the home front. Set in 1968, the story pivots on Jane Fonda as the wife of a gung-ho Marine Corps officer (Bruce Dern), who is on active duty in Vietnam. While he's away, Fonda does volunteer work at a local V.A. hospital, where she begins an affair with dove Jon Voight, a veteran whose legs have been paralyzed by enemy shrapnel. "The girl I play gradually becomes aware of the war through her relationships," explained Fonda, whose perseverance got the film produced. "She never

COMING HOME: Bruce Dern and Jane Fonda, who won a best actress Oscar for her performance.

becomes radicalized, though. If anything, she only moves from A to C and is curious about this war that's destroying a lot of people's lives. She's not political like me."

To the military, Fonda's name still evoked the image of "Hanoi Jane" smiling with enemy officers during a visit to North Vietnam. And the powers-that-be at the Pentagon had not forgotten or forgiven. When permission was requested for location shooting at military installations, the producers were turned down flatly by the Navy, the Army, the Marines, and the National Guard. Later, the Veterans Administration reversed its decision and opened the doors of its Long Beach, California, facility to the film crew.

For all its dramatic merits, however, *Coming Home* falls short of being the definitive Vietnam-era movie. Purporting to be an "examination of the effect on the war on people at home," it seems curiously rooted in the confusion of the time in which it takes place. Its thoughts are rambling, there is too much talk and too many guilt-ridden suicides. According to Fonda, the film's antiwar point of view was toned down by producer Jerome Hellman, who told her, "You get up on a soapbox and we'll sink like a rock. They're going to be looking for that from you." Fonda and Voight won Oscars for their unusually touching performances, as did scriptwriters Waldo Salt, Robert C. Jones and Nancy Dowd.

For an insight into how much America had changed in 32 years, see *The Best Years of Our Lives*, the definitive "coming home" movie of World War II.
***

## COMMAND DECISION (1948)

MGM   Sam Wood (Black & white)
With Clark Gable, Walter Pidgeon, Van Johnson, Charles Bickford, Brian Donlevy, John Hodiak, Edward Arnold, Richard Quine

What goes on in the minds and hearts of top military brass who dispatch troops on dangerous missions that will kill many of them? Draftees probably could have cared less, but viewers will be absorbed by this behind-the-scenes glimpse of military decisionmaking and the political pressures involved.

Clark Gable heads an all-star, all-male cast as an Army Air Corps general who is faced with the dilemma of whether to send his pilots on high-risk raids on German jet factories to hasten the end of the war, or to bow to political pressure in Congress (several representatives are visiting his command post) to cut high losses. If Gable stops the attacks, later missions may face hordes of superfast, heavily armed jet fighters and suffer even greater losses. If he continues, more of his men will die, and Congress may

pass legislation harmful to the Air Corps.

The players are first-rate, especially Walter Pidgeon as a superior officer who recalls the shortsighted era of aviation pioneer Billy Mitchell, when the Air Corps was seriously underfunded and thereby compromised. It's Gable who shines, however, in his best postwar role. One of the cinema's strongest male role models, Gable adds a new dimension to his usual macho image by struggling with matters weightier than the usual 110-pound blonde. *Command Decision* was adapted from a hit Broadway play of the same title that still was running when the film was produced. There are no action scenes, but you won't be disappointed.
***1/2

## COMMANDO (1985)

20th Century-Fox   Mark Lester (Color)
With Arnold Schwarzenegger, Rae Dawn Chong

Massively built Arnold Schwarzenegger does a credible Rambo impersonation in this exciting but redundantly violent action-exploiter. Schwarzenegger is Colonel Matrix, the retired commander of an elite American special operations unit, whose young daughter is kidnapped by Latin American rebels intent on returning their leader to power in the imaginary country of Val Verde. By holding his daughter, they hope to blackmail Matrix into assassinating the current ruler of the country. With the help of "innocent bystander" Chong, the ex-commando locates their hideout and becomes an unstoppable force of one. He invades the island lair with a napalm-firing rocket launcher, a machine gun, a submachine gun, a shotgun, a pistol, hand grenades, claymore mines, a Bowie knife and—at one point—even a buzz saw. Schwarzenegger, outclassing Stallone with his Mr. Universe physique, plays his character with a sense of humor, which keeps the film from becoming too absurd.

**1/2

## COMMANDOS STRIKE AT DAWN (1943)

Columbia   John Farrow (Black & white)

With Paul Muni, Anna Lee, Lillian Gish, Cedric Hardwicke, Ray Collins, Robert Coote, Richard Derr, Rosemary de Camp, Alexander Knox, Rod Cameron

Elite Allied units launched their first screen action in this fairly accurate account of a commando raid on Nazi-occupied Norway. Academy Award-winning actor Paul Muni, who appeared only in prestige movies, plays Torensen, a local resistance leader who escapes to England and returns with a commando unit. Torensen guides the men through a secluded fjord to a German airfield near his village. After an intense firefight, they destroy the field and release the hostages imprisoned in town. He dies during the raid, but the film ends hopefully with hostages and commandos sailing to England as the screen fades to Allied flags fluttering in the wind.

Filmed in Newfoundland, with Canadian soldiers impersonating the raiders, the movie focuses on the character of Torensen and how he changes from a thoughtful pacifist to a ruthless resistance fighter. That most Norwegians were violently opposed to the Nazis is reflected in the script by novelist Irwin Shaw, then serving in the army as a private, first class. Also addressed is the problem of Vidkun Quisling, leader of Norway's Nazis, whose detested name has become synonymous with "traitor" in just about every language of the world. The American equivalent of British commandos in World War II were Rangers, The First Special Service Force, Merrill Marauders, Marine Raiders, and beginning in 1952, The Green Berets of the Special Forces.

***

## CONFESSIONS OF A NAZI SPY (1939)

Warner Bros. Anatole Litvak (Black & white)

With Edward G. Robinson, Francis Lederer, George Sanders, Paul Lukas, Henry O'Neill, Lya Lys, Sig Rumann

Hollywood launched an all-out propaganda attack on Nazi Germany with this punchy, flag-waving thriller—a *cause célèbre* in its time. Essentially a hate-group expose, the film pits a crafty and reassuring G-man (Edward G. Robinson) against a network of ruthless Goebbels-trained spies operating through the German consulate and the German-American Bund in New York. Trapped by Robinson, jittery foreign agent Francis Lederer breaks down and blows the whistle on the entire operation, whose function, it turns out, is to fan the flames of racial and labor discord in America.

Warner Brothers decided to make the film, against the advice of studio executives, after the company's Berlin representative was trampled to death there in a riot. An effective primer on the policies and techniques of the Nazi government, the script was tailor-made by Milton Krims and John Wexley from a best seller written by a former FBI agent who had broken a German spy ring two years before. Selected to direct was Anatole Litvak, a Russian-born Jew who had been forced out of a promising movie career in Germany by the country's race laws.

Although the movie was a hit, isolationism still was a factor in the United States, and the House Un-American Activities Committee saw fit to criticize the studio for daring to express antifascist sentiments in a declaredly neutral country. (After the war the HUAC investigated the film again for not condemning communism as well.) Moreover, so outraged was the right-wing Bund that it instituted a $5 million libel suit against Warner Brothers. Robinson was briefly placed under guard after his family received anonymous death threats, and Jack L. Warner—according to his autobiography—got an honorable mention on Hitler's death list. Warner Brothers in turn countersued, but by September (the film was released in April) the controversy was rendered obsolete by the outbreak of World War II in Europe.

***

## THE CONSPIRATORS (1944)

Warner Bros.   Jean Negulesco (Black & white)
With Hedy Lamarr, Paul Henreid, Sydney Greenstreet, Peter Lorre, Victor Francen, Carol Thurston, Kurt Katch, Joseph Calleia, Vladimir Sokolov, George Macready

Warner's follow-up to *Casablanca* casts Hedy Lamarr (originally set for that film's Ingrid Bergman role) as a *femme fatale* in wartime Lisbon. Paramour Henreid supplies the pivotal intrigue, again as a freedom fighter, only this time it's for Holland. Villains Lorre and Greenstreet allegedly disliked the contrived script so much that they played their parts for comedy. It shows.
*1/2

## CORNERED (1946)

RKO   Edward Dmytryk (Black & white)
With Dick Powell, Walter Slezak, Micheline Cheirel, Morris Carnovsky, Nina Vale, Luther Adler

Settling old scores was on a lot of minds immediately after World War II—including RKO's. *Cornered* marks the beginning of Hollywood's enduring cycle of revenge films in which vanished war criminals are ferreted out and finally punished. The plot has tough guy Dick Powell fulfilling a vow to find the Nazi collaborators who killed his French wife. Cast as a demobilized Canadian airman, Powell follows the trail from France to Switzerland, and then to the insidious ambience of Buenos Aires. There he is greeted warmly by a *femme fatale* before being beaten and left for dead. Justice is finally served, however, as Powell gets what he came for in an edge-of-the-seat climax.

**1/2

## CORVETTE K-225 (1943)

Universal   Richard Rosson (Black & white)
With Randolph Scott, James Brown, Ella Raines, Barry Fitzgerald, Andy Devine, Noah Berry, Jr., Fuzzy Knight

Somewhere in size between a destroyer

and a gunboat, the swift little convoy vessels called corvettes helped keep supply lines open to England during World War II. Helping to win the Battle of the Atlantic is Randolph Scott as the skipper of a spanking new Canadian corvette that resists everything the Germans can throw at it, including bombers and the U-boat that previously sank his subchaser. Basically a primer on how convoy escorts operated in action, the film is as instructive as it is entertaining. The ship's crew is comprised of some of Hollywood's more colorful character actors, and they bounce their lines off each other with humor and style. If the battles seem harrowingly real, it's because many of them were actually photographed in combat.
\*\*\*

## THE COUNTERFEIT TRAITOR (1961)
Paramount   George Seaton (Color)
With William Holden, Lilli Palmer, Hugh Griffith, Eva Dahlbeck, Werner Peters

Writer/director George Seaton wrings every bit of suspense from this low-key espionage story based on Alexander Klein's allegedly factual book. Businessman William Holden, a naturalized Swede born in America, agrees to act as a spy for the British while pretending sympathy for Nazi Germany. Free to come and go between neutral Sweden and Germany, Holden falls in love with local spy Lilli Palmer, giving them a convenient cover for their clandestine activities. Overlong perhaps, but the story is compelling, and the instructions in espionage are fascinating.
\*\*\*

## COUNTERPOINT (1968)
Universal   Ralph Nelson (Color)
With Charlton Heston, Maximilian Schell, Anton Diffring, Leslie Nielsen, Kathryn Hays

Charlton Heston supplies the only bright note in this flattened-out version of Alan Sillitoe's novel *The General*. Maximilian Schell harkens back to wartime propaganda movies as a Nazi officer who captures USO orchestra conductor Heston and forces him to play a private concert. (Once again Nazi perfidy is equated with classical music.) The concert won't put you to sleep, but the story and direction will.
1/2\*

## THE COURT-MARTIAL OF BILLY MITCHELL (1955)
**Also titled** *One Man Mutiny*

Warner Bros.   Otto Preminger (Color)
With Gary Cooper, Charles Bickford, Ralph Bellamy, Rod Steiger, Elizabeth Montgomery, James Daly, Darren McGavin, Jack Lord, Fred Clark

Visionaries always are a problem, especially to closed military minds, and no one was more troublesome than General William Lendrum "Billy" Mitchell. Commander of the air force of the American Expeditionary Force in 1917-18, Mitchell was the leading proponent of a strategic, independent air force, which, he asserted, would determine the victor in a future war. Recognized now as a prophet, he advocated a separate U.S. air force, the development of bombers (along with bomb shelters), and the formation of paratroop assault forces. Among his accurate predictions were routine transoceanic flights; use of the Arctic route to cut distances; planes that fly at 1,000 mph; and, most surprisingly, in a letter dated December 14, 1923, the likelihood of a Japanese air attack on Hawaii, probably at Pearl Harbor.

The film recounts Mitchell's celebrated court-martial for "conduct prejudicial to good order and military discipline" after he accused his superiors of criminal negligence. Cast as Mitchell, Gary Cooper fails to convey much emotional depth, but the staging of the trial is powerfully detailed. Cooper, himself recuperating from an attack of malaria while on the stand, recalls Mitchell's past glories and failed experiments in a series of flashbacks, provoked by the cross-examination of a crack Army lawyer (Rod Steiger). Although General Douglas MacArthur is accurately presented as one of his judges, the script fails to point out that the men had been close friends for years (probably because MacArthur still was alive when the film was made).

The testimony of World War I heroes Andrew Spaatz, Hap Arnold, and Eddie Rickenbacker fails to sway the court, and, after President Calvin Coolidge advises a swift end to the trial to minimize embarrassment to the Army, Mitchell is demoted to colonel. At the fadeout, the aviator walks from the courtroom a civilian (Mitchell chose to retire instead). In military lore, of course, Mitchell has since been enshrined as a founding father of the Air Force, the service branch that was established after World War II. The film's release was timed to coincide with the opening of the new U.S. Air Force Academy in Colorado.

***1/2

## THE CRANES ARE FLYING (1957)

U.S.S.R.   Mikhail Kalatozov (Black & white)
With Tatiana Samoilova, Alexei Batalov, Vasili Merkuriev, A. Shvorin

A happy surprise, this powerful Russian character study dispenses with any ideological statements. The story reconstructs the home front during World War II in terms of a warmhearted but unsentimental story involving a young woman who marries her lover's cousin when she hears he has been killed in battle. Suffering through the unhappy marriage and wartime deprivations, she eventually learns the truth, but it is too late to help either of them. Named best picture at the Cannes Festival, this much-acclaimed movie indicated that the Russian cinema was coming back to life during the brief liberal respite that took place after Stalin's death in 1953. The black-and-white photography is stunning, and Ms. Samoilova is a world-class actress.

***1/2

## CRASH DIVE (1943)

20th Century-Fox   Archie Mayo (Color)
With Tyrone Power, Anne Baxter, Dana Andrews, James Gleason, Dame May Whitty, Henry Morgan, Minor Watson, Frank Conroy

A study in war movie cliches, this flashy melodrama features a love triangle among the three leads, a supporting cast representative of every American ethnic group, submachine guns that never run out of ammo, suicidal heroics—and some terrific battle scenes. Disgruntled Tyrone Power would rather be on a PT boat than a submarine, but eventually he sees the light and becomes a model officer. A raid on a German refueling island in the North Atlantic allows for some fancy commando work and a blazing finale, with burning fuel spewing out of sabotaged underwater tanks. It's all unbelievable but fun, especially in Technicolor, which rarely was used in movies of the war era. Special-effects men Fred Sersen and Roger Heman won Oscars for the combat scenes.

**½

## CROSSFIRE (1947)

RKO   Edward Dmytryk (Black & white)
With Robert Young, Robert Ryan, Robert Mitchum, Gloria Grahame, Sam Levene, Paul Kelly, Steve Brodie

Controversial in its time (and hence a big moneymaker), this tough report on homegrown anti-Semitism remains one of the forties' finest films. Its source is *The Brick Foxhole*, a novel by Richard Brooks that focuses on a sadistic soldier unsure of his manhood and whose homophobia leads him to murder a homosexual. Since sexual inversion was then taboo in Hollywood, screenwriter John Paxton changed the subject to anti-Semitism, a problem recently brought home by the Nazi attempt at genocide.

Plunging headlong into the plot, *Crossfire* opens with a shadow-drenched scene in which a man is being brutally beaten to death. Local police detective Robert Young visits a seedy bar where the Jewish victim (Sam Levene) was last seen; the trail leads him to a group of soldiers on leave. More of a "whydunit" than a "whodunit," the film soon reveals that the killer is one of the soldiers, an alcoholic bully (Robert Ryan) who committed the crime while in a prejudice-inflamed rage. The suspense derives from the facts that clever detective Young doesn't yet know the killer's identity and that neither he nor we know the motive behind the crime.

Shot on a low budget in a record 22 days, the film transcends its B-picture ghetto with a fine script, crisp ensemble performances and a compelling milieu of corruption and evil. Director Dmytryk transformed standing sets into a poetically heightened night world of seedy hotels, cheap bars, and wet city streets, which, like other grimy cityscapes, take on a peculiar ambience during late-night hours. Film historians consider the movie to be a classic example of *film noir*, a term applied to crime films of the 1940s that take place at night in shadowy, claustrophobic settings.

If *Crossfire* has a flaw, it's in Young's simpleminded plea for tolerance and the revelation that the murdered Jew had served honorably in the U.S. Army (Ryan had thought him to be a draft-dodger or a war profiteer). Morally, of course, it would be wrong to kill him no matter who he was. But the film is so well made that it probably would have been effective even if it were in favor of Nazism.

****

## CROSS OF IRON (1977)

Great Britain/West Germany   Sam Peckinpah (Color)
With James Coburn, James Mason, Maximilian Schell, David Warner, Senta Berger, Klaus Lowitch

German soldiers are the surprise heroes here. Nearly burned out and running on empty, a German battalion suffers great losses while fighting a fierce no-quarter battle on the Russian Front in 1943. Action-adventure expert Sam Peckinpah cleverly cast popular American actor James Coburn against type as a German NCO to make the character sympathetic. The other leads also are *simpático* types, placing the audience in the unusual position of rooting for the Wehrmacht (the film was a big hit in Germany). As you might expect from the director who made slow-motion death a fine art, there are a number of gory scenes, which usually are excised for television screenings. The most shocking is a throat-grabber that involves a Russian woman soldier and her German guard. The inconclusive ending probably will leave you grumbling.

**1/2

## THE CROSS OF LORRAINE (1944)

MGM   Tay Garnett (Black & white)
With Gene Kelly, Jean-Pierre Aumont, Cedric Hardwicke, Peter Lorre, Hume Cronyn, Joseph Calleia, Richard Whorf

While the ladies were busy next door with *Cry Havoc*, MGM simultaneously filmed this all-male pep talk. Gutsier than its celluloid sister, the movie follows a group of Frenchman through a too-easy surrender to the Nazis and their realization, after torture, of what the Boche really are up to. Dancer Gene Kelly is impressive in a dramatic role (as one of the prisoners), and the cast performs enthusiastically. Gnomish Peter Lorre doesn't look very Aryan, but he tortures with typical Nazi gusto.

**1/2

## THE CRUEL SEA (1953)

Great Britain   Charles Frend (Black & white)
With Jack Hawkins, Donald Sinden, Stanley Baker, John Stratton, Denholm Elliott, John Warner, Virginia McKenna, Moira Lister

Eric Ambler's uncompromising screenplay does full justice to Nicholas Monsarrat's rugged novel about convoy duty during World War II. Jack Hawkins is a standout as the commander of the *Compass Rose*, a British corvette battling Nazi subs in the North Atlantic. The emphasis is on the psychological—the emotional toll exacted by the experience of naval warfare. A sterling cast contributes fine vignettes (which actually are miniature character studies) of the stressbound crew. There are enough action scenes to satisfy the combat buff, however, and the British sub-hunting technique is shown to good advantage. Ambler's screenplay was nominated for an Oscar but lost to the "big" war movie of 1953, *From Here to Eternity*.

***1/2

## CRY HAVOC (1943)

MGM   Richard Thorpe (Black & white)
With Margaret Sullavan, Ann Sothern, Joan Blondell, Fay Bainter, Marsha Hunt, Ella Raines, Frances Gifford, Connie Gilchrist, Heather Angel

A rarity among war-era movies, this theatrical tear-jerker features an all-female cast. Based on the Broadway play *Proof thro' the Night* by Allen R. Kenward, Paul Osborn's manipulative script has some leading MGM players impersonating doomed nurses trapped on Bataan during the Japanese invasion of the Philippines. Touching occasionally, the film is an entertaining

fantasy version of what really happened. (One critic noted that "the girls seemed to have found a beauty salon on Bataan.") The other Bataan-nurse movie of 1943 was *So Proudly We Hail.*
**1/2

## CUBA (1979)

United Artists   Richard Lester (Color)
With Sean Connery, Brooke Adams, Chris Sarandon, Jack Weston, Hector Elizondo

Richard Lester manages to make Cuba's recent history as dull as Richard Fleischer's movie biography *Che!* Sean Connery plays a mercenary hired in 1958 by the decadent Batista regime to contain Fidel Castro's rebels. After taking a good look at the sex parties and wide-open gambling dens that earned Havana its reputation as "Sin City," Connery begins to have doubts about the morality of his mission. If macho Connery can't decide what side he should be on, who cares? The story is of interest only if you don't know which side won.
*

## THE DAM BUSTERS (1954)

Great Britain   Michael Anderson (Black & white)
With Michael Redgrave, Richard Todd, Derek Farr, Basil Sydney, Raymond Huntley, Ursula Jeans, Ernest Clark

Armchair pilots will want to fasten their seat belts for this replay of a daring RAF raid on the heart of the Fatherland. Told in stark semidocumentary style and colored with fascinating technical details, the movie lets the facts speak for themselves and thankfully dispenses with the usual vapid love interest.

The time is 1943. The British urgently need to slow down the mighty German war machine by taking out factories in the industrial Ruhr Valley. But how to do it? Precision radar bombing is a thing of the future, and bombers are generally unable to hit anything smaller than a large town. The "mission impossible" falls to the daredevil 617 Squadron, under plucky Wing Commander Guy Gibson. In May his 19 Lancasters swoop into Germany. The planes dive to a suicidal height of 60 feet and release their payloads of specially designed spherical bombs over the Moehne and Eder dams, which are thought to control the water supply for local industry. Although eight Lancasters are lost and damage to the Ruhr Valley is not critical, the mission nevertheless goes down in RAF history as "perhaps the most accurate bombing attack ever carried out in the whole of the Second World War."

Economical and spare, *The Dam Busters* overcomes its limited budget with first-rate models and miniature work. (It was nominated for a special-effects Oscar but lost to *The Bridges at Toko-Ri*, which depicted air battles of the subsequent Korean War.) Stalwart Richard Todd based his characterization on real-life Wing Commander Gibson, and Michael Redgrave is an eccentric free-form version of bomb-builder Barnes Wallis.
***

## DARBY'S RANGERS (1957)
## Also titled *The Young Invaders*

Warner Bros.   William Wellman (Black & white)

DARBY'S RANGERS: Combat survivors are awarded medals for gallantry.

With James Garner, Etchika Choureau, Jack Warden, Edward Byrnes, David Janssen, Venetia Stevenson

A driving, courageous leader of men, William O. Darby commanded the original 1st Ranger Battalion as a lieutenant colonel and, later, three Ranger battalions as a brigadier general. (Rangers, of course, are the American equivalent of British commandos.) The unit that carried his name, Darby's Rangers, waged a glorious effort against the Germans in North Africa, Sicily and Italy and now has become part of combat lore. This movie biography is strictly routine, however. Director Wellman made a tactical error when he cast James Garner as the general, who comes across as a laid-back, let's-get-this-over-with Hollywood layabout. Only Jack Warden, a former combat paratrooper, manages to breathe life into the film, as a battle-weary top sergeant.

**

DARBY'S RANGERS: Jack Warden (left) and James Garner (right), who played the American Ranger leader.

## THE DARK ANGEL (1935)

United Artists   Sidney Franklin (Black & white)

With Fredric March, Merle Oberon, Herbert Marshall, John Halliday, Janet Beecher, Frieda Inescort

"Creaky" is the word for this hearts-and-flowers melodrama, which was a big hit way back then (as was a 1925 silent version starring Ronald Colman and Vilma Banky). Merle Oberon, making her American film debut, plays the fiancee of English officer Fredric March, who returns from World War I blinded and with the intention of selflessly breaking off the engagement. Meanwhile, thinking he has died at the front, Oberon has made plans to marry his friend (Herbert Marshall). Oberon, in her prime, is a stunning beauty.

**

## DARK OF THE SUN (1968)

**Also titled** *The Mercenaries*

Great Britain   Jack Cardiff (Color)

With Rod Taylor, Yvette Mimieux, Kenneth More, Jim Brown, Calvin Lockhart, André Morell, Peter Carsten

Audiences in the United States and Europe liked this two-fisted Western-*cum*-war movie, which took advantage of the rising public interest in soldiers for hire. Mercenary Rod Taylor energetically rescues citizens of a Congo village from rebel attacks, claiming a large hoard of diamonds in the bargain. Here, Simba tribesmen fill in for rampaging Indians, and mercenaries sub for the cavalry. Director Jack Cardiff moves at a brisk pace, with lots of exciting action, including strafing runs on a train, hand-to-hand combat worthy of Bruce Lee and various kinds of violent death. It was more than censors would allow, however, and some scenes were trimmed back, especially for screenings in Great Britain.

**1/2

## DAS BOOT (THE BOAT) (1981)

West Germany Wolfgang Peterson (Color)
With Jürgen Prochnow, Herbert Grönemeyer, Klaus Wenneman, Erwin Leder, Hubertus Bengsch, Martin Semmelgrogge

Since World War II there has been a certain hesitancy on the part of German filmmakers to make war movies about the war. For this reason *Das Boot* received a lot of attention when it was released. But it's not as a curiosity that it will be remembered. On the face of it, this exceptional war movie doesn't seem so exceptional. It has the standard "men-at-war" story of a submarine (U-boat) crew on a mission in the North Atlantic. It even has the standard mixed-bag crew, complete with one loyal Nazi, a few "good German" crewmen who badmouth Hitler, and a stoic, heroic Captain who may not agree with his country's leaders but nevertheless is going to do his job and get his men back alive. But that's all that's standard about this film. This is

white-knuckle, stomach-churning suspense of the highest caliber. The depth-charge attacks, as the sub has to sink silently, deeper and deeper to avoid destruction, are astounding. The tension, as the pressure builds and the rivets holding together the U-boat's metal plates begin to pop, is almost too much to bear. Director Peterson makes the U-boat a metaphor for all war, concentrating, in its small confines, all of war's horrible, uncertain dread, its anticipation, and its occasional moments of sheer terror. Truly one of the great war films.

****

## THE DAWN PATROL (1938)

Warner Bros.   Edmund Goulding (Black & white)
With Errol Flynn, David Niven, Basil Rathbone, Donald Crisp, Barry Fitzgerald, Melville Cooper, Carl Esmond

Errol Flynn, the screen's top swashbuckler, is at the controls in this vigorous tale of Britain's Royal Flying Corps during World War I. It's all here: the forced gaiety of doomed pilots; commanding officers who send their men to almost certain death; individual heroics worthy of the Crown; and a blackboard roster that changes every time a man is lost. These cliches, old hat even in 1938, were previously seen in the original 1930 version of the film, directed by debuting Howard Hawks, with Richard Barthlemess and Douglas Fairbanks, Jr., playing the leads. Its exciting aerial photography was used in this remake.

***

## DAYS OF GLORY (1944)

RKO   Jacques Tourneur (Color)

With Gregory Peck, Tamara Toumanova, Alan Reed, Lowell Gilmore, Hugo Haas, Maria Palmer

Russian guerrillas are the heroes of this humanist war romance, made in the pro-Soviet tradition of Hollywood's *North Star* and *Mission to Moscow* (both 1943). Producer Casey Robinson attempted to heighten the realism by casting unfamiliar faces as Russian partisans hiding behind Nazi lines south of Moscow. The star unknown is Gregory Peck, making his screen debut as the leader of the group who falls in love with aloof dancer Tamara Toumanova. Tossing hand grenades during the big Russian counteroffensive against the Germans, they eventually go on to their eternal glory. Overwrought perhaps but suspenseful nevertheless, the film failed to click at the box office, probably because of its lack of star names and its downbeat ending. After the war it was given another knock by American anti-Communists for being overly pro-Soviet.

**1/2

## D-DAY, THE SIXTH OF JUNE (1956)

20th Century-Fox   Henry Koster (Color)

With Robert Taylor, Richard Todd, Dana Wynter, Edmond O'Brien, John Williams, Jerry Paris

Be prepared to wait and wait for the title event; American Captain Robert Taylor and British Colonel Richard Todd don't get around to it until the last 40 minutes or so. Until then, you'll have to sit through a three-way wartime romance involving the above-named officers and lovely Dana Wyn-

ter. (Why aren't there ever enough girls to go around in these movies?) London never was the way it seems here, and the firefight finale resembles a beach-party cookout. Wait instead for Fox's other D-Day movie, *The Longest Day*.

*1/2

## DECISION BEFORE DAWN (1951)

20th Century-Fox   Anatole Litvak (Black & white)

With Oskar Werner, Richard Basehart, Gary Merrill, Hildegarde Neff, Dominique Blanchar, Helene Thimig, O. E. Hasse, Hans Christian Blech

Keyed to a new national attitude toward our anti-Soviet ally West Germany, *Decision Before Dawn* offered American audiences a sympathetic German soldier troubled by his conscience. Austrian actor Oskar Werner, in his American debut, plays Happy, a POW who, disillusioned with the Nazis, agrees to be parachuted back home in 1944 to spy for the Allies. Wandering through the war-ravaged countryside (where the film was shot), he sees his country falling to pieces as the Allies begin to tighten the circle. Although Werner's odyssey is sometimes confusing, his sensitive portrayal transcends the dull spots, and it's a must-see.

**1/2

## THE DEEP SIX (1958)

Warner Bros.   Rudolph Mate (Color)

With Alan Ladd, William Bendix, Dianne Foster, Efrem Zimbalist, Jr., James Whitmore, Keenan Wynn, Joey Bishop

Quaker Alan Ladd, looking a bit over the hill, can't fathom the need to sink Nazi vessels from aboard a Navy submarine, and the crew can't fathom him. The dishonest script has Ladd's lieutenant being ashamed of his pacifist beliefs, which are redeemed by an act of military heroism. There's a good premise here, but there's also a slipshod production and grainy, purplish Warnercolor.

*1/2

## THE DEER HUNTER (1978)

United Artists   Michael Cimino (Color)
With Robert De Niro, Christopher Walken, Meryl Streep, John Cazale, John Savage

Blood-vivid and profoundly disturbing, *The Deer Hunter* is one of the few Vietnam movies released during the late 1970s that doesn't take a potshot at America. Set in the fictitious town of Clairtown, Ohio, the story follows three young steelworkers from a satisfying life at home to service in a war they can't understand or relate to. In Vietnam the three pals are captured by Viet Cong guerrillas, who subject them to psychological torture games of Russian roulette. The only one to survive the ordeal intact is Mike Vronsky (De Niro), a former deer hunter with a strong moral code (he had always refused to take the animal unless he could kill it in one shot).

After their escape, Steven (John Savage) loses the use of his legs and seems

THE DEER HUNTER: Robert DeNiro and John Savage attempt to board a helicopter after escaping a Viet Cong torture camp.

destined to spend the rest of his life as a mental and physical cripple in a veteran's hospital. Meanwhile, Nick (Christopher Walken) has remained in Vietnam, where he works in a sleazy Saigon gambling casino. De Niro later returns during the fall of Saigon and finds him a drugged-out wreck, playing a game of Russian roulette to win a large bet.

All the performers are outstanding, including Meryl Streep as the girl who transfers her affections from Walken to De Niro. Among the memorable scenes is a hunting excursion (filmed in Washington State); the exotic milieu of Saigon's red-light district; the squalor of a Viet Cong POW camp; and the surreal fall of Saigon. There are a few military errors, however: Special Forces teams never would carry a 40-pound flamethrower on patrol; and the Russian roulette torture is a fantasy out of World War II. But the movie succeeds in its allegorical replay of how the Vietnam War wounded the spirit of America. The Motion Picture Academy gave it three Oscars, including best picture and best director. The irony of Walken winning as best supporting actor for portraying yet another drug-crazed GI wasn't lost on veterans.

***1/2

## THE DELTA FORCE (1986)

Cannon   Menachem Golan (Color)

With Lee Marvin, Chuck Morris, Martin Balsam, Joey Bishop, Hanna Schygulla, Susan Strasberg, Bo Svenson

This brisk revenge fantasy, inspired by the front-page skyjacking of TWA

THE DEER HUNTER: Robert DeNiro has all the right equipment as a Special Forces Long Range Reconnaissance Patrol (LRRP) member.

Flight 847 from Athens in 1985, struck box-office gold by replaying the incident as a successful U.S. rescue effort. Rather than have the American government negotiate for the hostages' release, the film sends in the Delta Force, America's real-life counter-terrorist unit. Leading the ultra-commandos are Lee Marvin and Chuck Norris, who blast into Beirut and massacre the terrorists with the latest in weaponry and technology. Less interesting are the semi-star hostages who people the jet in the manner of countless *Airplane* movies; only Hanna Schygulla as a resolute stewardess and Bo Svenson as the pilot are convincing.

Wisely, the filmmakers here let the automatic weapons, fast assault vehicles (FAVs) and rocket launchers carry most of the action. The dialogue is used merely to set up the next explosion of violence. Shot in Israel, the film not surprisingly depicts Arabs as stereotyped villains of the worst sort. But skewed politics aside, the film prophetically read the temper of the times: Barely three months after its release, the U.S. bombed Libya in response to mounting terrorist attacks against Americans.

**\*\*\***

### DESERT ATTACK (1959)
**Also titled** *Ice Cold in Alex*

Great Britain   J. Lee Thompson (Black & white)
With John Mills, Anthony Quayle, Sylvia Sims, Harry Andrews

It's 1942 in sweltering Libya, and British tank commander John Mills is treading across the sand dunes trying to get to safety through treacherous German minefields. Complicating the journey is an eccentric passenger list that includes two lost nurses and a Nazi spy. Although suspenseful and surprisingly involving (stay with it), the film was edited for American release, making it occasionally confusing. The clever British title refers to the ice-cold beer the men look forward to when they arrive safely in Alexandria.

**\*\*1/2**

### THE DESERT FOX (1951)
**Also titled** *Rommel—Desert Fox*

20th Century-Fox   Henry Hathaway (Black & white)

With James Mason, Jessica Tandy, Cedric Hardwicke, Luther Adler, Everett Sloane, Leo G. Carroll, Richard Boone

Six years after the war, Hollywood paid its first tribute to the fallen enemy with

THE DESERT FOX: James Mason (left) as Rommel comforts his wife, Jessica Tandy, as Richard Boone looks on.

this vividly realistic screen biography of Field Marshal Erwin Rommel. James Mason does full justice to the man, playing him as a "good German"—in contrast to the usual cold-blooded Nazi stereotype. A cultivated military genius with a sense of higher moral purpose, Rommel became a popular national hero when his Afrika Korps inflicted a series of defeats on the British Eighth Army in 1942. He later served in the Italian campaign and was responsible for strengthening the "Atlantic Wall" against the Allied D-Day invasion of Europe. The film hews closely to the facts, opening prior to the credits with the rout of a British commando unit in Africa and culminating in Rommel's disillusionment and his involvement in the July plot to assassinate Hitler.

Mason reprised the role in *The Desert Rats* (1953), which offers more of Rommel's brilliance on the combat field. Other actors who have impersonated Rommel include Erich von Stroheim, as the hateful Hun of *Five Graves to Cairo* (1943), and Wolfgang Preiss, as the calm intellectual of *Raid on Rommel* (1971).

***1/2

## THE DESERT RATS (1953)

20th Century-Fox   Robert Wise (Black & white)
With Richard Burton, James Mason, Robert Newton, Torin Thatcher, Robert Douglas

A solid World War II action-drama that offers a gritty re-creation of the rigors of desert warfare. The title is the nickname of the Australian 7th Division, which made a brave defensive stand against Rommel's superior Afrika Korps at Tobruk, an important harbor in Libya. Richard Burton is impressive as a British officer who commands one of the division's battalions. He leads some well-staged antitank defense tactics, then launches commando raids behind enemy lines to keep the Germans off balance.

Wounded and captured, he meets Rommel before escaping in time for a final cinematic battle. James Mason, in a cameo role, plays Rommel, re-creating his sterling performance in *The Desert Fox* (1951), of which this film is nominally a sequel. Less effective versions of the campaign are depicted in *Tobruk* (1967) and *Raid on Rommel* (1971), in which Burton again gets to meet the legendary general.

***

## DESPERATE JOURNEY (1942)

Warner Bros.   Raoul Walsh (Black & white)
With Errol Flynn, Ronald Reagan, Arthur Kennedy, Alan Hale, Raymond Massey, Nancy Coleman, Sig Rumann, Ronald Sinclair, Albert Basserman

Without razzmatazz heroes like Errol Flynn the Allies could never have won World War II. (In reality, the actor was classified as 4-F when he tried to enlist, because of a heart murmur, latent tuberculosis and a touch of malaria.) Flynn (Australian), future President Reagan (American) and Kennedy (Canadian) bail out of their disabled RAF bomber over Germany's Black Forest into the clutches of sneering Nazi officer Raymond Massey. Escaping to Holland, the boys manage to blow up a factory and travel aboard Goring's personal train before flying back to England in a captured Luftwaffe plane. The night bombings and sabotage scenes, achieved with scale models and animation, look real, and Raoul Walsh's steam-roller direction will keep you cheering. Last line in the film is, "Now for Australia and a crack at those Japs!"

**1/2

## DESTINATION TOKYO (1943)

Warner Bros.   Delmer Daves (Black & white)
With Cary Grant, John Garfield, Alan Hale, John Ridgely, Dane Clark, Warner Anderson, William Prince, Tom Tully, John Forsythe, Faye Emerson, Peter Whitney

Good of its kind, this popular under-water thriller takes place aboard an American submarine, the *Superfin*. Aristocratic skipper Cary Grant soberly glides his craft through the Aleutian Islands toward Tokyo, with John Garfield on hand as a rebellious, womanizing torpedoman. Their mission is to check the weather to guide Lieutenant Colonel James Doolittle's B-25s to the first bombing raid on Tokyo (see *Thirty Seconds Over Tokyo*). The heavy-handed propaganda and religious messages are annoying, but the voyage is enjoyable overall. Later submarine movies have almost always followed *Destination Tokyo* as a model.

***

DESTINATION TOKYO: Cary Grant (third from left), helps John Garfield (right), John Forsythe (second from right) and John Ridgely (third from right) prepare to land in Japan with obsolete Winchesters.

### DEVIL DOGS OF THE AIR (1935)

Warner Bros.   Lloyd Bacon (Black & white)

With James Cagney, Pat O'Brien, Frank McHugh, Margaret Lindsay, Helen Lowell, Robert Barrat, John Arledge, Ward Bond

Cagney and O'Brien have a noisy, gung-ho time as a maverick trainee and his best friend/rival fighting for the same girl (Margaret Lindsay) and top honors in the Marine Corps air wing. You've seen it all before in dozens of peacetime service movies (most recently in 1986's high-tech *Top Gun*), but this is one of the best and brightest. *"Devil Dogs of the Air* is loaded with pictorial dynamite,"* wrote a contemporary reviewer, "even if it is only an advertisement for the preparedness boys."

**1/2

### THE DEVIL'S BRIGADE (1968)

United Artists   Andrew McLaglen (Color)

With William Holden, Cliff Robertson, Dana Andrews, Carroll O'Connor, Vince Edwards, Andrew Prine, Richard Jaeckel, Claude Akins

CO William Holden, looking tired and worn, recruits various American misfits to work with superior Canadian troops for the First Special Service Brigade behind German lines. After the usual brawls and tough training, the men finally shape up and storm into Italy and Norway, proudly flashing their red berets. Although full of sound and fury, the film is only a smudged carbon of its model, *The Dirty Dozen* (1967).

**

### THE D.I. (1957)

Warner Bros.   Jack Webb (Black & white)

With Jack Webb, Don Dubbins, Jackie Loughery, Lin McCarthy, Monica Lewis

Director Jack Webb, stars as a tough Marine drill instructor (or D.I., as they are more commonly known), attempting to turn awkward Don Dubbins into a real gyrene. Webb looks the part as he heaps abuse on recruit Dubbins while putting him through the brutal paces of basic training. But his delivery soon becomes monotonous and was better suited to his long-running TV series *Dragnet*. The Army trained its men more enjoyably in *Take the High Ground* (1954).

**

### THE DIRTY DOZEN (1967)

MGM   Robert Aldrich (Color)

With Lee Marvin, Jim Brown, Ernest Borgnine, John Cassavetes, Robert Ryan, Charles Bronson, Donald Sutherland, Telly Savalas, George Kennedy, Richard Jaeckel, Clint Walker, Trini Lopez, Robert Webber, Ralph Meeker

A bona fide classic almost from the time of its release, this ultraviolent winner has all the right ingredients: a terrific title, and a cast, script and director that live up to it. Lee Marvin is the major in command who rounds up 12 soldiers sentenced to life imprisonment and death for such crimes as rape and murder. In return for a pardon (if they live), each agrees to undergo a rigorous training routine that will further refine their violent skills for a suicide attack on a chateau filled with high-ranking German officers on leave.

Unleashed on the eve of D-Day, the "dirty dozen" commit every war crime in the book as they stealthily invade the ancient building and eventually destroy it. Nearly all are killed during the attack, a punishment that doesn't seem quite enough for their mass atrocities. In one of the film's most gripping and morally disturbing scenes, the GIs lock innocent civilians in a bunker with the officers, then drop grenades through the above-ground air vents—a reminder, of course, of Nazi gas chambers. The vicious red carnage, the most graphic yet seen in a war movie, offended many critics, including one who wrote, "in war the scum is brought to the surface; it seems that this applies to the cinema also." For reasons unknown, the film was also a big hit in Germany, where audiences cheered as loudly as their American counterparts when scores of their helpless countrymen were killed. ****

## DIVE BOMBER (1941)

Warner Bros.   Michael Curtiz (Color)

With Errol Flynn, Fred MacMurray, Ralph Bellamy, Alexis Smith, Robert Armstrong, Regis Toomey, Craig Stevens, Gig Young, Allen Jenkins, Moroni Olsen, Charles Drake

Director Michael Curtiz plows up the skies with the strident cry of dive bombers in this often exciting tale of U.S. Navy pilots attempting to overcome their physical limitations. Errol Flynn, not quite right for the part, is a Navy doctor working to eliminate pilot blackout. The medical problem is obsolete now, and the romantic interest is a bore, but you'll like the aerial scenes, the first to be shot in color with a new portable Technicolor camera. **1/2

## THE DOGS OF WAR (1980)

United Artists   John Irvin (Color)

With Christopher Walken, Tom Berenger, Helen Shaver, Colin Blakely, Hugh Millais, Paul Freeman, Jean François Stevenin, JoBeth Williams

One of the first of a new breed of mercenary movies, *The Dogs of War* retains all the good points of Frederick Forsyth's how-to soldier-of-fortune

DIVE BOMBER: Regis Toomey (left), Fred MacMurray (center) and Errol Flynn portray aviation pioneers.

THE DOGS OF WAR: Christopher Walken drives a small group of mercenaries to safety after a failed mission.

novel. Discarded is Forsyth's numbing overlay of esoteric trivia. Walken, fresh from his Oscar-winning performance for best supporting actor in *The Deer Hunter*, is impressive as Shannon, a "merc" hired by a shadowy international corporation that has discovered a rich vein of platinum in a certain West African country. To excavate the mineral, the corporation needs to be in control, which is why they hire a private army to overthrow the legitimate regime and set up a puppet government. Included in the cast are Tom Berenger as Shannon's close friend Drew, Helen Shaver as Drew's bitchy wife, and Colin Blakely as North, a BBC-TV reporter who meets an untimely end when he gets in the way.

Director Irvin attempts to get under the skin of his military adventurers by presenting Shannon with moral as well as tactical problems. A reflection of the feelings of many alienated Vietnam veterans, he eventually looks beyond his gun sight and begins to wonder if murder is worth $100,000 in a Swiss bank account. This is a brutal film about unlikable characters committing criminal acts against people who are sometimes even more despicable.

***

## DON'T GIVE UP THE SHIP (1959)

Paramount   Norman Taurog (Black & white)
With Jerry Lewis, Dina Merrill

Jerry's at half mast in this so-so service comedy, tailored to his frenetic talents. The brass is upset when sailor Jerry, clumsy as always, somehow loses a Navy destroyer.

*1/2

## DON'T GO NEAR THE WATER (1957)

MGM   Charles Walters (Color)
With Glenn Ford, Anne Francis, Gia Scala, Mickey Shaughnessey, Romney Brent, Fred Clark, Kennan Wynn, Eva Gabor, Russ Tamblyn, Earl Holliman

A big moneymaker in 1957, this high-gloss version of William Brinkley's best seller must have seemed funnier in the days before *M*A*S*H* (1970). U.S. Navy press officer Glenn Ford and assorted misfits are a rear-guard public-relations unit whose mission is to make friends on an occupied Pacific island. Fred Clark has some hilarious scenes as the pompous CO, but sailor Mickey Shaughnessey steals most of the scenes by continually uttering that (then) unmentionable word, bleeped on the sound tract.

**

## DRAGON SEED (1944)

MGM   Jack Conway (Black & white)
With Katharine Hepburn, Walter Huston, Aline MacMahon, Turhan Bey, Akim Tamiroff, J. Carroll Naish, Agnes Moorhead, Hurd Hatfield, Frances Rafferty

Taping her eyelids isn't quite enough to transform the sophisticated Ms. Hepburn into a convincing Chinese peasant. Adapted from Pearl Buck's best seller, the film was Hollywood's attempt to show the suffering of China during the Japanese occupation. The situation is seen from the point of view of a family of remote farmers, played by a mixed bag of actors with varying accents. Well intentioned, the story has the peasants slowly coming to the realization that the invaders can be routed only by meeting fire with fire. Lionel Barrymore supplies the unnecessary off-screen narration.

**

## DR. STRANGELOVE: OR, HOW I LEARNED TO STOP WORRYING AND LOVE THE BOMB (1964)

Columbia   Stanley Kubrick (Black & white)
With Peter Sellers, George C. Scott, Peter Bull, Sterling Hayden, Keenan Wynn, Slim Pickens, James Earl Jones, Tracy Reed

Just as topical today, more than 20 years after its release, Stanley Kubrick's bizarre black comedy depicts the launching of World War III by a rabid anti-Communist American military officer. The film begins with crazy American General Sterling Hayden sending bombers to Russia because he thinks they are behind a plot to deprive him of his precious "body fluids." As the bombers head for their fail-safe point, the president of the United States convenes an emergency meeting with his top advisers, who include former Nazi scientist Dr. Strangelove and gung-ho General Buck Turgidson (George C. Scott). Sellers gives an absolute tour de force in three roles: as a dashing RAF officer, the U.S. president; and the demented Strangelove, now working for our side, who can't prevent his artificial arm from automatically giving a Nazi salute. Also memorable is Slim Pickens as the "down home" bombardier on the stray B-52 that manages to get through. He rides the Bomb like a bucking bronco as it falls on Russia to the strains of Vera Lynn's old World War II recording of "Till We Meet Again." Watching the film is something like standing in front of a firing squad peopled by hilarious comedians. But cancel your plans and tune in.

\*\*\*\*

### DUNKIRK (1958)

Great Britain   Leslie Norman (Black & white)
With John Mills, Richard Attenborough, Bernard Lee, Robert Urquhart, Ray Jackson, Sean Barrett

Great Britain wrested a victory of sorts from defeat when British warships and hundreds of civilian vessels managed to evacuate 335,490 officers and men from Dunkirk within seven days, after France fell to the Nazis. This authentic-looking version boasts excellent credits all around, with touching performances from England's best movie soldiers. John Mills is one of the rescued troops, and Bernard Lee (James Bond's boss, "M") is one of the volunteer boatowners. The detailed script is based on *The Big Pick-up* by Elleston Trevor and *Dunkirk* by Ewan Butler and J. S. Bradford.

\*\*\*

DR. STRANGELOVE: Peter Sellers (bottom right) "feeds" Sterling Hayden's .30-caliber machine gun.

THE EAGLE HAS LANDED: Michael Caine (center) and his men, who are disguised as Allied Polish paratroopers, take over a British town in an attempt to assassinate Churchill.

## THE EAGLE HAS LANDED (1976)

Great Britain   John Sturges (Color)

With Michael Caine, Donald Sutherland, Robert Duvall, Donald Pleasence, Jenny Agutter, Anthony Quayle, Treat Williams, Larry Hagman, Jean Marsh, Judy Geeson

Director John Sturges has brewed a weak tea from Jack Higgins' suspenseful novel, which depicts a group of German soldiers parachuting into England to assassinate Winston Churchill. Disguised as Free Polish paratroopers training in Britain, they nearly pull it off but finally are trapped in a church by a U.S. Army Ranger unit. Sturges compounds the improbable events by portraying his Germans (led by cockney Michael Caine) as just a bunch of very regular chaps acting in good faith. (He saves a Jewish girl from a death train, at least temporarily.) You're meant to be placed in the uncomfortable position of rooting for the enemy, but you're made merely uncomfortable.

**

THE EAGLE HAS LANDED: Michael Caine, who served in Korea as an infantryman, strikes a professional pose with a Sten submachine gun.

### EIGHT IRON MEN (1952)

Columbia   Edward Dmytryk (Black & white)

With Bonar Colleano, Lee Marvin, Arthur Franz, Richard Kiley, James Griffith, Dick Moore

Director Dmytryk pumps a fair amount of suspense into this standard actioner, produced by Stanley Kramer's "B" unit at Columbia. A cast of relative unknowns (back then) brings fresh characterizations to a squad of American soldiers pinned down by enemy fire in Italy. The constricted sets and back-lot countryside look shoddy, however.

**1/2

### THE ENEMY BELOW (1957)

20th Century-Fox   Dick Powell (Color)

With Robert Mitchum, Curt Jurgens, Theodore Bikel, Al (David) Hedison

German actor Curt Jurgens is the enemy below and Robert Mitchum is the enemy above, who are engaged in an exciting cat-and-mouse duel between their German U-boat and American destroyer. The two parry for advantage, matching move with countermove in the deep blue of the South Atlantic. Each manages to escape a death blow from the other until the sensational final battle. The film is all the more powerful for eschewing Nazi stereotypes and playing the drama as a contest of wills and expertise between two top professionals. Director Dick Powell (who also produced) fills his canvas with telling detail—notably, a brutal scene in which a young seaman fails to move his hand in time as depth charges roll into the sea.

***

### THE ENEMY GENERAL (1960)

Columbia   George Sherman (Black & white)

With Van Johnson, Jean-Pierre Aumont, Dany Carrel, John Van Dreeland, François Prevost

Van Johnson brings a note of pathos to his role of an American officer on the European Front, where he searches for the Nazi general who murdered his wife-to-be. The production looks tatty, however, and the brief action scenes are nothing new.

**

### ENSIGN PULVER (1964)

Warner Bros.   Joshua Logan (Color)

With Robert Walker, Jr., Burl Ives, Walter Matthau, Millie Perkins, Kay Medford, Tommy Sands, Larry Hagman, Al Freeman, Jr., James Coco, James Farentino

Since the title character had died at the end of *Mister Roberts* (1955), Warner was hard-pressed to come up with a sequel—and maybe it shouldn't have. Jack Lemmon had pretty much claimed the role of lazy survivor Ensign Pulver, played here by Robert Walker, Jr., son of the famous actor (and Jennifer Jones). Walker really isn't bad, it's just that he's not quite good enough to hold the slapstick together. On board Mr. *Roberts'* rusty old tub are pros Burl Ives and Walter Matthau doing what they can to bail water.

*1/2

### ESCAPE (1940)

**Also titled** *When the Door Opened*

MGM   Mervyn LeRoy (Black & white)

With Robert Taylor, Norma Shearer, Conrad Veidt, Nazimova, Felix Bressart, Bonita Granville, Philip Dorn, Albert Basserman

MGM decided to name names in this well-played follow-up to the studio's

*The Mortal Storm*, released earlier that year. The country is definitely Germany now (not "somewhere in Europe"), visited by American-born Mark Preysing (Robert Taylor) to find his widowed mother, a famous German actress known as Emmy Ritter (Nazimova). Helping Preysing is an American-born countess (Norma Shearer), whose Nazi boyfriend (Conrad Veidt) is the commandant of the concentration camp where the woman is being held. The farfetched ending has a doctor injecting a coma-inducing drug into Ritter so she can be secreted to safety as a dead body.

As in so many of its prewar movies, Hollywood equated Nazi atrocities with the concentration camp and the Gestapo interrogation, being unaware of the worse horrors taking place. Conrad Veidt, a refugee German, made his American debut here, and Nazimova, one of the big stars of the World War I era, returned to the screen after an absence of 20 years. The film's source is Ethel Vance's runaway best seller of 1939. As a result of this film, Hitler banned all MGM products in Germany and the occupied countries.

***

## ESCAPE FROM EAST BERLIN (1962)
**Also titled** *Tunnel 28*

Germany/U.S. Robert Siodmak (Black & white)

With Don Murray, Christine Kaufmann, Werner Klemperer, Ingrid van Bergen

Topical in its time, this escape thriller took advantage of headlines garnered by East German's recent construction of a concrete wall across Berlin (that perennial Cold War hot spot) to stop the manpower drain from East to West. The plot is based on an actual incident in which 28 East Berliners escaped by tunneling under the Wall. Although Don Murray turns in a fine high-strung performance as the group's leader, director Robert Siodmak doesn't wring much suspense from the proceedings. The film is still worth a look, however, for its on-location photography and its intriguing view of a city with a split personality.

**

## ESCAPE TO ATHENA (1979)

Great Britain George Pan Cosmatos (Color)

With Roger Moore, David Niven, Elliott Gould, Telly Savalas, Richard Roundtree, Claudia Cardinale, Stephanie Powers

Filmed in Greece, this preposterous World War II caper movie lies in an abyss somewhere between slapstick and noisy melodrama. Moore plays a Nazi officer who wears designer leathers; Niven, Gould and Roundtree are among the POWs forced to excavate an archaeological site. Savalas/Kojak is on hand as a bejeweled, bullet-headed Greek guerrilla in charge of sabotaging German installations. Save your popcorn for another night.

1/2*

## ESPIONAGE AGENT (1939)

Warner Bros. Lloyd Bacon (Black & white)

With Joel McCrea, Brenda Marshall, Jeffrey Lynn, Shirley Ridges, George Bancroft, James Stephenson

Warner was turning out these propagandistic thrillers by the dozen during Germany's prewar expansion into Middle Europe. Joel McCrea stars as an American diplomat whose actress-wife (Brenda Marshall) had previously sold her service to the Gestapo as a spy when in need of money. Outraged, McCrea decides to return to Europe to expose the danger of Nazi espionage to the complacent American public. The story is tersely handled and bears a similarity to the studio's *Confessions of a Nazi Spy*, also made in 1939, and Hitchcock's *Foreign Correspondent*, in which McCrea would star the following year.

**

## EXODUS (1960)

United Artists   Otto Preminger (Color)

With Paul Newman, Eva Marie Saint, Ralph Richardson, Peter Lawford, Lee J. Cobb, Sal Mineo, John Derek, Hugh Griffith, Jill Haworth, Gregory Ratoff, Felix Aylmer, David Opatoshu

Otto Preminger shifted the emphasis of Leon Uris's best seller about the birth of Israel from politics to historical pageant (to avoid what he considered "propaganda"), and the result is a mixed blessing. The plot follows the escape to Palestine of displaced Jews interned on the island of Cyprus in 1947. Embroiled in the action is a fine cast of international stars, including Paul Newman as a brave underground leader and Sal Mineo as a fiery young terrorist (the role got him an Oscar nomination). Uniformly wooden are John Derek as a friendly Arab and Peter Lawford as a movieland British officer.

Despite excellent on-location color photography and a number of vivid battle scenes, *Exodus* is often as sluggish as a caravan of camels. Overlong at nearly 3 1/2 hours, it reportedly prompted comedian Mort Sahl to stand up at a screening and cry, "Let my people go!" Fortunately, the film usually is shown in two consecutive parts on television. Scriptwriter Dalton Trumbo finally got screen credit under his own name for this one, after having been blacklisted (and imprisoned) as one of the "Hollywood Ten," convicted of contempt of Congress by the HUAC in the late 1940s.

**1/2

## EYE OF THE NEEDLE (1981)

United Artists   Richard Marquand (Color)

With Donald Sutherland, Kate Nelligan, Anthony Andrews

Marble-eyed Donald Sutherland makes a convincing psychopath in this fine adaptation of Ken Follett's best seller, filmed in England and Ireland. The plot has Sutherland as a cold-blooded killer recruited by the Nazis to slip into London and steal the D-Day invasion plans. Sutherland, one step ahead of security agents, makes his way to a remote island in the North to await the boat that will take him to occupied France. While there he stirs the affections of a love-starved housewife (Kate Nelligan), whose husband (Anthony Andrews) has been crippled during the Battle of Britain. Director Marquand handles the suspense with finesse, and the love scenes, more mature than those usually found in war movies, should appeal to men and women alike. Best scene: Sutherland and the wheelchair-bound Andrews locked in mortal combat on a cliff overlooking the sea.

***

## FAIL SAFE (1964)

Columbia   Sidney Lumet (Black & white)
With Henry Fonda, Dan O'Herlihy, Walter Matthau, Larry Hagman, Frank Overton, Fritz Weaver

Based on the World War III chiller by Eugene Burdick, *Fail Safe* is one of the best of a slew of American political films released in the early 1960s. (The list includes *The Manchurian Candidate*, *Seven Days in May*, *Advise and Consent*, *The Best Man* and *Dr. Strangelove*.) Unfortunately, this high-pressure dooms-day melodrama was overshadowed by Stanley Kubrick's *Dr. Strangelove*, which treated the same subject as a malicious black comedy.

Here, the crisis results from a computer malfunction at an American air base that sends a fleet of fictional Vindicator bombers, armed with nuclear bombs, to Russia. Before Henry Fonda (as the U.S. President) can cancel the mission, the planes have passed their fail-safe point and can no longer be recalled. Moscow is destroyed, and, to make amends, Fonda calls the Soviet premier and tells him he has ordered the bombing of New York. Thus an all-out war has been avoided—at the expense of the unsuspecting citizens of New York.

Unbearably tense at times and convincingly acted, the film eschews splashy special effects in favor of showing the action from a bomber cockpit, and a large projected map of the world that resembles a mammoth video game, in the Pentagon. A product of the country's first ban-the-bomb movement, *Fail Safe* presents a good case for arms control. Although it has a disclaimer stating that Air Force weapon control systems are infallible, it's obvious that such assurances are what the film is all about.
***1/2

## A FAREWELL TO ARMS (1932)

Paramount   Frank Borzage (Black & white)
With Helen Hayes, Gary Cooper, Adolphe Menjou, Mary Philips, Jack La Rue, Blanche Frederici, Henry Armetta

The youthful Gary Cooper and Helen Hayes are touching as a World War I ambulance driver and the ill-fated nurse he falls in love with. The production looks dated now, but the war scenes retain their stylized effectiveness, with the legendary stars managing to suggest that spiritual love can transcend its often short-lived earthly counterpart. Oscars went to cinematographer Charles Bryant Lang, Jr., and sound recordist Harold C. Lewis. This is the first of Ernest Hemingway's many novels to reach the screen; the story was pirated in *Force of Arms* (1951) and filmed again in 1957.
***

## A FAREWELL TO ARMS (1957)

20th Century-Fox   Charles Vidor (Color)
With Rock Hudson, Jennifer Jones, Vittorio de Sica, Alberto Sordi, Kurt Kaznar, Mercedes McCambridge, Elaine Stritch, Oscar Homolka, Victor Francen

Producer David O. Selznick, maker of the landmark *Gone with the Wind*, made a cropper with this bloated version of Ernest Hemingway's autobiographical classic, previously filmed in 1932. Jennifer Jones (Selznick's wife) is an appealing Catherine, an English nurse who falls in love with Frederic (Rock Hudson), an American serving with an Italian ambulance unit during World

A FAREWELL TO ARMS: Gary Cooper and Helen Hayes are the romantic couple. The love scenes created quite a stir when the film was first released in 1932.

War I. Reportedly, Hudson lost interest in the film when he realized Selznick was throwing it to Jones. Director John Huston resigned early on, and substitute Charles Vidor had to contend with the producer's insistence on epic production values unsuited to the intimate story. Although Hemingway had long ago sold the movie rights, Selznick cabled the author and magnanimously offered $100,000 from the expected profits. Hemingway, displeased with the movie, cabled back that he doubted there would be profits and that if there were Selznick should change the dollars into nickels and "shove them" until he filled himself.

*1/2

## FATHER GOOSE (1964)
Universal  Ralph Nelson (Color)
With Cary Grant, Leslie Caron, Trevor Howard, Jack Good

Cary Grant casts aside his usual sartorial splendor for a winning portrayal of a seedy beachcomber named Walter, secretly spotting enemy planes for the Australians during World War II. Into his lonely tropical Eden drifts schoolmarm Leslie Caron with her prepubescent brood. Grant has some amusing moments as a W. C. Fields-like child-hater (although you know he isn't really), and Caron is a good comedy foil and romantic match. The script won best screenplay Oscars for S. H. Barnett, Peter Stone and Frank

Tarloff. A bit coy now, perhaps, but a film the entire family can enjoy.
**1/2

## 55 DAYS AT PEKING (1963)

U.S./Spain   Nicholas Ray (Color)

With Charlton Heston, David Niven, Ava Gardner, Paul Lukas, Flora Robson, Leo Genn, Robert Helpmann, Harry Andrews, John Ireland, Elizabeth Sellars, Jacques Sernas

One of the big road-show attractions of the early 1960s, this star-studded spectacle suffers when seen on the small home screen (it was filmed in 70m). The title refers to the siege of Peking's international diplomatic quarter in 1900 by a secret organization called "The Society of Harmonious Fists," more popularly known as "Boxers." Reinforcements from the six nations that had carved up China eventually arrived to put down the rebellion, which nevertheless paved the way for Sun Yat-sen's nationalist movement.

Dealing with the antiforeign violence is American major Charlton Heston, with Ava Gardner, David Niven and others supplying the decadence and intrigue. The script, by Philip Yordan and Bernard Gordon, hews closely to the facts, but viewers not interested in Chinese political history may be bored between the extravagant battle scenes, crammed with masses of extras.
**

## FIGHTER SQUADRON (1948)

Warner Bros.   Raoul Walsh (Color)

With Edmond O'Brien, Robert Stack, Henry Hull, John Rodney, Walter Reed, Tom D'Andrea, Shepperd Strudwick, Rock Hudson

Good air action scenes highlight this paean to the hot fighter jocks who shot up the Luftwaffe with batteries of eight .50-caliber machine guns mounted to barrel-shaped P-47 Thunderbolts. Some of the footage is the real thing and shows Nazi planes, locomotives, trucks, fuel tanks and buildings disintegrating under heavy American gunfire. The barracks chatter is a bit like dormitory dialogue, but it's believable since the majority of fighter pilots were of college age.
**1/2

## THE FIGHTING LADY (1945)

20th Century-Fox   William Wyler (Color)

no cast credits

An official war production, this early color documentary was shot by famed photographer Edward Steichen, USNR, aboard the aircraft carrier *Fighting Lady*. The film documents daily life on the high seas and includes rare footage of action in the Pacific off the Marianas and Guam. There's also a kamikaze attack on the vessel and breathtaking shots of pilots trying to maneuver tight landings in burning and damaged planes. Lieutenant Robert Taylor provides the off-screen narration.

Army Air Corps Colonel William Wyler edited the footage at the Hal Roach Studio in Culver City, which had been requisitioned by the U.S. War Department and redubbed "Fort Roach" (its staff of writers was jokingly referred to as "The Flying Typers"). Wyler, who won Oscars for directing *Mrs. Miniver*, *The Best Years of Our Lives* and *Ben Hur*, also filmed the prize-winning documentary *Memphis Belle*, the name of a famous B-17 bomber.

****

### THE FIGHTING SEABEES (1944)

Republic   Edward Ludwig (Black & white)

With John Wayne, Dennis O'Keefe, Susan Hayward, William Frawley, Leonid Kinskey, Duncan Renaldo, Addison Richards, Paul Fix

The Seabees, known officially as the U.S. Navy Construction Battalion (CBs), have never gotten their due for the many airfields, landing and other facilities they hastily built in combat areas during World War II. This film does what it can, but it's primarily an action vehicle for John Wayne. Cast as a construction worker in the Pacific, he fights a hand-to-hand battle with Japanese invaders when they attack one of his buildings during the early days of the war. Later commissioned into the Seabees, he again leads his men in search of snipers while the enemy overruns the base. Interesting-ly, it's Wayne's only film in which his character is responsible for unnecessary casualties.

Dennis O'Keefe is surprisingly good in his role as a levelheaded naval officer with the thankless job of keeping Wayne on a leash, but the rest of the cast is as guilty as Wayne when it comes to false bravado. Although there are two well-choreographed combat scenes, don't look for realism here: In one sequence an enemy tank is knocked out by a mortar shot, and in another construction workers don't even lose their hats when strafed by Zeros. Starlet Susan Hayward adds a bit of anachronistic glamor—and a further guffaw—as a reporter visiting the battlefront in designer dresses.

**1/2

### THE FIGHTING 69TH (1940)

Warner Bros.   William Keighley (Black & white)

With James Cagney, Pat O'Brien, George Brent, Alan Hale, Dennis Morgan, William Lundigan, Jeffrey Lynn, Frank McHugh, Dick Foran

THE FIGHTING 69TH: Tough guy James Cagney (right) is counseled by the chaplain, Pat O'Brien.

You'll have a good time curling up with this entertaining period piece. Those great old Warner actors, are almost like friends of the family, fighting in the trenches of World War I as members of the "Fighting 69th," an all-Irish regiment from the streets of New York. Cagney, switching from crime to war, turns yellow when the bullets start to fly. Luckily, chaplain Pat O'Brien is on hand to instruct him in courage under fire, allowing Cagney to become a hero in the last reel. Warner's intention was an all-star World War II recruiting poster, but the film survives nicely as an escapist adventure.

**1/2

## THE FINAL COUNTDOWN (1980)

United Artists   Don Taylor (Color)
With Kirk Douglas, Martin Sheen, Katharine Ross, James Farentino, Ron O'Neal, Charles Durning

An entertaining mix of science fiction and first-rate battle action, *The Final Countdown* marks the movie debut of the *U.S.S. Nimitz*, the world's largest nuclear-powered aircraft carrier. On a shakedown cruise in the Pacific near Hawaii, the mighty warship runs into what appears to be a violent electrical storm. Actually, the carrier has gone through a time warp that propels it back to the morning of December 7, 1941. F-14A Tomcats are quickly scrambled to intercept unidentified planes flying their way, which turn out to be—believe it or not—Japanese Zeros. The dilemma faced by the Nimitz's skipper (Kirk Douglas) is whether to sink the Japanese fleet thus preventing the sneak attack on Pearl Harbor, and altering the course of history. (The Pearl Harbor footage was lifted from *Tora! Tora! Tora!*.)

The real show is the footage of carrier in action and the technological wonders that keep it working. A seagoing Goliath, the *Nimitz* is more than 30 stories high and can stay at sea for 13 years before coming in to refuel its reactors. It carries a regular crew of 5,500 officers and men, with 10 squadrons of eight different aircraft and four catapults that can throw one into the air at 160 mph every 20 seconds. For a close-up look at the mighty vessel at work, this movie is a must.

***

## FIRES ON THE PLAIN (1959)

Japan   Kon Ichikawa (Black & white)
With Eiji Funakoshi, Osamu Takizawa, Micky Curtis

Nauseatingly graphic, this celebrated antiwar movie is often hopelessly arty, but it's fascinating nevertheless. The Leyte action in the Philippines is seen from the point of view of a Japanese private suffering through the last weeks of a losing war. Cut off from his unit, he senselessly murders a Filipino girl frightened by his ragged appearance, then shoots a starving soldier who is in the act of cannibalizing his buddy. At the finale, he attempts to give himself up to advancing GIs but is shot instead. By implication the movie is harshly critical of the military clique that brought Japan into the war.

**1/2

## FIRST BLOOD (1982)

Orion   Ted Kotcheff (Color)
With Sylvester Stallone, Richard Crenna, Brian Dennehy

The noncommunicative, demented

Vietnam veteran called Rambo first blazed into our memories in this ultra-violent revenge thriller. Having been wrongly jailed and brutalized by a sheriff (who drew "first blood"), Sylvester Stallone wreaks havoc on a small town by calling on his skills as a former Green Beret. The muscular superstar resorts to violence only when he has to, of course, which in his case means shooting, stabbing and stomping several deputies before he surrenders. (In the novel by David Morell, Rambo kills the deputies rather than wounds them.)

As usual in movies of this kind, the story is secondary to the special effects and combat scenes. You get karate chops, a car-motorcycle chase, a helicopter pursuit, lots of kill-crazed National Guardsmen, and enough explosions for several war movies. In one notable boo-boo a Guardsman takes out a mine shaft with an M-72 light antitank weapon that packs unbelievable explosive force as opposed to its actual small-scale power. Despite the fact that he has been wronged, it's difficult to identify with Rambo and his one-man blitzkrieg, although flashbacks to his treatment as a POW add a note of sympathy. The character manages to perpetuate the stereotype of the Vietnam-bred psychotic that veterans have been trying to live down since they came home. Apparently, veterans who overcame their problems are not good box office.

***

## FIRST TO FIGHT (1967)

Warner Bros.   Christian Nyby (Color)

With Chad Everett, Dean Jagger, Marilyn Devon, Gene Hackman, Claude Akins, Bobby Troup

Good battle scenes on Guadalcanal might hold your interest in this otherwise routine psychological melodrama. The synthetic macho belongs to Chad Everett as the winner of a Congressional Medal of Honor who, after being feted at home, loses his nerve when returned to the front lines (at his own request, yet). There's also a flashback telling how he fell in love with his wife while the couple watched *Casablanca*, of which several clips are shown to the detriment of this later Warner product.

*1/2

## FIVE BRANDED WOMEN (1960)

Italy/U.S.   Martin Ritt (Black & white)

With Jeanne Moreau, Silvana Mangano, Barbara Bel Geddes, Vera Miles, Van Heflin, Richard Basehart, Harry Guardino, Steve Forrest, Alex Nichol

Shorn of their hair for consorting with Nazis, five Yugoslavian women hide out in the hills, where they meet a band of male Partisans. Joining forces with the guerrillas, the women clear their names and gain a place of honor by heroically ambushing the invading Germans. While the rigors of underground life are shown in detail—including childbirth in the filth of a decaying hideout—the female stars are much too refined to make the tale believable.

**

## FIVE FINGERS (1952)

20th Century-Fox   Joseph Mankiewicz (Black & white)

With James Mason, Danielle Darrieux, Michael Rennie, Walter Hampden, Herbert Berghof, Oscar Karlweiss, Michael Pate

James Mason, who had portrayed Field Marshall Rommel in *The Desert Fox* the year before, turned Axis spy in this taut, well-oiled thriller, which ranks with the best of Hitchcock. Michael Wilson's script is based on L. C. Moyzich's factual book *Operation Cicero*, with Mason as the real-life, trusted valet of the British ambassador to Turkey. Code-named Cicero by the Gestapo, Mason steals valuable decoded information concerning the European campaign and sells it to the Germans (his motive is money). There's a thrilling chase through the streets of neutral Ankara when the British discover his treachery, and a triply ironic finale: The Germans dismissed the information as unreliable and Cicero, now safe in Rio, bemusedly learns that the Nazis double-crossed not only him but also the haughty countess (Danielle Darrieux) who stole his blood money. *Five Fingers* is one of those films that can be seen again and again.
***1/2

## FIVE GATES TO HELL (1959)

20th Century-Fox   James Clavell (Black & white)
With Neville Brand, Patricia Owens, Dolores Michaels

Neville Brand, usually a competent actor, is preposterous as a guerrilla warlord in French Indochina prior to the Vietnam War. Several of his victims are gorgeous Red Cross nurses (never plain ones, of course) unexpectedly surrounded by the enemy. At the very least the movie is good for a laugh. Clavell did better as the director of *To Sir with Love* and as the author of the best sellers *Tai-Pan* and *King Rat*.
1/2*

## FIVE GRAVES TO CAIRO (1943)

Paramount   Billy Wilder (Black & white)
With Franchot Tone, Akim Tamiroff, Erich von Stroheim, Anne Baxter, Peter van Eyck, Miles Mander

An espionage thriller rather than a combat movie, this wartime fantasy is set in the Libyan campaign. One of director Wilder's also-rans, it has two redeeming features: the stunning desert locale (actually California's Mojave Desert) and Erich von Stroheim as a sneering Rommel (a reprise of the actor's general in *Grand Illusion*). Franchot Tone stars as a British spy who saves the day at the Battle of El Alamein. It's an incredible premise, of course, since Rommel and his staff were extraordinarily conscious of security and would never have let a double agent (Tone) in on their plans. In reality, Britain's Field Marshal Montgomery did have an intelligence windfall before the battle, but this came from the supersecret "Ultra" communications intercept of Rommel's orders.

Released during Montgomery's march across North Africa, the film was remarkably timely and cleaned up at the box office. It's best enjoyed now for the performance of horrible Hun von Stroheim complaining to hotel maid Anne Baxter that he has an aversion to women in the morning.
**1/2

## FIXED BAYONETS (1951)

20th Century-Fox   Samuel Fuller (Black & white)

With Richard Basehart, Gene Evans, Richard Hylton, Craig Hill, Michael O'Shea

Good characterizations fail to lift this Korean War adventure out of the ordinary. Richard Basehart is a corporal who becomes a hero during the difficult winter of 1950-51, when enemy troops attach his cut-off squad. Director Sam Fuller provides some nice documentary-style touches, but he did better in Korea earlier that year with *The Steel Helmet*.

**

### FLIGHT FOR FREEDOM (1943)

RKO   Lothar Mendes (Black & white)

With Rosalind Russell, Fred MacMurray, Herbert Marshall, Eduardo Ciannelli, Walter Kingsford, Richard Loo

Perennially fascinating is the mystery disappearance of American aviator Amelia Earhart over the Pacific during a 1937 attempt to fly around the world. Movie career girl Rosalind Russell does a competent job of impersonating "Lady Lindbergh" in this highly fictionalized biography, which doesn't identify her by name (at the request of Earhart's widower George Palmer Putnam). Also included are incidents from the career of pioneer flier Jacqueline Cochran, wife of the film's producer, Floyd Odlum.

While the mystery has never been solved, recent researchers theorized that Earhart made a forced landing on a Pacific island being fortified by the Japanese, who executed her to guard their secret World War II plans. The film comes remarkably close to this view by having Russell crash-land to bring Navy searchers to the area,

FLIGHT FOR FREEDOM: Rosalind Russell as a female pilot who disappears over the Pacific while spying on the Japanese just prior to World War II. The film was loosely based on Amelia Earhart's similar disappearance. Courtesy of RKO Pictures, Inc. Copyright © 1943 RKO Pictures, Inc. All Rights Reserved.

where she had previously photographed enemy installations with a hidden airborne camera. There are some effective early flight sequences, but too much of the story is taken up by romantic interludes between Russell and ace pilot Fred MacMurray.

**

### FLYING LEATHERNECKS (1951)

RKO   Nicholas Ray (Color)

With John Wayne, Robert Ryan, Don Taylor, Jay C. Flippen, Janis Carter, William Harrigan, James Bell

Once again at the head of a fighter squadron, only this time it's the Marines, not *The Flying Tigers* (1942), John Wayne may have gotten older, but

FLYING LEATHERNECKS: Marine Corps Hellcat is ready for takeoff. Courtesy of RKO Pictures, Inc. Copyright © 1951 RKO Pictures, Inc. All Rights Reserved.

FLYING LEATHERNECKS: John Wayne (left) and Robert Ryan (right) are commanding officer and executive officer respectively. Courtesy of RKO Pictures, Inc. Copyright © 1951 RKO Pictures, Inc. All Rights Reserved.

he's the same no-nonsense leader, the stickler for discipline he played in *Sands of Iwo Jima* (1949), a much better outing for the typecast star. In between arguments with resentful Robert Ryan, the Duke gets to fight in Technicolor for the first time. There are also some good air combat scenes with real Hellcats and Corsairs and some footage shot in action by Marine Corps photographers. Almost stealing the picture is Jay C. Flippen's sergeant, who steals from other companies to make sure his own is well supplied.

**1/2

## FLYING TIGERS (1942)

Republic   David Miller (Black & white)

With John Wayne, John Carroll, Anna Lee, Paul Kelly, Gordon Jones, Gregg Barton, John James, Mae Clarke

Having rocketed to stardom in *Stagecoach* in 1939, after years of toiling in low-budget Westerns, John Wayne added the military to his legend with

this tribute to the "Flying Tigers." Properly known as the American Volunteer Group (or AVG), the unit was a Chinese Air Force unit organized by Colonel Claire Chennault, with 100 pilots and fighters from the U.S. Navy and Army. Their mission was to repel the country's Japanese invaders. The film's plot is the old "What are we fighting for?" routine, with Wayne fighting to save democracy (for the first time), while buddy John Carroll is strictly cash and carry. There are some effective aerial combat scenes whenever the pair isn't fighting for the love of Red Cross nurse Anna Lee. Carroll, like many reluctant cinematic warriors before him, atones for his greed by saving Wayne's life and sacrificing his own on a suicide mission. The altruistic turnaround is the picture's dramatic highlight, but it's Wayne's charismatic presence that holds the film together.
**1/2

## FOLLOW THE BOYS (1944)

Universal   Edward Sutherland (Black & white)
With George Raft, Vera Zorina, Grace MacDonald, Charley Grapewin, George Macready, Elizabeth Patterson. Guest stars: Orson Welles, Marlene Dietrich, Jeannette MacDonald, Donald O'Connor, Dinah Shore, W. C. Fields, Peggy Ryan, the Andrews Sisters, Arthur Rubenstein, Sophie Tucker

A dancer (George Raft) turns patriotic and organizes a big musical show to entertain the troops. This all-star flag-waver was one of a number of musical comedy revues turned out by Hollywood during the war years (a booth selling war bonds always was prominently displayed in theater lobbies). Paramount had *Star-Spangled Rhythm*(1942), MGM had *Thousands Cheer* (1943) and Warners, the most war-minded of studios, had *This Is the Army* (1943) and *Hollywood Canteen* (1944). There are a few good bits in *Follow the Boys*, notably the rare sight of amateur magician Orson Welles sawing Marlene Dietrich in half, and a very funny routine by W. C. Fields.
**1/2

## FORCE OF ARMS (1951)

Warner Bros. Michael Curtiz (Black & white)
With William Holden, Nancy Olson, Frank Lovejoy, Gene Evans, Dick Wesson, Paul Picerni

Army officer William Holden falls in love with ingenue WAC Nancy Olson, who had been badly hurt in a previous romance. The couple has a difficult time keeping their minds on the Italian campaign, and you'll probably feel the same about their affair. Director Curtiz (*Casablanca*) pours on the suds with a liberal hand, and you may not recognize Ernest Hemingway's *A Farewell to Arms* updated to World War II in Richard Tregaskis's short story. The film was conceived as a follow-up to *Sunset Boulevard*, in which the two stars had appeared to better effect the year before.
**

## FORCE 10 FROM NAVARONE (1978)

Great Britain   Guy Hamilton (Color)
With Robert Shaw, Harrison Ford, Edward Fox, Franco Nero, Barbara Bach, Richard Kiel

A sequel in name only to the exciting *Guns of Navarone* (1961), this tepid wartime fantasy has two of the characters from Alistair MacLean's novel leading a daring sabotage mission in Nazi-occupied Yugoslavia.

There are liberal and sometimes inappropriate leavenings of humor as the men go about blowing up a vital bridge, with far too many garish on-screen casualties. Robert Shaw, looking drawn and tired, died of a heart attack soon after shooting was completed.
**

## A FOREIGN AFFAIR (1948)

Paramount   Billy Wilder (Black & white)

With Jean Arthur, Marlene Dietrich, John Lund, Millard Mitchell, Stanley Prager, Peter Von Zerneck

Like vintage champagne, Billy Wilder's dry comedy about wartime morals seems to become headier with age. Filmed on location in war-ravaged Berlin, the film concerns a naive female congresswoman (Jean Arthur) visiting Germany to investigate the suspected low morale of U.S. troops stationed there. Instead, she falls in love with a manipulative Army captain (John Lund) who is having an affair with a beautiful ex-Nazi (Marlene Dietrich).

To Wilder, the gloom and misery of the ruined, partitioned city is a canvas against which survivors and victors alike are forced to show their true and often hilarious natures. Russian soldiers are depicted as boobs being hustled by GIs selling them cheap Mickey Mouse watches, while both enjoy the riches of the black market and the local women, who can be had for a few chocolate bars and a pair of nylons. Dietrich, who gets to sing a few of her trademark songs, is perfect as a worldly opportunist whose beliefs change with the political winds. Arthur, learn-

ing to play dirty, ultimately captures Lund and has Dietrich hustled off to a de-Nazification center, but not before Marlene tells the congresswoman "what silly shrews American women are."
***1/2

## FOREIGN CORRESPONDENT (1940)

United Artists   Alfred Hitchcock (Black & white)

With Joel McCrea, Laraine Day, Herbert Marshall, Albert Basserman, George Sanders, Edmund Gwenn, Robert Benchley, Eduardo Ciannelli, Harry Davenport, Martin Kosleck

After debuting in Hollywood with the Academy Award-winning *Rebecca* earlier that year, Hitchcock undertook this wartime espionage thriller (at the urging of British authorities) to help counter American isolationism. Released in August 1940, it coincided with the fall of France and the German blitz of London. One of the director's best films, it resembles *The 39 Steps*, *Saboteur* and *North by Northwest* in that the hero's mission to solve a mystery results in a new maturity and a deepened trust in his allies.

The complex plot concerns a likable but not very bright journalist (Joel McCrea) sent to cover a story in England. There he falls in love with the beautiful daughter of a Nazi spy (Herbert Marshall) posing as the head of a pacifist organization. The chain of intrigue leads McCrea to Holland and a secret rendezvous point for Nazi fifth columnists. After several attempts are made on his life, he loses his innocence and becomes dedicated to exposing the spy ring. When his Clipper flight to the

States is shot down by the enemy, he survives and returns to England. At the finale, McCrea is shown broadcasting to America and delivering a ringing plea, as bombs fall on London, to prepare for the coming war against fascism.

The film's impressive design is the work of William Cameron Menzies, who had re-created the Old South for *Gone with the Wind*. Among Hitchcock's breathtaking scenes is a murder committed on the crowded steps of a town hall (the killer escapes under a sea of umbrellas), an escape from an Amsterdam hotel by creeping along a narrow outside ledge, a seemingly innocent Dutch windmill whose sails revolve in the wrong direction, and a truly "smashing" plane crash. Shot entirely in Hollywood, the film was augmented with background shots from London and Holland and looks remarkably authentic.

Among the admirers of *Foreign Correspondent* was Dr. Joseph Goebbels, Hitler's minister of information and propaganda, who probably got a print from Switzerland. The film's one flaw, in Hitchcock's view, was the casting of open-faced Joel McCrea as his common man. Gary Cooper, his first choice, later regretted turning down the project because it was a thriller.

****

## THE 49TH PARALLEL (1941)
**Also titled** *The Invaders*
Great Britain   Michael Powell (Black & white)

With Laurence Olivier, Raymond Massey, Anton Walbrook, Eric Portman, Glynis Johns, Leslie Howard, Nial MacGinnis, Finlay Currie, Raymond Lovell, John Chandos

An outstanding success in its time, this well-crafted exercise in anti-Nazi propaganda was conceived by the British government as yet another sneaky prod to get the United States into the war. Filmed on location in Canada with international-caliber stars, it's a "prestige" movie in every sense of the word: Kenneth Clark, head of the country's Films Division of the Ministry of Information, oversaw the production, which was edited by future director David Lean and scored by classical composer Ralph Vaughan Williams. Scriptwriter Emeric Powell won an Oscar for best original story.

The plot has six German U-boat survivors attempting to journey to the neutral United States after their vessel has been sunk in the Gulf of St. Lawrence by the Royal Canadian Air Force. Led by super-Aryan Eric Portman, the group kills several trappers to steal their plane and later hides out at a Hutterite community of pacifists who have fled Nazi Germany. When one of their number decides to defect to the community, they kill him, too. After destroying the manuscript of an intellectual he finds camping in the woods (Leslie Howard), lone survivor Portman overcomes a Canadian soldier (Raymond Massey) on a train bound for New York. He appears to be destined for safety, but with the help of American railroad workers willing to bend the law a little, he is finally captured.

The photography of the vast Canadian wilderness is stunning, and there are some exciting set pieces, including a nighttime journey across ice-clogged Lake Ontario. Particularly effective is Portman's performance as the head Nazi, which avoids the Hollywood caricature common to the period. His unique brand of evil, it is made clear, is born of a blind and fanatical loyalty that also engenders cold-blooded violence. Howard, a big star in the United States after *Gone with the Wind* (1939), is meant to represent anyone (read, America) who isolates himself from the Nazi threat by adopting a cynical pacifist philosophy. Howard does fight back, however, once he learns the score.

***1/2

## FOR WHOM THE BELL TOLLS (1943)

Paramount   Sam Wood (Color)

With Gary Cooper, Ingrid Bergman, Katina Paxinou, Akim Tamiroff, Arturo de Cordova, Joseph Calleia, Vladimir Sokoloff, Mikhail Rasumny, Victor Varconi

Among the youthful idealists and writers attracted by the Spanish Civil War was Ernest Hemingway. He drove an ambulance for the Loyalists and later wrote *For Whom the Bell Tolls* based on his long and passionate adherence to the Republic. One of the great writers of his time, Hemingway wanted his readers to experience the tragedy of the fascist victory in Spain (which was a prelude to World War II) and to understand the universal crisis of the modern world.

Not much is left of Hemingway's subtext in this expensively mounted, overlong screen adaptation, reportedly because Paramount feared interference from Franco's fascist government. (Although technically neutral as a "nonbelligerent," Spain supported Hitler and Mussolini.) While it's clear who the enemy is, the film is essentially a love story that uses the war as a backdrop. What's best are the performances of the four leads, who seem to spring from Hemingway's pages. Cooper, playing his second Hemingway hero, is perfection as Robert Jordan, an American fighting with the Lincoln Brigade, one of several volunteer foreign units warring against Franco. Joining forces with a band of partisans led by the fiery Pilar (Katina Paxinou in her Oscar-winning role), Jordan falls in love with the displaced Maria (Ingrid Bergman) and later dies in a suicidal defense of a critical bridge.

Hemingway's message of compassion and nobility is expressed in the title, which is a quotation from John Donne: ". . . any mans death diminishes me, because I am involved in Mankinde; and therefore never send to know for whom the bell tolls; It tolls for thee."

***

## THE FOUR HORSEMEN OF THE APOCALYPSE (1961)

MGM   Vincente Minnelli (Color)

With Glenn Ford, Ingrid Thulin, Charles Boyer, Paul Henreid, Lee J. Cobb, Paul Lukas, Yvette Mimieux, Karl Boehm

With a few more expensive flops like this one MGM would have gone into receivership. Glenn Ford awkwardly essays the role that made Rudolph Valentino a star in the 1921 silent version, and Sweden's Ingrid Thulin, so moving in the films of Ingmar Bergman, is badly handled by all concerned (her lines were redubbed by Angela Lansbury). The story, based on an antique novel by Vincente Blasco-Ibanez, has to do with an Argentine playboy who goes against his family to work for the French Resistance during World War II (originally World War I). The titled Four Horsemen—plague, war, famine and death—hoof through as visions among the bombs and concentration camps. Preview audiences laughed at these sequences, presumably before they nodded off.

1/2*

## FOUR SONS (1940)

20th Century-Fox   Archie Mayo (Black & white)

With Don Ameche, Eugenie Leontovich, Alan Curtis, Mary Beth Hughes, Robert Lowery, Sig Rumann, George Ernest, Lionel Royce, Ludwig Stossel

Hollywood cast the Nazi annexation of Czechoslovakia as a tear-jerker in this update of a 1927 antiwar silent directed by John Ford (his cast included amateur actor Archduke Leopold of Austria). The story centers on a Czech mother with four sons: One travels to America, another becomes a Nazi, the third is a patriot and the fourth joins the Wehrmacht. Only the son in America survives the Nazi invasion of his country and Poland, leaving the mother to express her sorrow at their gravesites before departing for the United States.

Static and talky, the film sacrifices action for rhetoric, but it's an occasionally effective reminder of the suffering Germany imposed on civilians in conquered territories. Released at the peak of the May 1940 German offensive against France, *Four Sons* seemed awfully tame when compared to newsreels showing the Nazi blitzkrieg in action, and it failed at the box office.

**

## FRANCIS (1950)

Universal-International   Arthur Lubin (Black & white)

With Donald O'Connor, Patricia Medina, Ray Collins, Zasu Pitts, John McIntyre, Robert Warwick, Eduard Franz, Chill Wills (as the voice of Francis)

This is the first of a series of popular comedies about a talking mule named Francis, discovered by Donald O'Connor while serving as a private in the U.S. Army. During his seven outings (six with O'Connor), Francis found his pal in and out of uniform, one of which belonged to the WACS. Most are passably entertaining, especially for the kids. Director Lubin went on to create the TV series *Mr. Ed*, about a wisecracking horse.

The sequels include *Francis Goes to the Races* (1951), *Francis Goes to West Point* (1952), *Francis Covers Big Town* (1953), *Francis Joins the WACS* (1954), *Francis in the Navy* (1955) and *Francis in the Haunted House* (1956 [with Mickey Rooney]).

**

## THE FROGMEN (1951)

20th Century-Fox   Lloyd Bacon (Black & white)

With Richard Widmark, Dana Andrews, Jeffrey Hunter, Robert Wagner, Gary Merrill, Harvey Lembeck, Warren Stevens

Amphibious members of the U.S. Navy's Underwater Demolition Team, popularly known as frogmen, sabotage obstacles on Japanese-held islands to aid an American invasion. Surprisingly free of patriotic cant, the film is a bit sluggish, but it offers a detailed look at how the divers do it and some sparkling underwater photography—for those who care. Contract players Robert Wagner and Jeffrey Hunter still had a lot to learn.

**

## FROM HERE TO ETERNITY (1953)

Columbia   Fred Zinnemann (Black & white)
With Burt Lancaster, Montgomery Clift, Deborah Kerr, Frank Sinatra, Donna Reed, Ernest Borgnine, Philip Ober, Michey Shaughnessy

One of the best films of the 1950s, *From Here to Eternity* offers a reasonable approximation of James Jones's no-holds-barred novel about the Army in peacetime. Set in an Army camp at Pearl Harbor in 1941, the plot centers on a young soldier (Montgomery Clift), a bugler who gave up his boxing career after blinding an opponent. Described as a "hardhead," he steadfastly refuses to box in a company match, even after being cruelly hazed by the other men. When his buddy (Frank Sinatra) is beaten to death by the stockade sergeant (Borgnine), Clift murders him and goes AWOL, hiding out at the apartment of his lover, a local dancehall girl (Donna Reed). Meanwhile, the company's first sergeant (Burt Lancaster) is having a dangerous affair with the CO's neglected and bitter wife (Deborah Kerr).

The film ends with the Japanese attack on Pearl Harbor, which echoes—and channels—the festering

FROM HERE TO ETERNITY: Burt Lancaster (fourth from left) and Jack Warden (third from left) fire Browning Automatic Rifles from the hip against Japanese planes bombing Pearl Harbor. Note that Warden's BAR doesn't have a magazine.

FROM HERE TO ETERNITY: Montgomery Clift (center) defends himself against a company bully.

undercurrents of love, hatred and violence of the drab, monotonous peacetime routine. Carefully limned is a gallery of classic military types: The CO (Philip Ober) is pompous and ineffectual; Clift's naive corporal becomes as brutal as the system; and stockadekeeper Ernest Borgnine is a frothing sadist. Only Lancaster's first sergeant survives, having catered to his superiors and manipulated the system with pragmatic contempt. Also effective are Kerr and Reed, cast against type, as women who retain the capacity to love even while being exploited by their selfish macho lovers.

As strong as it is, the film would have been even more powerful if Hollywood's former production code (and the U.S. Army) hadn't insisted on bowdlerizing Jones's book. Donna Reed's whorehouse has been tidied up and changed into a dance hall; Kerr's character is no longer a thrill-seeker, and Sinatra's character no longer picks up loose change by hustling homosexuals. Jones's hothouse eroticism is captured in one famous scene, however, when Lancaster and Kerr hungrily make love on a beach as the surf washes over them.

A critical and popular favorite, *From*

*Here to Eternity* captured eight Oscars: for best picture, best director, best supporting actor (Frank Sinatra), best supporting actress (Donna Reed), best screenplay (Daniel Taradash), best cinematography (Burnett Guffey), best sound recording and best film editing (William Lyon). In 1979 Columbia produced a six-hour miniseries based on the book, with Natalie Wood and William Devane in the Kerr-Lancaster roles. Longer doesn't mean better, however, and the studio's hoped-for television series was short-lived.

\*\*\*\*

## THE GALLANT HOURS (1960)

United Artists   Robert Montgomery (Black & white)

With James Cagney, Dennis Weaver, Richard Jaeckel, Carl Benton Reid, Ward Costello

James Cagney gives a fine performance in this otherwise disposable biography of Admiral William Frederick "Bull" Halsey, Jr., one of the key Navy commanders in the Pacific war. Cagney is a perfect choice for the scrappy, charismatic war hero, but the script isn't up to his abilities. Director Montgomery, who served in the Navy when he was an actor, coproduced with Cagney. If there aren't many battle scenes, that's because Halsey spent most of his time at headquarters.

\*\*

## GALLIPOLI (1981)

Australia   Peter Weir (Color)

With Mark Lee, Mel Gibson, Bill Hunter, Bill Kerr

Another minor gem from Australia, which had begun to turn out world-class products during the 1970s. Beautifully photographed, it numbingly evokes the horror and waste of lives resulting from Britain's badly planned, poorly executed amphibious invasion of Gallipoli, Turkey, during World War I. (It was First Lord of the Admiralty Winston Churchill's attempt to outflank the Central Powers.) Like most battles in the Great War, thousands of ANZAC troops lost their lives in mass frontal attacks against enemy machine-gun fire and artillery.

Peter Weir's highly personal version of the events focuses on the lives of the enlisted men. Lee, Gibson and Kerr are about as nice a group of "Aussies" ever seen on the screen, and they show their grit long before they see combat. Weir places the military and political aspects of the fiasco in the background and probes instead into why boys fought and died for their country without really knowing the reason. The climactic battle is very well handled, and you may find yourself ducking under the constant bombardment. The final mad charge against the clattering machine guns is unforgettable.

\*\*\*1/2

## A GATHERING OF EAGLES (1963)

Universal-International   Delbert Mann (Color)

With Rock Hudson, Rod Taylor, Mary Peach, Barry Sullivan, Kevin McCarthy

Former Air Force Colonel Sy Bartlett produced this paean to the Strategic Air Command, which bears a suspicious similarity to his script for Fox's far superior *Twelve O'Clock High* (1949). Rock Hudson is the hard-nosed CO this time around, with Rod Taylor

A GATHERING OF EAGLES: SAC group commander Rock Hudson (top, center) looks worried as maintenance sergeant Robert Lansing hurriedly repairs a malfunction in a B-52 cockpit. Kevin McCarthy (top, right), a SAC readiness inspector, keeps track of time elapsed from alert to takeoff.

bringing up the rear as his whining XO. The film gains momentum when B-52s take to the air, which isn't often enough. Hopefully, the performers aren't a reflection of the actual commanders, since both seem to be on the verge of a nervous breakdown.

**

## THE GENERAL DIED AT DAWN (1936)

Paramount Lewis Milestone (Black & white)

With Gary Cooper, Madeleine Carroll, Akim Tamiroff, William Frawley, Philip Ahn, Dudley Digges, Porter Hall

Gary Cooper plays a soldier of fortune fighting on the right side of revolutionary China in the 1930s. Along the way, he falls for blond spy Madeleine Carroll and grapples with nasty warlord General Yang, played with stock-company intensity by Akim Tamiroff. Director Milestone distills a musky intensity from playwright Clifford Odets's script, and there's an effective early use of split screen: To show simultaneous events, Milestone divided the screen into panels, each separated by a ceremonial Chinese sword.

**1/2

## GLORY AT SEA (1952)

Great Britain Compton Bennett (Black & white)

With Trevor Howard, Richard Attenborough, Sonny Tufts

British sailors on a Lend-Lease ship ferrying vital supplies from the United States to Britain see action in the Battle of the Atlantic. Trevor Howard has some good moments as a mis-understood captain who earns the respect of his cranky crew by trial and error. Nothing new here, but the story and battle scenes are competently handled in the understated British manner.

**

### THE GLORY BRIGADE (1953)

20th Century-Fox   Robert D. Webb (Black & white)

With Victor Mature, Lee Marvin, Richard Egan, Alexander Scourby

The title refers to the Greek forces that fought in the Korean War under the U.N. banner alongside American GIs. A homage to the contribution of these ferocious and determined fighters, the movie casts Victor Mature as a U.S. Army engineer of Greek descent whose outfit is attached to the Glory Brigade. Alexander Scourby, miscast as the Greek commander, may be more familiar to you as the resonant-voiced' narrator of the famous documentary *Victory at Sea*. Different, but whenever the action slows down the Cold War clichés take over.

**1/2

### THE GLORY GUYS (1965)

United Artists   Arnold Laven (Color)

With Tom Tryon, Harve Presnell, Senta Berger, Andrew Duggan, Slim Pickens, James Caan, Michael Anderson, Jr.

The great action director Sam Peckinpah wrote the script, based on Hoffman Birney's novel *The Dice of God*, which may have intimidated director Laven. A Western-*cum*-war movie, the plot centers on square-jawed Tom Tryon as a U.S. cavalry officer under orders to send untrained recruits into battle against the Sioux. Forget the story and performances and concentrate on the expensive, well-staged action scenes. The Indians are given slightly better odds than usual in this one.

**

### GOD IS MY CO-PILOT (1945)

Warner Bros.   Robert Florey (Black & white)

With Dennis Morgan, Dane Clark, Raymond Massey, Andrea King, Alan Hale, John Ridgely, Craig Stevens, Stanley Ridges

War movies often have been a forum for philosophical musings, especially about religion; usually such dialogue gives an added depth to the film's overall view of war and its human consequences. In *God Is My Co-Pilot*, however, the Deity has been turned into an invisible costar on the Allied side. The film actually is Hollywood's second homage to the Flying Tigers, and it's based on the experience of one of the unit's pilots, Col. Robert Lee Scott, Jr., as recounted in his popular novel. Raymond Massey plays commander Claire Chennault, and Dennis Morgan is the Doubting Thomas of a pilot. The film fails to answer an obvious question: Did God enlist, or was He drafted?

**

### GO FOR BROKE! (1951)

MGM   Robert Pirosh (Black & white)

With Van Johnson, George Miki, Lane Nakano, Akira Fukunaga, Warner Anderson, Don Haggerty, Gianna Maria Canale

The success of *Battleground* the year before prompted MGM to give Robert

Pirosh a chance to direct as well as to write another war movie, again with Van Johnson. Its unique plot documents the exploits of the 442nd Regimental Combat Team, a real-life Japanese-American infantry unit that saw action in the Italian campaign. It was the most decorated unit (in terms of its size) of World War II and also suffered the highest casualty rate.

Johnson plays a junior officer who grudgingly accepts his assignment to the unit. Like most movie soldiers, the native-born Americans (called Nisei) are happy-go-lucky fighters, and they not unexpectedly win over Johnson with repeated acts of courage. Their relief of a "lost battalion" of Texans, however, results in more losses for the rescuers than for the unit that was surrounded. Good performances, above-average action sequences and a factual script make this one not only a credit to the Nisei warriors but also to Hollywood for recognizing their contribution. The film's only drawback is the blind eye it turns to the home-front internment of the soldiers' families for the duration of the war.

\*\*\*

## GONE WITH THE WIND (1939)

MGM   Victor Fleming (Color)

With Clark Gable, Vivien Leigh, Olivia de Havilland, Leslie Howard, Thomas Mitchell, Barbara O'Neil, Hattie McDaniel, Butterfly McQueen, Victor Jory, Evelyn Keyes, Ann Rutherford, Laura Hope Crews, Harry Davenport, Jane Darwell, Ona Munson, Ward Bond

The Old South may not have been quite like this, but it hardly matters. As much a phenomenon as a movie, this Hollywood blockbuster still weaves a powerful spell nearly 50 years after its release. Although it's essentially a love story between hustlers Rhett Butler (Clark Gable) and Scarlett O'Hara (Vivien Leigh), many people remember the film as a Civil War epic with vast battle scenes. In fact, there are no battles, although it gives a powerful impression of the war by showing its effects on the leading players. When Atlanta is put to the torch by General Sherman, for example, we see only a few collapsing buildings as Scarlett drives through the burning ruins. And the KKK sequence takes place mostly offscreen, with the men coming home to tell their women what happened. The only really majestic scene is Scarlett's search for Ashley Wilkes (Leslie Howard) through thousands of wounded Rebs lying at the Atlanta railroad station.

The driving force behind *Gone with the Wind* was producer David O. Selznick, who spent a fortune to recall the era accurately, down to perfectly detailed Union and Confederate uniforms and replicas of weapons used during the conflict. Selznick was less successful when he tried to do the same for World War I in an expensive remake of *A Farewell to Arms* (1957), his last movie.

\*\*\*\*

## GO TELL THE SPARTANS (1978)

Spartan Company   Ted Post (Color)

With Burt Lancaster, Craig Wesson, Marc Singer, Joe Unger, Jonathan Goldsmith

Burt Lancaster, aging but better than ever, is first-rate as a burned-out, passed-over major who finds himself

GO TELL THE SPARTANS: Burt Lancaster plays an over-the-hill Army officer assigned to South Vietnam in the war's early years.

on active duty in Vietnam during the early days of the war, before the United States had decided what it was doing there. Lancaster's sardonic officer has little faith in his mission or his demoralized men, who comprise a small advisory team assigned to a rural outpost. A chain of events leads the men and the local militia they are "advising" to lose a battle with the Viet Cong. The details of guerrilla warfare are very realistic and include booby traps, an unseen enemy and a hostile population. Lancaster has a humorous moment, however, when he lewdly explains why he will never be promoted.

Graphically violent, the film has been shown uncut only on cable television. Both pro- and anti-Vietnam War viewers can enjoy it as a well-made war movie, and its political point is neither purposely complex nor naively simple. ***1/2

## GRAND ILLUSION (1937)

France   Jean Renoir (Black & white)

With Jean Gabin, Erich von Stroheim, Pierre Fresnay, Marcel Dalio, Dita Parlo, Julien Carette, Gaston Modot, Jean Daste

An eloquent statement about the absurdity of war and the illusions that bring it about, this seminal French film was directed by the son of famous Impressionist painter Pierre Auguste Renoir. The time is World War I and the place is a German POW camp. Three French prisoners of various backgrounds — an aristocrat, a workman and a Jew — attempt to convince themselves that their duty is to escape and rejoin the battlefront action (which is kept offscreen). During their confinement they discover they can no longer view the enemy as such. The aristocrat has become a friend of the camp's commandant (von Stroheim in a remarkably fine-tuned performance), the worker falls in love with a German woman who aids his escape, and the Jew has never identified with a class or nationality. The "grand illusion" is that patriotism should be an adequate reason for men to kill one another.

Although the prison life is realistically detailed, the film is suffused with a melancholy romanticism that adds a note of ambiguity to its message of pacifism, aimed at France and Germany alike. Mussolini apparently misunderstood the widely popular film when he applauded it. *Grand Illusion* won a special prize at Cannes in

1939; a year later, the Nazis marched into France and banned the film.

****

## THE GREAT DICTATOR (1940)

United Artists   Charles Chaplin (Black & white)

With Charles Chaplin, Paulette Goddard, Jack Oakie, Reginald Gardiner, Henry Daniell, Billy Gilbert, Maurice Moscovitz

It's ironic that Chaplin's screen persona, a put-upon, kindhearted little tramp, bore such a close physical resemblance to Adolf Hitler, one of the great archvillains of the 20th century. Taking full advantage of the similarity, Chaplin scores a direct hit on the "great dictator" in this classic burlesque. As a Jewish barber in the fictional country of Tomania who is mistaken for the country's ruler, one Adenoid Hynkel, Chaplin struts, swaggers, sputters, and speaks in fractured German: *"Und Garbitsch farshtunk of der Herring."* Also on hand is Jack Oakie as his baldheaded rival Benzino Napolini, a takeoff on Benito Mussolini.

This was Chaplin's first all-talkie, and it won him the New York Film Critics Award for best actor, which he declined because he was annoyed at the criticism of Hynkel's six-minute humanitarian speech at the finale. "They had had their laughs," Chaplin later explained. "Now I wanted them to listen. I wanted to ridicule their [the Nazis'] mystic bilge about pure-blooded race." Despite hostility from American isolationists and anonymous threats of personal violence against Chaplin, the film was a success wher-ever it played, except for fascist Argentina.

***1/2

## THE GREAT ESCAPE (1963)

United Artists   John Sturges (Color)

With James Garner, Steve McQueen, Richard Attenborough, Charles Bronson, Donald Pleasence, James Coburn, David McCallum, Gordon Jackson, John Leyton

Based on the mass escape of RAF prisoners from Stalag Luft North, documented in the book by Paul Brickhill, this heart-thumping adventure runs nearly three hours in length, but you'll hardly notice. It's the basic prison-break plot raised to the nth degree, with an all-star cast of everyone's favorite rebels. The preposterous but engrossing story is predicated on the idea that the German guards were lazy and corruptible and that the escapees were resourceful enough to pass as Germans. (In reality, the Nazis often headed off escapes by planting informers in the camps.) To effect the escape—through not one, but three tunnels—the men set up a secret tailor's shop and sewed several dozen military and civilian outfits, complete with matching identification papers for 250 POWs (which seems to indicate they've also manufactured a duplicating machine). Seventy-six manage to break free, 50 are captured and shot, 20 are returned to the camp and six make good their escape.

The players really seem to be enjoying their roles, especially Steve McQueen as an American soldier frequently in solitary confinement.

Assigned to distract the prison guards during the escape, he stages a spectacular motorcycle ride, which he filmed without a double. (He also did the stunt riding for one of the daring Germans who chases him.) Along with his wild drive through the streets of San Francisco in *Bullitt* (1968), McQueen's joyride is one of the best motorized chases ever put on film.
***1/2

## THE GREEN BERETS (1968)

Warner Bros.   John Wayne (Color)

With John Wayne, David Janssen, Jim Hutton, Aldo Ray, Raymond St. Jacques, Jack Soo, Bruce Cabot, Irene Tsu, Patrick Wayne, Jason Evers

Give John Wayne credit for sticking to his guns and having the courage to make a pro-Vietnam War movie in a year that opinion polls showed Americans wanted out of Southeast Asia. Critics blasted it for its hawkish

THE GREEN BERETS: John Wayne (center) and Aldo Ray (left) inspect a Special Forces outpost. Both were a bit too old and overweight for their roles.

THE GREEN BERETS: John Wayne, who codirected the film (with Ray Kellogg), behind the camera.

rected, with an assist from Ray Kellogg. The movie's source is a book by Robin Moore, who gave the Green Berets a better shake.

**1/2

"gung-ho" treatment, which seemed more appropriate to one of Wayne's old World War II epics, like *Sands of Iwo Jima* (1949).

As an action picture it's not bad, but don't expect the real war. At times Wayne seems to be in a Western, with the Viet Cong filling in for the Indians attacking an isolated outpost. The "A-Camp" resembles a cavalry fort, with barbed wire and claymore mines substituting for log fortifications and cannons. Moreover, at times the VC attackers seem to be Japanese soldiers high on sake while making a last *banzai* charge in the name of the emperor. Wayne, too old and overweight for his role as a Special Forces colonel, di-

## GUADALCANAL DIARY (1943)

20th Century-Fox    Lewis Seller (Black & white)
With Preston Foster, Lloyd Nolan, William Bendix, Richard Conte, Anthony Quinn, Richard Jaeckel, Roy Roberts, Lionel Stander, Reed Hadley, Minor Watson

A model of its kind, this stirring combat movie reenacts America's first victory against the Japanese, which had happened only a year before. Based on Richard Tregaskis's eyewitness account, it hews to the facts but concentrates on the glory rather than the horror of the invasion of the Solomon Islands. Among the cocky Marines of the First Division who land unopposed on Guadalcanal are Foster, Nolan, Bendix, Quinn and the teen-aged Jaeckel. As they soon learn, however, they're in for a long and grueling campaign against a determined enemy.

To the movie's credit, the stress and hazards of jungle warfare are authentically depicted, and the enemy is not the usual bespectacled, grinning and sadistic stereotype. As with scores of other wartime movies, the unit represents a cross section of American society. There is a Jew, a Catholic, a Hispanic, a black seaman and the inevitable infantryman from Brooklyn. In its time the film displayed a calm confidence that the Japanese soon would be defeated, since Guadalcanal was one of the few islands they evacuated instead of fighting to the last man. The Marines were so pleased with how they were portrayed that they used the film as an advertisement, with recruiting booths placed in theater lobbies. Others have tried to duplicate its winning mix of humor, pathos and explosive combat, but *Guadalcanal Diary* remains the best of its kind. It's as enjoyable now as it was then.

\*\*\*\*

## GUNGA DIN (1939)

RKO   George Stevens (Black & white)
With Cary Grant, Victor McLaglen, Douglas Fair-banks, Jr., Sam Jaffe, Joan Fontaine, Robert Coote, Montagu Love, Eduardo Ciannelli, Cecil Kellaway

Described as a "prime example of the cinema of exhilaration," this storybook favorite was inspired by Rudyard Kipling's rousing colonialist poem of the same title. The fabricated plot tells of three soldiers of the Royal Sappers, who are faced with a revolt in India by a vicious sect of religious fanatics called the Thuggees. This threat to the regiment, and to the Empire itself, prompts Fairbanks to call off his impending marriage (to Joan Fontaine) and return to the welcoming arms of mates Cary Grant and Victor McLaglen. After a battle royal in which each shows his dauntless courage, the regiment is saved by Gunga Din (Sam Jaffe), a water boy who blows a warning signal on his bugle. Repaying his loyalty, the soldiers make the Indian a corporal and bury him with full military honors.

India finally got its independence eight years later, of course, but it's easy to see why it took so long. Well trained and given the best weapons available, it was no great feat for British soldiers to fight off the natives at the rate of 10 to one, as Grant and company do in the movie. Only when the odds rise three times over are they capable of being subdued. The action scenes, especially when the British break up an ambush, are exceptional, as is the stalwart trio's display of unarmed combat.

Still a jolly good show!

(In 1963, Frank Sinatra, Dean Martin and Sammy Davis, Jr., starred in an occasionally amusing camp western remake titled *Sergeants Three*.)

\*\*\*1/2

## GUNG HO! (1943)

Universal   Raymond Enright (Black & white)
With Randolph Scott, Robert Mitchum, Noah Beery, Grace MacDonald, Alan Curtis, J. Carroll Naish, David Bruce, Peter Coe

Hollywood was fighting mad in 1943 and so were the movie Marines reenacting this diversionary raid on Makin Atoll in the Gilbert Islands. Lucien Hubbard's script is based on the wartime experiences of Captain W. S. LeFrançois, U.S.M.C., who served with the Marine Raiders, an elite attack force modeled on British commandos. Under the command of Lieutenant Colonel Carlson (Randolph Scott), the Raiders learn every dirty trick in the book, along with a phrase he picked up while working with Mao Tse-tung's guerrillas: "gung-ho." (It originally meant "work together" but since has come to describe any overly zealous or enthusiastic action.)

Like its title, the film is fast, hardworking and enthusiastic. The early training sessions and the actual strike are detailed step by step and are on a par with more expensive war movies. Among the scenes that will keep you on the edge of your seat is a grenade attack by a track star, an assault on a Japanese radio station, and a clever ruse that has the Japanese bombing their own men.

\*\*\*

## THE GUNS OF NAVARONE (1961)

Columbia   J. Lee Thompson (Color)

With Gregory Peck, David Niven, Anthony Quinn, Stanley Baker, Anthony Quayle, James Darren, Irene Papas, Gia Scala, James Robertson Justice, Richard Harris, Bryan Forbes

One of the most dazzling war films ever, *The Guns of Navarone* has something for everyone: a compelling story, epic action, stunning photography, first-rate performances and a provocative debate on the nature of loyalty and courage. The story, based on Alistair Maclean's best seller, has to do with the Allied sabotage of two mammoth German guns standing guard over a fortress in the Aegean Sea. Leading the top-secret mission is commando Gregory Peck, accompanied by explosive expert David Niven, who are guided to their destination by a group of Greek partisans, one of whom is a traitor. Unlike their patriotic counterparts in other war films, these soldiers are fearful and doubtful rather than stoically determined. A telling moment comes when Peck, no supersoldier, finds that he can't bring himself to execute the petrified woman who gave them away. Instead, she is shot without remorse by a female partisan who can't understand why Peck could be so foolishly sentimental.

The suspense builds steadily as the commandos scale the massive concrete fortifications that hold the cannons, which are impervious to aerial and naval bombardments. The Germans, portrayed as arrogant but equally dedicated soldiers, fail to notice until too late that the saboteurs have slipped inside and have wired their charges. By the time the payoff comes, you're more than ready for it; the explosion is so powerful that it seems likely to destroy the screen as well. (The special effects won Oscars for Bill Warrington and Vivian C. Greenbaum.) War may be hell, according to producer/screenwriter Carl Foreman, who wrote the script for *The Bridge on the River Kwai* (1957), but it also can be highly entertaining and enlightening.

\*\*\*\*

## A GUY NAMED JOE (1943)

MGM   Victor Fleming (Black & white)

With Spencer Tracy, Van Johnson, Irene Dunne, Lionel Barrymore, Esther Williams, Ward Bond, Barry Nelson

In addition to religious delvings into the meanings and effects of death, which was on everyone's mind during World War II, Hollywood tackled the subject in a softer, idealized fashion, as in this propagandistic ghost movie. Spencer Tracy plays the specter of a fighter pilot killed in action and sent back to Earth by heavenly general Lionel Barrymore to help guide rookie Van Johnson. (As a bonus, Tracy gets to say good-bye to wife, Irene Dunne.) Dalton Trumbo's script and Victor Fleming's expert direction somehow make the mixture of comedy, love, drama and combat jell, and the players are appealing. Johnson, interrupted in the midst of his first starring role by an automobile accident, was allegedly going to be fired until Tracy insisted that production be halted until he recovered. Producer Everett Riskin also made the memorable ghost story *Here Comes Mr. Jordan* (1941), filmed again as Warren Beatty's *Heaven Can Wait* (1978).

**1/2

## HALLS OF MONTEZUMA (1951)

20th Century-Fox    Lewis Milestone (Color)

With Richard Widmark, Jack Palance, Robert Wagner, Reginald Gardiner, Karl Malden, Richard Boone, Richard Hylton, Skip Homeier, Jack Webb, Neville Brand, Martin Milner

When he said "The Marine Corps . . . have a propaganda machine that is almost equal to Stalin's," Harry S. Truman may have been thinking of this movie. As usual, they are the roughest, toughest, meanest warriors who ever died in the Pacific for Old Glory, and they can't abide slackers and wimps. Lewis Milestone, who directed *All Quiet on the Western Front* (1930) and other winners, will make you believe it, with a little help from Widmark and company.

Plagued by intense headaches (from the stress of combat), commander Widmark kills the pain with drugs illegally obtained from medical corpsman Karl Malden, who prefers not to report his supervisor's drug abuse. The grunts in the unit are an unusual mix that consists of a kill-crazy Jap-hater (because his sister married one) called

HALLS OF MONTEZUMA: Reginald Gardiner (left) and Richard Widmark check out a Japanese position on a South Pacific island. Gardiner's uniform and pearl-handle revolver weren't government issue but fit his role as a decidedly unmilitary Japanese-language interpreter.

Pretty Boy (Homeier), a youngster being blooded by the war (Wagner), a peculiar translator (Gardiner) who sports a pearl-handled revolver, and a journalist (Webb) who is writing a novel about it all. The Marines again do the impossible—they locate the rocket launching sites of the dug-in Japanese and, later, destroy it to the sound-track strains of the Marine Corps anthem.

**1/2

## HEARTBREAK RIDGE (1986)

Warner Bros. Clint Eastwood (Color)
With Clint Eastwood, Marsha Mason, Everett McGill, Eileen Heckart, Bo Svenson

Eastwood does his usual competent directorial work, and his usual better-than-competent acting job in his somehow-likeable-tough-guy role. In this one he's Gunnery Sergeant Tom Highway. He's been decorated for valor in Korea and Vietnam, and now finds that his type of two-fisted, drinking, foul-mouthed Marine is going out of style. He's assigned the task of whipping young recruits into shape. For conflict, there's his by-the-book Major (Everett McGill), and for character dimension, his equally profane ex-wife (Marsha Mason). Films like these require real combat near the end for the men to prove themselves. In *Heartbreak Ridge* they end up in Grenada, where Clint and his boys can mow down some Cubans and learn some hard lessons (as one pundit has noted, the running time of the movie is longer than the real invasion). In the end, Clint resolves matters with the major and with his ex-wife. This movie is exactly what one would expect—a mix of good war action, fistfights, humorous obscenities, jingoistic patriotism and a happy ending. As such, it's hard to be disappointed.

**1/2

## HEAVEN KNOWS, MR. ALLISON (1957)

20th Century-Fox   John Huston (Color)
With Deborah Kerr, Robert Mitchum

Another two-character tale that unites a gruff, worldly male with an innocent female. This time it's a Marine corporal and a nun stranded on a Pacific island occupied by the Japanese. Huston did it before in *The African Queen*, but despite the redundancy this is a pleasant motion picture with two good performances. Ms. Kerr was nominated for an Oscar for her portrayal of a woman of the cloth.

**1/2

## HELL AND HIGH WATER (1954)

20th Century-Fox   Samuel Fuller (Color)
With Richard Widmark, David Wayne, Bella Darvi

This Cold War exercise pits an elite sub crew against Chinese Communists plotting to start World War III. If you can get by the absurd plot and politics, it's an enjoyable viewing experience. The acting is above par, and the special effects were nominated for an Oscar. The underwater photography is fine, too.

**1/2

## HELL IN THE PACIFIC (1968)

Cinerama   John Boorman (Color)
With Lee Marvin, Toshiro Mifune

A Marine and a Japanese airman are stranded on yet another uninhabited Pacific island, where they wage a miniwar. After both prove themselves equally inept as victor and defeated, they decide to cooperate to ensure their mutual survival. Marvin's and Mifune's forceful acting isn't enough to save this World War II allegory. The film's fantasy beginning and inconclusive ending leave the viewer with a sense of loss—of two hours.
*1/2

## HELL IS FOR HEROES (1962)

Paramount   Don Siegel (Black & white)

With Steve McQueen, Bobby Darin, Fess Parker, Harry Guardino, Bob Newhart, James Coburn, Nick Adams, Mike Kellin

This spirited war movie is representative of Siegel's early low-budget films—*Riot in Cell Block 11*, *Baby Face Nelson* and *Invasion of the Body Snatchers*—which have become B-movie classics. The hardboiled hero here, who is an effective soldier on the front line but has problems with authority, preceded another Siegel hero, *Dirty Harry*, by several years.

The story has a small squad led by Guardino positioned on the Siegfried Line (the fortified border between Germany and France) during the winter of 1944. Left to defend an area usually covered by a platoon, the men have to hold out until help comes. The attacks and counterattacks are vigorous and have a sense of realism rarely seen in war movies. And there is no shortage of men and equipment for the picture's final assault on a pillbox.

There are three former television stars: McQueen, Adams and Parker; three excellent character actors: Coburn, Guardino and Kellin; a comedian, Newhart; and a singer, Darin, all turning in peak performances. McQueen's character, a former master sergeant busted to private for drinking and fighting in back areas, is one of the actor's best.

A small war movie compared to epics of the era, *Hell Is for Heroes* is a monumental achievement in its own way. Although the violence is more graphic than in most war movies, it is within the story's context and not gratuitous. It's clear why Siegel's action-adventure films were ahead of their time.
****

## HELL TO ETERNITY (1960)

Allied Artists   Phil Karlson (Black & white)

With Jeffrey Hunter, David Janssen, Vic Damone

This film purports to be the life story of Guy Gabaladan, an American interpreter of World War II who was fluent in Japanese. As a combat interpreter, Gabaladan uses his language skills to great advantage during the Saipan campaign by convincing diehard Japanese soldiers to surrender. He also saves some civilians by talking them out of committing suicide. Hunter handles the role quite well, and Janssen's best-buddy performance is consistent with his other journeyman parts. Damone, well known for his singing, should have stayed away from acting. There are several good action scenes, but the story is good enough without them.
**1/2

## THE HEROES OF TELEMARK (1965)

Columbia　Anthony Mann (Color)

With Kirk Douglas, Richard Harris, Ulla Jacobsson, Michael Redgrave, Anton Diffring, Eric Porter

During World War II, the Nazis as well as the United States were investigating the use of atomic power for a weapon. One of the ingredients then necessary for nuclear research was heavy water, which Germany could obtain only from occupied Norway. However, a coordinated series of British commando raids and local guerrilla sabotage kept this vital material from getting to the Third Reich.

Douglas plays one of the Norwegians and acts, of course, heroically, while the German security forces are seen as the epitome of evil. The infiltration and demolition of a heavy-water plant by the commandos are textbook perfect. And the suspenseful ending is a surprising one that was based on a true story; it isn't a scriptwriter's invention. Mann gets to work with an excellent cast, beautiful Norwegian scenery and plenty of special effects. Yet the film lacks the emotional impact of his earlier war effort, *Men in War* (1957).

**1/2

## THE HILL (1965)

MGM　Signey Lumet (Black & white)

With Sean Connery, Harry Andrews, Ossie Davis, Michael Redgrave

Sean Connery portrays an inmate in a British high-security stockade in North Africa during World War II. The discipline is just as tough as in an enemy POW camp and creates many problems for the prisoners. One of the stockade's many punishing drills is the climbing of a manmade hill, under the oppressive heat of the desert sun. The unbearable conditions inevitably lead to a prison riot, which is as exciting as any filmed. Lumet evokes not only the brutal physical hardships of military captivity but also the psychological toll exacted by penal servitude. Connery is at his gritty best, and the fine supporting cast is believable and sympathetic in their respective roles as prisoners and guards. The beauty of the desert also shines through the barbed wire and gunposts.

***

## HITLER (1962)

Three Crown　Stuart Heisler (Black & white)

With Richard Basehart, Mario Emo, Martin Kosleck, John Banner

This B-movie biography follows the life of Hitler from World War I to his last days in Berlin. Basehart doesn't quite capture the spirit of the infamous dictator, and although the facts are all here, they've been documented before. This Hitler is a real loser.

*1/2

## HITLER'S CHILDREN (1943)

RKO　Edward Dmytryk (Black & white)

With Kent Smith, Bonita Granville, Tim Holt, Otto Kruger, Hans Conreid, H. B. Warner

*Hitler's Children* is a lurid representation of German life under the Nazis. Produced at the height of World War II, it doesn't pull its hard-hitting punches, like other early films on the subject. Germany is seen as a country that brainwashes its children, condones the breeding of illegitimate children, the

HITLER'S CHILDREN: An indoctrination session in a film that only hinted at the actual horrors then taking place in Nazi Germany. Courtesy of RKO Pictures, Inc. Copyright © 1943 RKO Pictures, Inc. All Rights Reserved.

sterilization of "unfit" women and the torture of those who don't cooperate. Although the film was considered overwrought propaganda when it was released, later events proved that Dmytryk's sensationalism wasn't even close to the real horror. The sleeper hit of 1943, it made the then unheard-of sum of $3 million; it cost only $200,000 to produce.

A steamy, potboiler B-movie that's worth seeing if you don't expect more than this.

\*\*\*

## HITLER'S MADMEN (1943)

MGM   Douglas Sirk (Black & white)

With Patricia Morrison, John Carradine, Alan Curtis, Ralph Morgan, Ludwig Stossel, Howard Freeman

This one is about the assassination of Reinhard Heydrich. Carradine is brilliant as the cruel Nazi overlord of Czechoslovakia, but the rest of the cast, particularly Curtis as an underground hero, is mediocre.

The film depicts the German occupation as being shockingly brutal; the Nazis shown here are hooligans of the worst sort. Although some of the anti-German sentiment rampant throughout the film seems dated and trite, it was a powerful statement during the middle years of the war, when information about the "final solution" was finally reaching the Allies.

A B-movie melodrama in every way, from acting to back-lot sets, but Carradine's performance makes it worth viewing.

**

## HOLLYWOOD CANTEEN (1944)

Warner Bros.   Delmar Daves (Black & white)
With Jack Benny, Eddie Cantor, Joan Crawford, Bette Davis, John Garfield, Sydney Greenstreet, Paul Henreid, Peter Lorre, Ida Lupino, Eleanor Parker, Roy Rogers, Alexis Smith, Barbara Stanwyck, Jane Wyman

Don't expect much of a story here, since Dane Clark and Robert Hutton are the only actors not playing themselves. The pair visits the Canteen and runs into every Warner Brothers star under contract (the other studios refused to let their stars participate). Nice cameos, good music and harmless chatter make it a fun movie with some insight into Hollywood's campaign to keep up the boys' morale.

**1/2

## HOME OF THE BRAVE (1949)

RKO   Mark Robson (Black & white)
With Frank Lovejoy, Lloyd Bridges, James Edwards, Jeff Corey, Steve Brodie

A powerful, often moving drama about friendship, racism and psychology, *Home of the Brave* was the first postwar film to address the problem of racial segregation. It's based on a Broadway play by Arthur Laurents about a little-known incident during the war. The play had a Jewish protagonist, but producer Stanley Kramer and writer Carl Foreman felt that the time was ripe for a film about blacks, since several films about anti-Semitism had already been made.

The story concerns a five-man reconnaissance team infiltrating a Japanese-held island to survey the terrain and beach. One, a black (Edwards), immediately faces racist taunts from a disgruntled soldier (Brodie) and is defended by a former schoolmate (Bridges). Their assignment is scrubbed after they make unexpected contact with the enemy. Bridges is killed, but not before he, too, insults Edwards, who immediately becomes psychosomatically paralyzed. The events leading up to his paralysis on the island are told in flashback. The soldier, suffering from amnesia, is cured by a friendly Army doctor (Corey) with drugs and psychiatry.

*Home of the Brave* is a powerful story that's just as enthralling and entertaining today as it was in 1949.

***1/2

## HORNET'S NEST (1970)

United Artists   Phil Karlson (Color)
With Rock Hudson, Sylva Koscina

An American paratrooper (Hudson) agrees to train a gang of young Italian boys after they help him survive a German ambush. The boys quickly master the Schmeissers and MG-42s in their stockpile of captured weapons. Eventually they destroy the local German garrison and an important dam all by themselves, before an American relief column arrives.    *Hornet's Nest* tries to show how war brutalizes children, but the only ones hurt by this film are the audience. Ludicrous in every way.

1/2*

## HOTEL BERLIN (1945)

Warner Bros.   Peter Godfrey (Black & white)
With Faye Emerson, Helmut Dantine, Raymond Massey, Andrea King, Peter Lorre, Alan Hale

World War II was winding down when Warner Bros. made this poor imitation of *Grand Hotel*. This hotel is a large, cosmopolitan establishment in Germany's capital city and a meeting place for the Nazi elite. Socializing in its sumptuous rooms are politicians, high-ranking officers and beautiful actresses, some of whom live there.

Complications arrive with the entrance of an escaped political prisoner (Dantine), who has the Gestapo on his tail. Dantine, who finally gets to play a good German after portraying the Nazi thug in *Edge of Darkness* and the downed German in *Mrs. Miniver*, is reasonably good as the democracy-loving concentration camp escapee. Lorre, in a bit part, also delivers a commendable performance, but the others, particularly Hale as a corrupt Nazi Party member, are horrendous.

*Hotel Berlin* is as unbelievable as its characters are unreal.

**

## HOW I WON THE WAR (1967)

Great Britain   Richard Lester (Color)
With Michael Crawford, John Lennon, John MacGowan

This satire, set in World War I, has a young cast that seems preoccupied with matters other than acting. John Lennon, an icon of the pacifist movement of the late 1960s, doesn't measure up to the role of a young British solider who thinks war is a lark.

*How I Won the War* doesn't work as an antiwar picture because of its poor acting. As comedy, it simply isn't funny.

*1/2

## THE HUNTERS (1958)

20th Century-Fox   Dick Powell (Color)
With Robert Mitchum, Robert Wagner, Richard Egan, May Britt, Lee Evans

This colorful movie about jet combat in Korea boasts some colorful dogfights between American F-86 Sabre jets and MIG-15s (actually American F-84s modified for the film). Beautiful as well as exciting, the brightly painted fighters perform high-speed maneuvers against each other in an azure blue sky. Mitchum is terrific as a top American ace, but Wagner is mediocre as a hotshot rookie out to make his reputation. The love scenes between Mitchum and Britt in Japan slow the story's fast pace and aren't romantic in the least. Mitchum's characteristic stoical approach to acting and Britt's passionless performance make them an unlikely match.

*The Hunters* has another highlight: Mitchum and Wagner being shot down over North Korea and having to make their way back to friendly lines. Their escape and evasion maneuvers are as exciting to watch as the air battles. An entertaining movie whenever the camera focuses on the action, but the lukewarm performances of Britt and

THE HUNTERS: Robert Mitchum (left) and Robert Wagner must evade the enemy after being shot down over Korea.

Wagner and the trite romantic subplot keep it from being a great one.
***

### I AIM AT THE STARS (1960)

Columbia   J. Lee Thompson (Black & white)
With Curt Jurgens, James Daley, Herbert Lom, Gia Scala, Victoria Shaw, Adrian Hoven, Karel Stepanek

In 1960, landing on the moon before Russia was an American priority, and no one had done more for the country's space effort than Wernher von Braun. A national hero of sorts, von Braun was paid tribute in this Hollywood biography (shot in Germany), with Curt Jurgens impersonating him in the noblest of terms. As entertainment the film is passable, but what's intriguing is how the filmmakers tidied up von Braun's past to suit his present popular image. Von Braun, of course, developed Hitler's infamous V-2 rocket at Peenemünde on the Baltic Sea to launch against recalcitrant Great Britain. (The "V" stood for *Vergeltung*, the German word for reprisal.) At war's end, von Braun was not charged with war crimes but instead was "invited" to join the U.S. rocketry team. In the amazing finale, a character whose children had been killed in a V-2 raid says, "Good-buy, von Braun, and good luck with the universe."

As might be expected, the film was not a success in England, where a viewer suggested the following addendum to its title: *I Aim at the Stars (but Sometimes Hit London and Points West).*
**

### ICE STATION ZEBRA (1968)

MGM   John Sturges (Color)
With Rock Hudson, Ernest Borgnine, Patrick McGoohan, Jim Brown

*Ice Station Zebra*'s thin plot pits an elite American submarine crew against Russian paratroopers at the North Pole. During a fight over a spy satellite and the information it contains, they eventually face each other down in a shoot-out straight out of a Western B-movie. Story aside, the action and photography leading to the final explosive contact between the Reds and the supersubmariners, led by Hudson, will keep viewers from falling asleep. Hudson, finally living up to the promise of his early career, delivers a balanced performance that meshes quite well with the overall production.

The underwater photograph, North Pole sets and the combat scenes between the two superpowers makes it a good viewing selection despite a poor script. The camerawork earned Daniel L. Papp an Oscar nomination, as did the special effects of J. McMillan Johnson (he lost to *2001*).

*Ice Station Zebra* would make a great double bill with Sam Fuller's *Hell and High Water* (1954), which had a U.S. Navy submarine battling the Chinese Communists.

**1/2

## IMITATION GENERAL (1959)

MGM   George Marshall (Black & white)
With Glenn Ford, Red Buttons, Taina Elg

Glenn Ford plays the title character, a sergeant who assumes command when the real general is hit by a burst of German MG-42 machine-gun fire while trying to organize a counter-attack. Buttons, an Academy Award winner for *Sayonara*, plays his faithful corporal sidekick who helps perpetuate the deception. Marshall has a knack for directing comedy, and the film is funny, but it's a bit embarrassing to laugh at someone's life-threatening experience. Although humor and satire are important to war movies, this one uses slapstick only to get easy laughs.

If you're a burlesque fan, give it a try. As a war movie it's only worth a snicker.

*1/2

## INDIANA JONES AND THE TEMPLE OF DOOM (1984)

Paramount   Steven Spielberg (Color)

With Harrison Ford, Kate Capshaw

This sequel to *Raiders of the Lost Ark* was just as popular as the original. Instead of Germans, this time Jones is pitted against the enemies of the British Empire in India in a takeoff of the old colonial war movies of the 1930s. The action is more akin to an amusement park outing, with the camera substituting for the joyrides. The rescue of Jones by a contingent of Indian levies under the command of a British officer offers a great demonstration of an antique rapid-fire drill with bolt-action Enfield rifles.

**1/2

## IN HARM'S WAY (1965)

Paramount   Otto Preminger (Black & white)
With John Wayne, Kirk Douglas, Patricia Neal, Patrick O'Neal, Dana Andrews, Burgess Meredith, Brandon De Wilde, Henry Fonda, Franchot Tone

Wayne is an admiral in this all-star epic about the U.S. Navy in the Pacific. The time is the early, trying days of World War II, when each battle meant the difference between surviving to fight again or possibly losing the war. Once again, a good story is waylaid by exaggerated performances, especially those of Douglas, Meredith, O'Neal and De Wilde as Navy officers who are more in tune with political in-fighting than the war. Nice try but it misses, despite the broadside.

**

## THE INN OF THE SIXTH HAPPINESS (1958)

20th Century-Fox   Mark Robson (Color)
With Ingrid Bergman, Curt Jurgens, Robert Donat, Athene Seyler

IN HARM'S WAY: John Wayne courts Patricia Neal. Wayne and Neal were lovers in an earlier war movie, *Operation Pacific*.

Former servant girl Ingrid Bergman hears the call and becomes a missionary who opens a home for orphans in war-torn China. A touching tearjerker with fine performances by Bergman and Donat in his last film role. But be warned: The picture is overly long at 158 minutes and the acting and plot become overdone at the two-hour mark.
**

## INVASION U.S.A. (1985)

Cannon   Joseph Zito (Color)
With Chuck Norris, Richard Lynch, Melissa Prophet, Alexander Zale

Chuck Norris, a karate expert who became the poor man's Sylvester Stallone with 1984's *Missing in Action* and *Missing in Action Part II*, takes a turn at routing a terrorist invasion of the United States. Once again he's an indestructible one-man army, and once

again the terrorist organization (unnamed) is a substitute for the "Red
threats" of the 1950s and the fascist
fifth columnists of the 1940s. The final
battle between National Guard troops
and massed terrorists is unique and
well-filmed—with enough special-
effects violence for several war movies.
But don't expect good acting or a well-
developed story line. Strictly a B-movie
outing that is best enjoyed as a comic-
book fantasy.

**1/2

## IS PARIS BURNING? (1966)

Paramount    Rene Clement (Black & white)
With Jean-Paul Belmondo, Charles Boyer, Leslie
Caron, Jean-Pierre Cassel, Alain Delon, Kirk Douglas,
Glenn Ford, Yves Montand, Anthony Perkins, Michel
Piccoli, Simone Signoret, Jean-Louis Trintignant,
Orson Welles, Robert Stack, Daniel Gelin

"*Brennt* Paris?" Hitler reportedly
asked. The answer is that Paris never
was put to the torch, as the Nazis intended, but the answer here is a long time
coming—almost three hours. The film
takes a historical look at the liberation
of Paris in August 1944, with a cast of
stars playing cameo roles based on real
people who took part in the event. The
players       deliver       competent
performances, although we are given
only fleeting glances as they make their
contribution and depart from the
screen. The ultra-detailed story is a
complicated one that requires
foreknowledge of the event to follow it.

As with most multipart films, *Is Paris
Burning?* is only as strong as its weakest
link; a host of writers, including young
Francis Ford Coppola, rarely match
their styles, and some of the episodes
seem to come from different books.

A few good episodes aren't enough
to make the film work.

**

## I WANTED WINGS (1941)

Paramount    Mitchell Leisen (Black & white)
With Ray Milland, William Holden, Wayne Morris,
Brian Donlevy, Constance Moore, Veronica Lake

This pseudorecruiting film for the
Army Air Force was the prototype of
many to follow. The plot centers on a
new class of air cadets and follows
them through pilot training. Along the
way, Milland, Holden and Morris
become involved with Constance
Moore and Veronica Lake, appearing
in her first film. The romances immediately ground the picture every
time it manages to take off, but the excellent aerial sequences (filmed with
the full cooperation of the Army Air
Corps) keep the picture above sea level.
The special effects won an Oscar.

The patriotic cant and stylized acting
are typical of the late prewar years.
Forty-five years later, however, the
quaint training sequences and tepid
love scenes are unintentionally
hilarious.

**1/2

## I WANT YOU (1951)

RKO    Mark Robson (Black & white)
With Dana Andrews, Farley Granger, Dorothy
McGuire, Peggy Dow

Producer Samuel Goldwyn's success
with *The Best Years of Our Lives* prompted him to make this tale of family life
and personal strife during the Korean
War. Not much of it works, however,
and overall the story is a drawn-out
look at an American family going

through changes because of the conflict. Andrews, playing a World War II veteran, volunteers for duty in Korea because he wants his children to be proud of him. His brother, played by Farley Granger, is hesitant about going off to war.

The reasons are soon made clear why they are duty-bound to fight in Korea, along with several "us-versus-them" pro-American speeches filled with paranoid visions of enemy bombings and an invasion of the United States. A product of Hollywood's swing to the conservative, promilitary war movies often associated with the McCarthy years, *I Want You* is little more than a propaganda film with good performances.
**

## JET PILOT (1957)

RKO   Josef Von Sternberg (Color)

With John Wayne, Janet Leigh, Jay C. Flippen, Richard Rober, Paul Fix, Roland Winters, Hans Conreid, Ivan Tresault

Begun in 1949 and released in 1957, this $5 million production stands as one of the most eccentrically made clinkers ever to come from a major Hollywood studio. The brainchild of billionaire Howard Hughes (then the owner of RKO), it was completed in 1951 and tinkered with for the next six years. Hughes recut the film several times, had aerial scenes shot several ways, and then junked the musical score and commissioned a new one from Bronislau Kaper. The result is a jumble of Cold War melodrama, low comedy and some wonderful jet fighter footage. Leigh, looking out of date back then in her circa 1949 outfits and hairstyles, plays a sexy Russian pilot who escapes in a MIG jet and defects to Colonel John Wayne at an air base in Alaska. Wayne marries her and *he* defects to Russia to spy for the Pentagon. Leigh, whose breasts are constantly thrust into the low-slung camera, realizes that the Commies are rats after all, and the pair escape to the creature comforts of the United States.
*

## JOE SMITH, AMERICAN (1942)

MGM   Richard Thorpe (Black & white)

With Robert Young, Marsha Hunt, Harvey Stephens, Darryl Hickman, Jonathan Hale

This back-home domestic melodrama stressed the contribution of blue-collar workers to the war effort. Robert Young plays an aircraft-factory assembly-line worker who is kidnapped and tortured by German spies to get the secret of a new bombsight. Not only does he escape, but he also leads the FBI to his captors' lair. It's an above-average suspense thriller, but don't expect Hitchcock.
**1/2

## THE KILLING FIELDS (1984)

Warner Bros.   Roland Joffé (Color)

With Sam Waterston, Hgaing S. Ngor, John Malkovich

Adapted from Sidney Schanberg's nonfiction best seller of the same title, this stark re-creation of genocide in Cambodia is a towering achievement that lingers long in the memory. Sam Waterston plays Schanberg, a *New York Times* reporter, and Ngor is his Cambodian assistant Dith Pran, who are trapped in the capital of Phnom Penh when the country falls to ruthless Khmer Rouge insurgents in 1975. After the battle, made breathtakingly real, Schanberg is one of a handful of Western reporters allowed to remain in the city. Pran, after sending his family to safety, stays with him.

Eventually the foreign reporters are forced to leave, and Pran is caught up in dictator Pol Pot's mad plan to turn the country into an agrarian utopia. (Historian Eric Hoffer described Pol Pot as "the true believer" who will kill you for your own good.) Cities are emptied, and the Khmer Rouge proceeds to exterminate approximately 2 million Cambodians—a quarter of the population—considered enemies of the state.

The film cuts between Schanberg's comfortable award-winning career in New York and Pran's desperate attempts to survive the hunger, beatings and executions inflicted on workers in the massive collective farms. Pran ultimately makes an exciting escape from endless days in the field and reaches safety in Thailand. Through the efforts of Schanberg, he comes to New York for a touching reunion and safe haven in a job at *The New York Times*. Surprisingly effective is amateur actor Ngor — another victim of the Khmer Rouge — who was rewarded with an Oscar for best supporting actor. *The Killing Fields* is a powerful human document, but be warned: It is a grisly motion picture.

****

# KING OF HEARTS (1967)

France   Philippe de Broca (Color)

With Alan Bates, Genevieve Bujold, Pierre Brasseur, Jean-Claude Brialy

The inmates literally inherit the asylum (and a town) in this whimsical comedy about the madness of war. Carrier pigeon expert Bates "volunteers" for a one-man mission during the final days of World War I to disarm a bunker filled with dynamite. If he fails, the asylum, the zoo and the entire town will be destroyed.

It takes a while for Bates to realize that all the villagers have fled and that the bizarre residents actually are patients freed from the asylum. The lovable loonies seem to come from a Lewis Carroll fantasy, and they live out their delusions as a general, a baron, a ballerina, several prostitutes, etc., against the backdrop of the war. When British and German forces arrive and kill off each other in battle, Bates sheds his uniform and, totally in the buff, joins the mad hatters at the asylum instead of continuing to fight.

Touching and delicate, the film is held together by an intelligent script, good ensemble acting and an incisive point of view. Unabashedly antiwar, it's funny, too.

***1/2

# KING RAT (1965)

Columbia   Byran Forbes (Black & white)

With George Segal, Tom Courtenay, James Fox, Denholm Elliott, James Donald, John Wills

Based on James Clavell's novel about his internment as a POW in Changi Prison, Singapore (he was captured on Java in 1942), *King Rat* grimly captures the dehumanization of prison exist-

KING RAT: Director Bryan Forbes (left) gives instructions to George Segal (center) and Tom Courtenay.

ence. Rather than depicting the usual physical abuse of Japanese captors, the film focuses on the neglect and physical starvation of the POWs. What desperate men will do to survive is explored in every squalid detail.

Segal is the title character, called simply "King," who is the camp wheeler-dealer. He trades among the POWs and the Japanese, dealing in food, medicine and jewelry, which allows him the luxury of laundered uniforms, a high-protein diet and even manicures. Segal is good in the role, and his likable screen persona makes his hustler almost sympathetic. Courtenay, as the camp's MP determined to halt the entrepreneurial schemes, and Fox, as a young British officer who becomes King's pawn, are

standouts in an impressive supporting cast. Best scene: King's salivating friends, invited to his cell to dine on a delicious meat stew, nearly gag when they find out what it's made of.

This is one of the better films to deal with Allied POWs, and it's not without a few humorous moments.
***1/2

## KINGS GO FORTH (1958)

United Artists   Delmar Daves (Color)
With Frank Sinatra, Natalie Wood, Tony Curtis

Here's a love triangle with a twist: Wood is a young American woman living in the South of France as World War II winds down, and Sinatra and Curtis are soldiers in love with her. The twist is that Wood's father is a black millionaire and she has been passing for white. Both men heroically accept her heritage, and the triangle is resolved when heel Curtis dies in action. Good guy Sinatra, after losing an arm, gets to marry her. Curtis makes a credible attempt to give a performance, but Sinatra is Sinatra, and his overbearing screen presence keeps an otherwise good film from reaching its potential. Wood's casting as a black woman isn't her fault, and she gives the role a noble try.

An offbeat but original love story.

**1/2

## LAFAYETTE ESCADRILLE (1958)

Warner Bros.　William Wellman (Black & white)
With Tab Hunter, David Janssen, Etchika Choureau

A project close to director Wellman's heart, this film recounts the exploits of the famous Foreign Legion flying squadron in which he had served during World War I. Wellman ended his movie career here, and it's a lackluster send-off. Warner failed to give him a proper budget and compounded the error by forcing him to cast its young contract players. Hunter is out of place as an all-American boy who becomes a man as a result of the war, and he comes across as doltish and spoiled. The flying scenes are kept to a minimum. The story has potential, but it's unrealized in this assembly-line product.

**

## THE LAST BLITZKRIEG (1959)

Columbia　Arthur Dreifuss (Black & white)
With Van Johnson, Kerwin Mathews, Larry Storch, Dick York

This small-scale production focuses on a lesser-known aspect of the Battle of the Bulge. Johnson stars as the leader of a group of English-speaking German soldiers whose job is to sabotage communications among American troops. Johnson plays a Nazi with conviction, and there are several good action scenes. The film is entertaining and educational despite the obvious low-budget production values.

**1/2

## THE LAST DETAIL (1973)

Columbia　Hal Ashby (Color)
With Jack Nicholson, Otis Young, Randy Quaid, Carol Kane

Nicholson and Young have a field day as veteran petty officers who have drawn prisoner escort duty. While transporting naive young Quaid from Virginia to the hard-time Portsmouth Naval Prison in New Hampshire (he was convicted of thievery), the sentimental pair decides to give him a final, life-affirming spree. Their sailor-style night on the town consists mostly of boozing, brawling and broads, all wonderfully observed with pathos, comedy and drama.

Director Ashby knows the life and never condescends to service-comedy cliches. Especially good is Nicholson letting it all hang out as a hard-swearing, heavy-drinking gob who has a soft spot for cash-and-carry whores and for his bewildered but eager prisoner. Young, who died shortly after the film was released, was a steady professional whose composed performance allows Nicholson a buffer for his high energy. Providing a believable focus for their deep concern is Quaid, who plays the rural lad with an appealing understatement that holds its own against his more seasoned costars.

***1/2

## THE LAST OF THE MOHICANS (1936)

Edward Small   George B. Seitz (Black & white)

With Randolph Scott, Binnie Barnes, Bruce Cabot, Henry Wilcoxon, Heather Angel

Colonial America's French-Indian wars were actually conflicts between the British and French for control of frontier lands and parts of Canada, with local Indian tribes fighting for the French. This exciting chapter in America's history inspired James Fenimore Cooper to write his classic novel *The Last of the Mohicans* (1826), which remains the most popular of his Leatherstocking Tales. Filmed previously as a silent, the story comes to vigorous life in the hands of director Seitz and his robust young cast, who look perfectly at home in the wilderness of western New York State. The story is replete with battles and exciting pursuits as a family journeys across the frontier during the wars, resulting in the death of the older daughter at the hands of a nasty Indian. The magnificence of the pristine countryside, dotted with fir trees and crystal lakes, may make you wish Buffalo and Rochester had never happened. Brought on screen are Cooper's memorable Indian Natty Bumppo, a frontier scout also known as Hawkeye, who dispatches several Hurons, Delawares and a Mohican with a long rifle to save his white friends.

The novel was filmed again as *The Last of the Redmen* (1947), a forgotten B-feature with Jon Hall, and as a limp TV movie with Steve Forrest in 1977. Better was a Canadian miniseries that never aired in the United States.

***

## THE LAST TRAIN FROM MADRID (1937)

Paramount   James Hogan (Black & white)

With Lew Ayres, Dorothy Lamour, Gilbert Roland, Lionel Atwill, Karen Morley, Robert Cummings, Anthony Quinn

Hollywood's first treatment of the Spanish Civil War might just as well have been set in any other part of the world, for all its relevance to the actual conflict. The war is merely a backdrop for sorting out the personal relationships of a group of people attempting to leave war-torn Madrid. Neither the characters nor the actors playing them are worth your time. Thriller writer Graham Greene said, "It is probably the worst film of the decade and should have been the funniest.

*1/2

## LAWRENCE OF ARABIA (1962)

Columbia   David Lean (Color)

With Peter O'Toole, Omar Sharif, Arthur Kennedy, Anthony Quinn, Alec Guinness, Jack Hawkins, Claude Rains, Donald Wolfit, Anthony Quayle, José Ferrer, Michael Ray

David Lean's epic adventure literally excites the senses with its enormous sweep and intimate penetration of character. It's the true story, intelligently scripted by Robert Bolt, of the legendary T. E. Lawrence, a British adventurer-turned-soldier who united Arab tribes to oust the Turks during

LAWRENCE OF ARABIA: Arab horsemen sweep across a Turkish camp.

World War I. The truth is stretched a bit in the portrayals of several characters, but it's all as it happened, and there are no phony heroics. All the genre conventions are superbly used here: There is a difficult terrain (the desert); plenty of danger (from guerrillas of both sides); bravery (Lawrence walks barefoot across the Sinai desert); an impossible assignment (to take 'Aqaba from the rear); ruthlessness (he must kill a man he rescued to conform with Arab justice); and heroism (he personally leads many charges against the Turks).

O'Toole, then a newcomer, gives the performance of his life as the idealistic, introspective soldier-scholar who discovers his own dimensions by constantly testing himself. Also holding his own with a veteran cast is Egyptian Omar Sharif as Lawrence's friend Ali Ibn El Karish. Lending top support is the sun and the desert (which Lawrence calls the "sun's anvil"), photographed spectacularly on location in the Middle East. The various battles were painstakingly staged there and have a particularly authentic feeling.

Among the catalogue of memorable scenes is Lawrence moving through the desert on a camel as the figure of Karish slowly comes into focus through the distorting waves of heat; and Lawrence's horrifying discovery that he is caked with blood after a battle and the shock of recognition that barbarism lies under his civilized

LAWRENCE OF ARABIA: For the train ambush scene, director David Lean used several Browning air-cooled machine guns, which had yet to be developed when the event took place.

surface. At the finale Lawrence is something of a mystery—which he continues to be, more than 50 years after his death in a motorcycle accident.

*Lawrence of Arabia* got seven Academy Awards; for best picture, best director, best color cinematography (Fred A. Young), best color art direction (John Box, John Stoll and Dario Simoni), best sound, best music score (Maurice Jarre) and best editing (Anne Coates). Although the film is enjoyable on the home screen, it should be seen in its original wide-screen, stereophonic format for maximum impact.

****

## LION OF THE DESERT (1981)

Great Britain   Moustapha Akkad (Color)
With Anthony Quinn, Oliver Reed

When Italy decided to occupy Libya as a Johnny-come-lately colonial power, tribes of Bedouins rebelled and tied down the invaders from 1912 to 1931. Quinn, in one of his better ethnic impersonations, plays an aged Bedouin chieftain whose cavalry often outdoes Italy's tanks and armored cars. Reed, as one of Mussolini's pompous generals, also is good, but the supporting cast leaves much to be desired. The battle scenes are spectacular and show why the film reportedly cost $30 million to produce. There is an excess of pro-Arab rhetoric, which is rumored to be the reason this Arab-financed production was made.

**1/2

## THE LONGEST DAY (1962)

20th Century-Fox   Ken Annakin, Bernhard Wicki, Andrew Marton (Black & white)

With Eddie Albert, Paul Anka, Arletty, Jean-Louis Barrault, Richard Beymer, Richard Burton, Red Buttons, Sean Connery, Ray Danton, Fabian, Mel Ferrer, Henry Fonda, Steve Forrest, Gert Frobe, John Gregson, Jeffrey Hunter, Curt Jurgens, Peter Lawford, Roddy McDowell, Sal Mineo, Robert Mitchum, Kenneth More, Edmond O'Brien, Robert Ryan, George Segal, Rod Steiger, Tom Tryon, Peter Von Eyck, Robert Wagner, Stuart Whitman, John Wayne and others

A monumental achievement, this reconstruction of the D-Day invasion of Nazi Europe almost matches the event it chronicles in size, scope and success. Producer Darryl Zanuck, a war buff, personally supervised the battle scenes and directed several of them, although he is not given screen credit. As in Cornelius Ryan's best seller of the same title, the invasion is seen from the British, American, German and French viewpoints. The film begins with the massive Allied preparations for the assault and the coordination of troops, ships and aircraft. At the same time Dwight Eisenhower, the commander of Operation Overlord (code name of the operation), alerts the French Resistance to begin sabotaging railroad tracks and roads leading to Normandy. Meanwhile, Anglo-American bombers destroy every major bridge on the Seine.

The film then cuts to the German headquarters, which had believed the action to be a feint to draw attention from a landing further north. Caught unawares, and with defending Field Marshal Erwin Rommel away on leave, the Germans brutally fight for each inch of sand as Allied troops land on Utah, Juno, Gold, Sword and Omaha Beaches and as American airborne divisions drop from the sky. The battle action stops occasionally for the all-star multinational cast to portray the event's participants and to perform several unsung acts of heroism. Among the memorable scenes are Red Buttons hanging by his parachute on a church steeple as his unit is decimated; the emotional taking of a town by a Free French commando unit; and the Rangers assault on the formidable heights of Pont du Hoc.

For all its merits, the film drags somewhat with its attention to details of the French Resistance and Nazi strategic sessions. Moreover, the characterizations are mostly types rather than people: The Germans are cold-blooded Huns, the French are fighting for the glory of Mother France, and the Americans are just down-to-earth guys trying to save the world. At the time of its filming in 1961 *The Longest Day* also was criticized by political pundits for tying up more than a few U.S. Army troops as extras. It was the year that Soviet leader Nikita Khrushchev demanded Berlin to be turned over to East Germany and got an icy *nyet* from President John F. Kennedy. It seemed that World War III was about to break out until Khrushchev built the Berlin wall instead and permanently divided the city.

An immediate hit and a perennial favorite, the film won Oscars for cinematography (Jean Bourgoin, Henri Persin and Walter Wottiz) and special effects (Robert MacDonald and Jacques Maumont). It probably would have scored higher except for the concurrent release of *Lawrence of Arabia*, which made a grand sweep of Academy Awards that year.

\*\*\*\*

## THE LORDS OF DISCIPLINE (1982)

Paramount   Franc Roddam (Color)
With David Keith, Robert Prosky, G. D. Spradlin, Michael Biehn, Rick Rossovich, Mark Breland, John Lavachielli

One of a wave of military school and military training films that flowed from Hollywood in the early 1980s, *The Lords of Discipline* takes place in a South Carolina military academy that resembles The Citadel. The time is the early 1960s, before Vietnam made the military unpopular; the dramatic conflict is provided by a secret society of cadets called "The Ten." Having appointed themselves guardians of the school's traditions and standards, the group weeds out those they deem unfit for the academy by threatening and physically abusing them. Cadets selected for "special treatment" are the physically inept and those who don't conform to the life-style of the southern gentry. Among those singled out by "The Ten" is freshman Mark Breland, a black student who is the first of his race to attend the institution. Keith, charged with the protection of the

THE LORDS OF DISCIPLINE: A military school senior, David Keith (left), is ordered by Robert Prosky to protect the institute's first black cadet from other students.

THE MALTA STORY 133

cadet, spends an exciting hour and a half discovering the identities of the group. Breland, you may remember went on to become an Olympic Gold Medal winning boxer. The film is based on Pat Conroy's even better novel.

\*\*\*

## THE LOST COMMAND (1966)

Columbia   Mark Robson (Color)

With Anthony Quinn, Alain Delon, Claudia Cardinale, George Segal, Michele Morgan, Maurice Ronet

Good performances and well-staged battle scenes help compensate for the occasional pretentiousness of this antiwar tract. The soldiers this time out are French, fighting in Indochina during the 1950s and later in the colony of Algeria. Quinn stars as a French paratroop commander whose dedicated second-in-command is French actor Delon. Based on Jean Larteguy's novel *The Centurions*, the film reprises the shameful French defeat at Dien Bien Phu and the capture of officers and men. After their release from a POW camp, Quinn and Delon are assigned to Algeria, where the latter falls in love with beautiful revolutionary Claudia Cardinale. Delon, disillusioned by poor leadership and repelled when his unit resorts to torture to disarm the Algerian rebellion, eventually decides to leave the French Army.

Thought-provoking and solidly produced, the film was underrated by critics and filmgoers alike, probably because the subjects were unpopular at the time. The combat scenes are plentiful and take place mostly in exotic Algeria.

\*\*1/2

## MacARTHUR (1977)

Universal   Joseph Sargent (Color)

With Gregory Peck, Ed Flanders, Dan O'Herlihy, Dick O'Neill, Art Fleming, Ward Costello, Marj Dussay, Ivan Bonar

Romantic leading man Peck makes an impressive transformation into General Douglas MacArthur (1880-1964), one of the great military leaders of our century. Director Sargent tells the story chronologically and lets the general's words speak for themselves. Beginning with the desperate early years of World War II, the general recalls his defeat in the Philippines and the subsequent Death March of Bataan, then continues through his reconquest of the Pacific as commander of the Allied forces in the southwestern Pacific. After the surrender of Japan, he is made Supreme Allied Commander of the occupied country (some called him the "Emperor" because of his arrogant manner). Finally, after Korea and the Inchon landings, MacArthur is relieved of command of the U.S. and U.N. forces by his policy nemesis, President Harry S. Truman.

MacArthur was every bit as flamboyant and egotistical as Patton, but somehow this screen biography lacks the grandeur of George C. Scott's film. Best scenes: the general making good on his vow "I shall return" to the Philippines, and the signing of the Japanese surrender aboard the *U.S.S. Missouri*.

\*\*\*

## THE MALTA STORY (1954)

Great Britain   Brian Desmond Hurst (Black & white)

With Alec Guinness, Jack Hawkins, Anthony Steel, Flora Robson, Muriel Pavlow

A small-scale story about the defense of Malta during World War II. One of the crown colonies, the 95-square-mile island virtually controlled the central Mediterranean, which is why the British fought so hard to keep it out of German hands. This version of the battle has an RAF pilot enjoying a dull love affair with a local girl while German planes strafe the island. Not much else happens. Lord Guinness picked better roles later in his career.

*1/2

## MAN HUNT (1941)

20th Century-Fox   Fritz Lang (Black & white)
With Walter Pidgeon, Joan Bennett, George Sanders, John Carradine, Roddy McDowall, Heather Thatcher

German expatriate Lang weaves a compelling web of paranoia through this cat-and-mouse thriller, adapted from Geoffrey Household's novel *Rogue Male*. Pidgeon is a British hunter who deliberately muffs a chance to shoot Hitler while in Germany and is captured and tortured instead. Escaping to England, he finds that the tables have turned and that he is now the hunted man. Sanders is especially good as the cultivated but arrogantly brutal Gestapo head. The period propaganda doesn't get in the way here, although once again the British sense of fair play overcomes Germany's win-by-any-means approach.

***

## THE MAN WHO NEVER WAS (1956)

20th Century-Fox   Ronald Neame (Color)

With Clifton Webb, Gloria Grahame, Stephen Boyd

The acerbic Clifton Webb is less mannered than usual as Ewen Montagu, a real-life spy. Based on Montagu's memoirs, the film details how the British counterespionage agent carried out "Operation Mincemeat" to mislead the Germans during World War II. The instrument of deception is a dead body, dressed in a staff officer's uniform, which is left on the Spanish coast with bogus identification papers and orders placing the Allied invasion at Sardinia and Greece. This was a cover for the planned and eventual invasion of Sicily.

Director Neame adds spice to the proceedings by casting Boyd as an English-speaking German spy in England trying to ferret out the real details. Also getting involved is Gloria Grahame in one of her trademark tart roles. The story's believe-it-or-not quality is enhanced by crisp performances and makes for a thrilling and suspenseful film.

**1/2

## THE MAN WHO WOULD BE KING (1976)

Columbia/Allied Artists   John Huston (Color)
With Sean Connery, Michael Caine, Christopher Plummer, Saeed Jaffrey, Jack May, Shakira Caine

Kipling's grand fantasy adventure comes to the screen with all its glory and garishness intact. Connery and Caine are the story's two career soldiers, recently discharged, who found their own kingdom on the border of late 19th-century India. After years of faithful service to the British Crown, the pair have fallen on hard times and are making do as petty swindlers and blackmailers. Hearing tales of a treasure in an Afghan-like territory, they make their way there through blizzards, treacherous mountain terrain and attacks by bandits. In a stroke of luck, they make friends with an Indian soldier (Jaffrey), the sole survivor of a previous expedition, who becomes their Gunga Din. With the rifles they have brought along, Connery and Caine enlist a military force and establish their own kingdom, called Kafiristan. Connery, enthroning himself as a god-emperor, is about to take possession of the lost treasure of Alexander the Great when his all-too-human frailties give him away. The film comes to its tragic end with one final and gruesome battle to the death.

A pet project of director Huston, the film required a 20-year effort to get it made. His re-creation of Victorian India is marvelously tangible, as is the stark beauty of the ancient mountain communities. The small-scale but intense battles are right out of the drill manual, and often they are more comic than violent. Connery and Caine are perfectly cast as the brazen soldiers turned hustlers, and Jaffrey's performance as the loyal Indian servant is absolutely charming.

****

## THE MANCHURIAN CANDIDATE (1962)

United Artists   John Frankenheimer (Black & white)
With Frank Sinatra, Janet Leigh, Laurence Harvey, Angela Lansbury, Henry Silva, James Edwards, James Gregory

This well-crafted political thriller fully realizes the movie potential of Richard Condon's even better thriller. Laurence Harvey is the title character, a Korean War veteran who had been captured by the enemy and brainwashed in China before being released. A ticking time bomb, Harvey has been programmed to assassinate an important politician when given a certain subliminal signal—and he doesn't know it. His indoctrination is shown in flashbacks, but from here on, hold on to your seats! No one is exactly what he (or she) appears to be, and the plot is cleverly concealed like the surprise in a nest of Chinese boxes. The finale, at a crowded political rally in Madison Square Garden, is a stunner.

Director Frankenheimer's paranoid vision of Cold War politics seemed a bit farfetched when the film was reviewed. But a year later, after the assassination of President John F. Kennedy, the truth became stranger than Condon's fiction. Best is Angela Lansbury as an ambitious, meddling, duplicitous American "mom."
***1/2

## MARCH OR DIE (1977)

Great Britain   Dick Richards (Color)
With Gene Hackman, Terence Hill, Catherine Deneuve, Max Von Sydow, Ian Holm

American Gene Hackman, a major in the Foreign Legion, survives World War I with only 200 of 8,000 men left to fight in the Sahara. Seems there is a lost city there that possesses a treasure buried with the "Arab Joan of Arc," who apparently had stashed enough away to pay for France's war effort.

Along for the suicide mission are several ex-thieves, German POWs and some young adventurers, guided to their destination by two museum curators.

There's an attempt to bring a contemporary sensibility to the film by having a French minister say, "After all, they are only foreigners," accurately reflecting the country's attitude to its brave but dispensable Legionnaires. But as anyone knows who has seen this story in countless adventure films, you violate holy places only at your own peril.

**

## MARINES LET'S GO (1962)

20th Century-Fox   Raoul Walsh (Color)
With Tom Tryon, David Hedison, Tom Reese, Linda Hutchins, William Tyler

A blemish on the great Raoul Walsh's movie war record, this tepid tale of Marines on leave in Japan (from the Korean War) will either embarrass you or put you to sleep. Walsh was the original choice for *PT-109*, based on President John F. Kennedy's war record, but after the president saw this one he suggested another director. *What Price Glory?* it's not.

*1/2

## MARINE RAIDERS (1943)

RKO   Harold Schuster (Black & white)
With Pat O'Brien, Robert Ryan, Ruth Hussey, Frank McHugh, Barton MacLane

Pat O'Brien plays a fictionalized version of Lieutenant Colonel Merritt Edson, whose 1st Marine Battalion joined forces with Paramarines and defeated the numerically superior Japanese at Guadalcanal. The story begins with the battle named for him, Edson's Ridge. O'Brien's pal is airborne grunt CO Ryan, who looks quite "pretty," as a fellow officer puts it, in jungle fatigues. The action scenes soon dissolve into a love story, however, with O'Brien double-crossing the wounded Ryan and shipping him out while unconscious so he can't marry the pretty Australian (Ruth Hussey) he's in love with. The enemies become friends again in the last reel, when all is forgiven as they hit the beaches of New Georgia for a full-scale battle.

Although not as entertaining as *Gung Ho!*, this companion Raiders feature has a few good moments. Best scene: Ryan charging a Japanese dugout with a Reising submachine gun to avenge the torture death of a buddy. Notorious for jamming after only a few rounds, the Reising was discarded en masse by Marines, as it is here. Ryan's jams, too, and he angrily throws it away.

**1/2

## M*A*S*H (1970)

20th Century-Fox   Robert Altman (Color)
With Donald Sutherland, Elliott Gould, Sally Kellerman, Tom Skerritt, Robert Duvall, John Shuck, Jo Ann Pflug, Gary Burghof

Even after hundreds of episodes of its TV copy, this rudely funny original still holds its own. The title is an acronym for a Mobile Army Surgical Unit three miles behind the front lines of the Korean War. In between 12-hour tours of duty in bloodstained operating rooms, the doctors and nurses mix perfect martinis, enjoy poker sessions

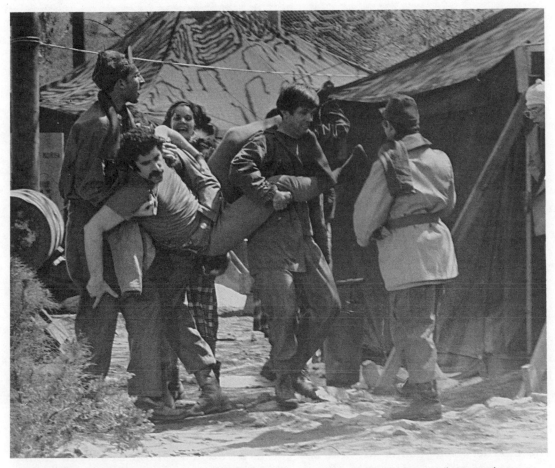

M*A*S*H: Elliott Gould is carried away by fellow M*A*S*H unit members in the hilarious service comedy.

and golf afternoons, have raucous parties and enjoy various sexual liaisons. As surgeons Hawkeye and Trapper John, respectively, Sutherland and Gould hilariously attempt to live the American Dream against the backdrop of the war, and their synchronized delivery flows smoothly in every scene. Duvall, in a supporting role, gleams with religious fervor, especially when he finally shacks up with WAC Major "Hot Lips" Houlihan (Kellerman) and their affair is broadcast over the company's loudspeakers.

Other standouts are Shuck as a dentist who decides on suicide because he's impotent, and Burghof, the only actor to repeat his role on the TV series, as Radar, the CO's telepathic clerk.

Altman and scriptwriter Ring Lardner, Jr., underline the charnel-house atmosphere of Richard Hooker's novel and make vividly graphic the futility of attempting to save young lives and repair battle casualties while their superiors are dedicated to killing people. Released when the shrill protest against the Vietnam War was

M*A*S*H: The crew assembles to settle a bet as to whether "Hot Lips" Houlihan is a true blonde.

reaching a crescendo, the film isn't only about Korea, in Lardner's words, but "a special kind of war, an American one on the Asian mainland, and our habit of taking our culture along with us and ignoring the local variety." Lardner expounded on Vietnam's effect on the genre in Julian Smith's book *Looking Away.* He won as Oscar for the best screenplay (based on material from another medium) of 1970, a year that *Patton* made a grand sweep of the Academy Awards.

\*\*\*\*

### THE MEN (1950)
**Also titled** *Battle Stripe*

United Artists   Fred Zinnemann (Black & white)

With Marlon Brando, Teresa Wright, Everett Sloane, Jack Webb

Brando proved he was a movie natural as a troubled paraplegic veteran in this, his first film, made while he was waiting to star in Hollywood's adaptation of his stage hit *A Streetcar Named Desire.* Brando's touching characterization as an emotionally raw veteran afraid of marrying a "normal" girl (Teresa Wright) ranks with the best of his career. Webb also is good as a similarly wounded victim of World War II whose optimism turns to disillusionment, but it's Brando's film all the way. Producer Stanley Kramer also made *Home of the Brave*, a similar film dealing with embittered men whose lives were changed by the war.

\*\*\*

THE MEN: Marlon Brando leads a patrol in his first motion picture.

## MEN IN WAR (1957)

Allied Artists   Anthony Mann (Black & white)
With Robert Ryan, Aldo Ray, James Edwards, Vic
Morrow, Nehemiah Persoff, Scott Marlowe

Everyone involved in this low-budget, small-scale Korean War movie does an excellent job. The time is the late summer of 1950, when American and South Korean forces made their initial retreat. Platoon leader Ryan attempts to lead his men out a pocket surrounded by the enemy, back to the 24th "Tropic Lightning" Division. Making their way past snipers, minefields and artillery fire to the last obstacle, they reach a hill held by North Koreans. Joining forces with a sergeant (Ray) and a shell-shocked colonel from the 1st Cavalry, they find themselves equipped with everything an infantryman can carry—Garands, Thompsons, BARs, Brownings, a flamethrower and plenty of grenades. The final assault, not unexpectedly, is a winner.

Ryan and Ray deliver good performances, although they are upstaged by Edwards as a stalwart squad leader and Morrow as a battle-wacky GI. The combat scenes are well staged and the script pays attention to detail and character development. A thoroughly exciting military adventure.

***1/2

## MEN OF THE FIGHTING LADY (1954)

MGM   Andrew Marton (Color)
With Van Johnson, Walter Pidgeon, Kennan Wynn,
Frank Lovejoy, Louis Calhern, Dewey Martin

The title "lady" is an U.S. aircraft carrier stationed off the coast of Korea. The all-male cast keeps it running as smoothly as their routine performances. A technically interesting look at carrier operations of the period, the film has little more to offer except for some documentary footage of carrier jets in action.

**

### MERRILL'S MARAUDERS (1962)

Warner Bros.   Samuel Fuller (Color)

With Jeff Chandler, Ty Hardin, Will Hutchins, Claude Akins, Peter Brown, Andrew Duggan

"Merrill's Marauders" was an organizational forerunner of today's Rangers and shared an elite status with the 1st Special Service Brigade and the Ranger battalions. Unlike their contemporaries, however, the Marauders undertook only one mission: a long-range, direct-action patrol deep behind Japanese lines in Burma in 1944. Although the mission was considered a success, its 3,000 men were incapable of further combat as a unit because the ranks had been heavily depleted by disease, casualties and exhaustion.

As Merrill, Chandler gives one of the best performances in his spotty career. But the remainder of the cast was drawn from the studio's television roster, and their heroics seem amateurish. The film manages to soak up the swampy terrain, however, and to convey the physical exertion of the three-month patrol. Moreover, Fuller gets to work with more men than usual in staging some exciting battle scenes.

**1/2

### MERRY CHRISTMAS, MR. LAWRENCE (1984)

Universal   Nagisa Oskima (Color)

With David Bowie, Tom Conti, Ryuichi Sukomoto, Takeshi, Jack Thompson

Outstanding performances make this POW film set in 1942 Java a cut above other Japanese prison camp movies. Audiences weaned on stereotypes of brutal Japanese guards may find director Oskima's treatment too sympathetic and Conti's role, as a translator who attempts to understand their reasons for inflicting pain on the prisoners, too collaborative, but it all rings true. Rock musician Bowie is surprisingly good as an Australian major captured while on a commando action. Equally impressive is fellow musician Sukomoto as the camp commandant, who applies a fitting punishment when Bowie takes a spiritual stand against him. (Sukomoto also wrote the film's electronic music score.)

The story meanders somewhat whenever it flashes back to prewar Australia and dwells on the erotic bond between the Australian prisoner and his Japanese captor. (Director Oskima previously made *In The Realm of the Senses*, an X-rated "art" film about the murder-castration of a Japanese businessman by his lover.) Like many POW films, this one is depressing, and when its wordy East-West culture clash turns physical, it becomes almost too brutal to watch. Definitely not for the squeamish.

***

### MISSING IN ACTION (1984)

Cannon   Joseph Zito (Color)

With Chuck Norris, M. Emmet Walsh, Lenoire Kastorf, James Hong

MISSING IN ACTION: Chuck Norris evokes a popular winning image of the Vietnam War veteran.

Chuck Norris picked up the rescue mission theme in *MIA* (1984). Norris, a martial arts expert who had had limited success in a string of karate B-movies, played a recent escapee from a POW camp in Vietnam. He returns to Vietnam and, after coercing the location of a still active camp from his previous captor, becomes a one-man army and rescues his fellow POWs from captivity.

Six months later, *MIA, Part 2* (1985) was released. This was more a preface than a sequel, since it explained how Norris escaped in the first place. Confusing? Certainly, but both films are surprisingly well-filmed action movies that have kept audiences and even critics enthralled, and the two low-budget features earned extremely high profits and made Norris a bankable Hollywood star.

**1/2

## MISTER ROBERTS (1955)

Warner Bros.    John Ford, Mervyn LeRoy
  (Color)

With Henry Fonda, James Cagney, William Powell, Jack Lemmon, Ward Bond, Betsy Palmer, Phil Carey, Ken Curtis, Harry Carey, Jr.

Thoughtful, touching and witty, this postwar classic summed up the feelings of a generation of Americans who had served in the military during World War II. Working in tandem, directors Ford and LeRoy effectively mounted a screen version of the smash-hit Broadway play (by the novel's author, Thomas Heggen, and

Joshua Logan), with Henry Fonda repeating his trademark role.

As the fair-minded Mister Roberts, Fonda now seems more like a 1950s middle-management type than a would-be hero, even though he longs to leave the safety of his cargo ship for action in the Pacific. Faring better more than 30 years later is Cagney as a hilarious Captain Bligh of a CO who cares more for his palm tree than for his crew. Lending fine support is Jack Lemmon as the lazy Ensign Pulver—the role that won him stardom and an Oscar—and William Powell as the ship's medical officer.

These immediately recognizable characters are symbols, of course: Cagney represents the seeming mindlessness of military authority; Lemmon speaks for all those bound by an arbitrary commander; and Mister Roberts is the rational mediator. But the film also honors those who served far behind the war front, whose enemies were boredom and a lack of female companionship but who nevertheless developed a strong sense of comradeship and did what was required of them. Heggen's story is so skillfully wrought that we never question Mister Roberts's sanity when he wins his transfer and finally goes off to war.

***1/2

MISTER ROBERTS: James Cagney (left) shows Henry Fonda his most prized possession—the commander's hat he hopes to wear when he's promoted.

## THE MOON IS DOWN (1943)

20th Century-Fox   Irving Pichel (Color)
With Henry Travers, Lee J. Cobb, Cedric Hardwicke, Dorris Bowden, Peter Van Eyck

Well-meaning but predictable, this talky wartime resistance drama takes place in occupied Norway, where an act of sabotage brings Nazi retribution to a normally peaceful village. Like its source, a propagandistic novel and play by John Steinbeck, Nunnally Johnson's script attempts to bring a rare (for its time) note of psychological insight into the cast of dutiful Nazi conquerors. Only Cedric Hardwicke as the commander convincingly elicits our sympathy, however; the others come across as the usual cultured swine who read Goethe and listen to Wagner before going off to torture and kill. The set, given a coat of whitewash, is the Welsh mining village of *How Green Was My Valley* (1941).

**

## THE MORTAL STORM (1940)

MGM   Frank Borzage (Black & white)
With James Stewart, Margaret Sullavan, Robert Young, Frank Morgan, Robert Stack, Bonita Granville, Maria Ouspenskaya, Dan Dailey

Similar to Fox's *Four Sons*, released the same year, this major MGM product exploited America's fascination with and fear of the Nazi regime marching through Europe. The script, based on Phyllis Bottome's novel about how fascism undermines the sanctity of the family, perfunctorily accedes to the United States' official neutrality by setting the story "somewhere in Europe." Former Wizard of Oz Frank Morgan plays a Jewish professor sent to a concentration camp at the time of Hitler's rise to power. His stepsons and his daughter's fiance (Robert Young) become ardent fascists, while his son and wife retain their independent views. His daughter (Margaret Sullavan) eventually comes to her senses and falls in love with a young farmer (James Stewart), who arranges their escape to Austria.

The film seems a bit melodramatic today, and only the aged Maria Ouspenskaya accurately reflects the country the film attempts to portray, but in retrospect it faithfully depicts Germany's dilemma in 1933. If anything, the Gestapo agents were even crueler than those portrayed here. The family's suffering is occasionally heart-rending, and the final scene, with Stewart and Sullavan valiantly attempting to ski to safety, shouldn't leave a dry eye in the house. (Stewart's character dies in the book, but since the actor was one of the studio's most popular stars, he was allowed to survive.) MGM took a harder swipe at Germany later that year with Mervyn LeRoy's *Escape*.

***

## THE MOUNTAIN ROAD (1960)

Columbia   Daniel Mann (Black & white)
With James Stewart, Glenn Corbett, Harry Morgan, Lisa Lu

A rather listless drama about the Burma Road and the U.S. Army Engineers working to keep supplies moving into China during World War II. Stewart is good as an officer whose personal problems include a disregard for the safety of the fleeing Chinese, but overall the film is as exciting as the picks and shovels he uses. The China/Burma/India Theater was called the "forgotten" one during the war, and this film doesn't help a bit.

*1/2

## MRS. MINIVER (1942)

MGM   William Wyler (Black & white)

With Greer Garson, Walter Pidgeon, Teresa Wright, Dame May Whitty, Reginald Owen, Henry Travers, Richard Ney, Helmut Dantine, Henry Wilcoxon, Rhys Williams

Unreal perhaps, this wartime tribute to British civilians who fought the war from their doorsteps may be thinly disguised propaganda but it's moving nevertheless. Greer Garson, then at the peak of her formidable popularity, is the perfect British housewife and mother and has a typically patriotic family. Her eldest son (Richard Ney) enlists in the RAF and participates in the Battle of Britain; husband Walter Pidgeon helps evacuate the troops from Dunkirk with his small pleasure boat; her daughter-in-law (Teresa Wright) dies in a German bomb attack; and she herself is menaced by a German pilot (Helmut Dantine) who has parachuted into the neighborhood.

A big hit in the United States, *Mrs. Miniver* helped marshal support for Great Britain when she was fighting Germany single-handedly. Also released in Britain, it was a shot in the arm for that country's morale, although some critics complained about its Hollywood falseness (it was shot entirely at MGM's Culver City lot). To some British it lionized the comfort-loving middle class, which had attempted to appease Hitler instead of opposing him at the outset. And while Garson and Pidgeon are overwhelmingly charming, their hirelings and other members of the working class are portrayed as comic oafs.

American viewers aren't likely to perceive this subtext of snobbery, however, and probably will be swept along by its well-oiled drama of an "ordinary" family nobly attempting to hold back Nazi barbarians. Overcome by sentiment, the Motion Picture Academy awarded the film six Oscars: for best picture, best actress (Garson), best supporting actress (Wright), best director, best screenplay (Arthur Wimperis, George Froeschel, James Hilton and Claudine West, based on Jan Struther's novel) and best cinematography (Joseph Ruttenberg). Garson made history of sorts when her patriotic acceptance speech ran on for more than 30 minutes, prompting the Academy to set a new limit.

***1/2

## THE NAKED AND THE DEAD (1958)

RKO   Raoul Walsh (Color)

With Cliff Robertson, Aldo Ray, Raymond Massey, William Campbell, Joey Bishop, Richard Jaeckel, James Best, Jerry Paris, Lili St. Cyr, Barbara Nichols

Norman Mailer's novel *The Naked and the Dead* rocketed the author to the top of the literary ladder, but this big-budget version is strictly bottom rung. Among the bowdlerizations required by Hollywood's former Production Code are the removal of all of Mailer's authentic four-letter words and the novel's more savage plot elements. But why did the scriptwriters inject inappropriate comedy and romantic flashbacks in a story that gets its points across with ugliness and brutality?

Only Aldo Ray suggests some of the novel's power in his portrayal of the sadistic Sergeant Croft, a reactionary who shoots Japanese and kills birds with equal pleasure (and who takes the gold from the teeth of Japanese dead). Croft probably is killed by one of his own men (it isn't made clear) after he leads them into an ambush. Massey, cast as a general who believes that enlisted men will fight harder if they hate their commanding officers, is shown to be as inept as he is authoritarian. Best are the exciting action scenes, including the platoon's defensive stand against a banzai charge (shot in Panama). But even better is Mailer's book.

**

THE NAKED AND THE DEAD: Aldo Ray's sadistic sergeant. Courtesy of RKO Pictures, Inc. Copyright © 1959 RKO Pictures, Inc. All Rights Reserved.

THE NAKED AND THE DEAD: Aldo Ray deploys a reconnaissance squad. Courtesy of RKO Pictures, Inc. Copyright © 1959 RKO Pictures, Inc. All Rights Reserved.

## NAZI AGENT (1942)

MGM   Jules Dassin (Black & white)
With Conrad Veidt, Ann Ayers, Frank Reicher, Dorothy Tree, Ivan Simpson, Martin Kosleck

Conrad Veidt, Hollywood's resident Nazi, gets to play the good guy as well as the bad one in this MGM quickie. The far-out plot casts him as twins, one of whom is a Nazi agent in the United States. The other twin is a naturalized American who hates the Nazis (as Veidt did himself). After killing his brother in self-defense, he impersonates him to expose the spy ring and finds himself falling in love with his late sibling's ex (Ann Ayers). In reviewing the film one critic described her as "the girl for whom two Veidts don't make a wrong." This was the first feature for director Dassin after having toiled in MGM shorts for several years.
**

## NEVER SO FEW (1959)

MGM   John Sturges (Color)
With Frank Sinatra, Gina Lollobrigida, Peter Lawford, Steve McQueen, Paul Henreid

Sinatra and Lollobrigida aren't the most convincing of lovers, what with Gina feigning passion for Frankie but seeming to be overcome by the jungle heat. The story is a fictionalized account of the famed OSS Detachment 101, which operated in Burma during World War II. Starting with only 25 men, the unit recruited Kachin tribesmen to wage guerrilla war against the Japanese, and by war's end more than 600 officers and enlisted men commanded a force of 11,000 Kachines. Since Sinatra isn't believable as a jungle fighter, the picture falls apart at its center, although McQueen, in his first important role, holds your interest throughout. The pluses include a few solid firefights and a large-scale assault on the guerrilla base camp. The film at least has the honesty to point out that Chiang Kai-shek's Nationalist Chinese government made a tidy profit selling U.S. weapons to the Japanese and local criminals.
**1/2

## NIGHT AMBUSH (1957)

Great Britain   Michael Powell (Black & white)
With Dirk Bogarde, Marius Goring

British commandos sneak onto the island of Crete and kidnap a German general. Well acted, but the cheap production values and cliche script undermine whatever excitement there is of the daring raid.
**

## THE NIGHT OF THE GENERALS (1967)

Columbia   Anatole Litvak (Color)
With Peter O'Toole, Omar Sharif, Philippe Noiret, Christopher Plummer, Tom Courtenay, Joanna Pettet, Coral Brown, Charles Gray, Donald Pleasence, John Gregson, Juliette Greco

Hans Helmut Hirst's fascinating novel gets trampled by director Litvak, whose impressive cast struggles vainly to keep him on course. O'Toole plays a Nazi SS general with a sadistic bent who likes to kill in bed as well as on the battlefield. When a prostitute is brutally murdered in Paris, detective Sharif narrows his search to O'Toole, who previously had murdered a Polish whore before destroying the Warsaw Ghetto. The time is 1944 and the setting

is Paris, so we get a glimpse of Rommel in a bullet-ridden car, a bit about the plot on Hitler's life, and some uninteresting lovemaking between Courtenay and Pettet. O'Toole's comeuppance, cleverly imagined, arrives after the war's end.
*1/2

## NIGHT PEOPLE (1954)

20th Century-Fox   Nunnally Johnson (Color)
With Gregory Peck, Broderick Crawford, Anita Bjork, Rita Gam, Buddy Ebsen, Peter Van Eyck

The title refers to multinational espionage agents fighting the Cold War in Berlin. Peck is an M.P. counterintelligence officer attempting to obtain the release of an American soldier kidnapped by persons unknown in the East. The young Pfc.'s father happens to be an industrialist (Crawford) who flies to the divided city to get his son back. Triple cross follows double cross as British intelligence encounters Russian security forces (made up of former Nazis) and American good old boys who would rather listen to a baseball game than deal in espionage. An intelligent script, good performances and on-location Berlin make it work.
**1/2

## NIGHT TRAIN TO MUNICH (1940)
**Also titled** *Gestapo; Night Train*

Great Britain   Carol Reed (Black & white)
With Rex Harrison, Margaret Lockwood, Paul Henreid, Basil Radford, Naunton Wayne

Similar to Hitchcock's *The Lady Vanishes* (1938), this spy melodrama shares the same leading lady (Lockwood) and stuffy upper-class comics Radford and Wayne. Harrison plays Bennett of the English Secret Service, who slips into Czechoslovakia to bring out a scientist who has invented a secret weapon. Helping the men escape into Switzerland are the scientist's daughter (Lockwood) and the two cricket-loving Englishmen. The train trip is an exciting one, almost as good as Hitchcock's.
**1/2

## 1941 (1979)

Paramount   Steven Spielberg (Color)
With Dan Aykroyd, John Belushi, Ned Beatty, Treat Williams, Robert Stack, Warren Oates, Slim Pickens, Toshiro Mifune

Everyone makes a mistake now and then, and *1941* is director Spielberg's. Never one to fumble on a small scale, Spielberg billed the studio $28 million for this anomaly in an otherwise brilliant career. The plot's inspiration was the sighting off the California coast

1941: John Belushi's frenetic performance failed to attract audiences.

of a Japanese submarine shortly after Pearl Harbor, and the comedy derives from Stanley Kramer's *It's a Mad, Mad, Mad, Mad World* (1963). It's all very unfunny, however, as numerous expensive sets are destroyed in the name of hysterical citizens panicking in Los Angeles. Belushi has his moments as a macho pilot zooming through the canyons of downtown L.A., although he was much better served with the script of *Animal House*. For a more enjoyable time, see the two big service comedies made during the year this film is named for: Abbott and Costello's *Buck Privates* and Bob Hope's *Caught in the Draft*.

\*

### NO MAN IS AN ISLAND (1962)
**Also titled** *Island Escape*

Universal-International  John Monks, Jr., Richard Goldstone (Color)
With Jeffrey Hunter, Marshall Thompson, Barbara Perez, Ronald Remy

Based on a true incident during World War II, this battle adventure boasts a good performance from Hunter and some convincing combat locales (actually the Philippines). Hunter plays a sailor trapped on Guam who turns to guerrilla warfare to survive while hiding out in a leper colony. After he settles down in a cave, however, not enough happens to alleviate his boredom—or the viewer's.

\*\*

### NONE BUT THE BRAVE (1965)
Warner Bros.   Frank Sinatra (Color)
With Frank Sinatra, Clint Walker, Tommy Sands, Tony Bill, Brad Dexter

Criticized in its time for being naive and too Hollywood glossy (perhaps because it's Sinatra's solo directing effort), this antiwar movie is never less than involving. Sinatra plays a Navy medic whose plane has crashed, along with a Marine platoon, on a Pacific island held by the Japanese. A miniwar

NONE BUT THE BRAVE: Clint Walker (left), Frank Sinatra (second from left) and Tommy Sands (second from right) starred in the film. Sinatra also directed it.

results between the two detachments until they finally reach a live-and-let-live truce. Sinatra even saves the life of a Japanese soldier, only to have the truce broken when contact is made with his superiors.

**

## NO TIME FOR SERGEANTS (1958)

Warner Bros.   Mervyn LeRoy (Black & white)
With Andy Griffith, Nick Adams, William Fawcett, Murray Hamilton, Myron McCormick

Homespun Andy Griffith got a lot of mileage from Mac Hyman's novel about a country boy who gets drafted into the Army and turns it upside down. Griffith first played the troublesome hillbilly on live television, then repeated the role in a long-running Broadway play. Out of its time, the film version seems more than ever like a one-joke play, although it's good for an occasional laugh.

**

## NORTH STAR (1943)

**TV title** *Armored Attack*

Samuel Goldwyn   Lewis Milestone (Black & white)
With Anne Baxter, Dana Andrews, Farley Granger, Walter Huston, Walter Brennan, Erich von Stroheim, Martin Kosleck, Ann Harding, Jane Withers

Intended as a tribute to America's World War II ally the Soviet Union, *North Star* was orphaned by producer Sam Goldwyn in 1947 when the House Un-American Activities Committee began an investigation into the alleged Communist infiltration of Hollywood. Later it was sold to television with a bit of redubbing and a "clean" new title: *Armored Attack*. Very much a propaganda piece, Lillian Hellman's script recounts the saga of a Russian village occupied by the Germans, whose ranks include leather-gloved general Erich von Stroheim and mad doctor Martin Kosleck, who bleeds Russia's children for transfusions for wounded German soldiers. The noble, long-suffering Hollywood peasants are given to spouting such well-meant slogans as "You cannot keel the spirit of a free people" and "For every one of us who falls, ten will rise to take his place." Director Lewis Milestone, working against the bias, delivers his usual competent job and makes some of the hyperbole ring true.

**1/2

## OBJECTIVE BURMA! (1945)

Warner Bros.   Raoul Walsh (Black & white)
With Errol Flynn, William Prince, James Brown, George Tobias, Henry Hull, Warner Anderson, John Alvin, Stephen Richards, Tony Caruso, Joel Allen

British critics and audiences were so angered by this worthy action drama that it almost caused an international incident. Excitingly staged and beautifully played by a cast of Warner stalwarts, the film stars Errol Flynn as the captain of a group of American paratroopers who drop behind enemy lines in Burma to destroy a Japanese radar station. There's the usual demographic cross section of American GI's (including one from Texas, one from Nebraska and another from Brooklyn), each of whom knows how to set booby traps, throw knives with amazing precision, and sweep the enemy with their devastating Thompsons. Providing the wartime motivational speeches

OBJECTIVE BURMA!: Errol Flynn briefs his paratroop platoon.

is an Ernie Pyle-type newspaperman. Typical of movies of the dwindling war years, the ending is somewhat downbeat, with only 12 of the original 50 men making it to safety on foot.

But what rankled the British was the film's outright neglect of their country's greater role in the Burma war. *Objective Burma!* was abruptly withdrawn after a brief showing in a London cinema, and didn't reappear until seven years later, with an apologetic prologue.

Among the film's memorable scenes is one that involves a Japanese infiltrator who lures his GI victims by calling out, "Where are you, Joe?" in perfect English. "Over here," answers a savvy paratrooper, who pulls the pin on a grenade and lays it in the soldier's

OBJECTIVE BURMA!: From left to right, George Tobias, Tony Caruso, Errol Flynn and Joel Allen.

path. "By the way, my name ain't Joe," he says after the grenade explodes.
***1/2

## AN OFFICER AND A GENTLEMAN (1982)

Paramount   Taylor Hackford (Color)

With Richard Gere, Debra Winger, David Keith, Lou Gossett, Jr.

Will arrogant, antisocial Navy brat Richard Gere realize his dream and become one of the best among the bravest—a Navy pilot? Well, do birds fly? (The question of how he ever got past the selection board and the psychological exams is left unaddressed.) The process from enlistment to flying off the deck of an aircraft carrier is an exhausting one, and the first step is 13 grueling weeks in officer candidate

AN OFFICER AND A GENTLEMAN: Lou Gossett, Jr., won a best supporting actor Oscar for his portrayal of a tough drill instructor.

boot camp. In charge is Marine drill instructor Lou Gossett, Jr.—who steals the picture from Gere and is as tough as they come. A professional from the peak of his Smokey the Bear hat to the tips of his spit-shined shoes, Gossett's D.I. does everything in his power to get Gere to quit, teaching him some valuable lessons in the process.

Debra Winger is perhaps too bright for the role of a blue-collar local looking for a way out of the backwater community near the base (she seems quite capable of taking care of herself). But she's an appealing actress, and her sexual passion for the flyboy is believable. A sort of *I Wanted Wings* crossbred with *The D.I.* and dressed in explicit language and sexuality, the film works well on its own terms, both as a love story and as an object lesson in dealing with military stress.

***1/2

AN OFFICER AND A GENTLEMAN: Richard Gere (left) and David Keith as aviation cadets.

## OFF LIMITS (1953)
**Also titled** *Military Policeman*

Paramount   George Marshall (Black & white)
With Bob Hope, Mickey Rooney, Marilyn Maxwell, Marvin Miller

Hope, *Caught in the Draft* once again, plays a fight manager drafted into the Military Police. Never one to miss an opportunity, hustler Hope decides to create a new champ out of naive recruit Rooney. Predictable, with blond Marilyn Maxwell supplying the curves and Rooney acting as straight man for Hope's one-liners.

**

## ON THE BEACH (1959)

United Artists   Stanley Kramer (Black & white)
With Gregory Peck, Ava Gardner, Fred Astaire, Anthony Perkins, John Tate, Lola Brooks, Donna Anderson

Made during Hollywood's first cycle of anti-Bomb films, this humanist overture for peace was an international success and helped set the stage for a short-lived détente between Russia and the United States a year later. The *Bulletin of Atomic Scientists*, which has been keeping track of the possibility of nuclear doom since 1945, moved back the hands of its ominous clock from two minutes to twelve to seven minutes to twelve. But then came the U-2 incident, the Berlin Wall and the Bay of Pigs fiasco, and the clock once again rushed precipitously foreward.

*On the Beach* takes place in Australia, the only inhabited continent not yet decimated by the effects of a nuclear war (which is not shown). The clouds are on their way down under, however, and the end of the human race is inevitable. Among those trapped are a scientist who plans to die in an automobile race, a young couple who decide to swallow government-issue suicide pills and administer one to their child, and a submarine commander and a divorcee who have just discovered their love for each other.

A second cycle of ban-the-Bomb and no-nuke films began in the late 1970s with the release of the science-fiction-oriented *Damnation Alley*. Although verbose at times, this entry—based on Nevil Shute's famous novel—remains one of the most powerful.

\*\*\*

## ONE MINUTE TO ZERO (1952)

RKO   Tay Garnett (Black & white)
With Robert Mitchum, Ann Blyth, William Talman, Charles McGraw, Margaret Sheridan, Richard Egan

All the clichés of World War II propaganda movies are on parade in this Korean War potboiler. Mitchum is cast as a combatwise Army colonel who happens to be on the spot advising the pro-American Republic of Korea when hostilities break out. After personally taking out a tank with a bazooka, Mitchum spars with hostile U.N. official Ann Blyth. Given command of a regiment, he shells a civilian refugee column being used as a cover by Communist guerrillas, an atrocity balanced (or so the studio thought) by shots of captured Americans executed with their hands tied behind their backs. There's some good documentary footage from the U.S. Army Signal Corps that has the effect of highlighting out the film's combat scenes.

\*\*

ONE MINUTE TO ZERO: Robert Mitchum and Ann Blyth fall in love while the Korean War wages around them. Courtesy of RKO Pictures, Inc. Copyright © 1952 RKO Pictures, Inc. All Rights Reserved.

## OPERATION CROSSBOW (1965)
**Also titled** *The Great Spy Mission*

Great Britain   Michael Anderson (Color)
With Sophia Loren, George Peppard, Tom Courtenay, John Mills, Lilli Palmer, Anthony Quayle, Patrick Wymark, Jeremy Kemp, Trevor Howard, Richard Todd, Paul Henreid, Sylvia Sims

The title refers to a fictional Allied espionage raid on the Nazi munitions factory at Peenemünde, on the Baltic Sea. It was here that Dr. Wernher von Braun and other leading German scientists created the infamous V-1 and V-2 rockets, which Hitler planned to shower on London at the rate of 5,000 a day. *Operation Crossbow* parachutes in Peppard, Courtenay and Kemp to destroy some of the launching sites, despite the presence of SS guards nearly everywhere and the lack of adequate intelligence information. Although the story is a pure flight of fancy, the comic-book action is thrilling and the ending really throws off sparks. (In reality, the Allies did their damage at Peenemünde with bombers in August 1944. Moreover, the remote-controlled rockets arrived too late in the war to prolong it.) Top-billed Sophia Loren makes only a cameo appearance, and the actors impersonating real-life characters (including Winston Churchill) seem to have come out of a wax museum.

**1/2

## OPERATION MAD BALL (1957)

Columbia   Richard Quine (Black & white)

With Jack Lemmon, Ernie Kovacs, Mickey Rooney, Arthur O'Connell, Kathryn Grant, James Darren

Lemmon and Kovacs have some amusing moments as an Army con artist and his bedeviled CO, respectively, in this fast-moving service comedy. The time and place are postwar occupied Germany, and the plot "hook" is a military rule forbidding fraternization with the nurses. No matter how he does it, Lemmon is determined to have a wild party right under his unit's brass noses.

**1/2

## OPERATION PACIFIC (1951)

Warner Bros.   George Waggner (Black & white)

With John Wayne, Patricia Neal, Ward Bond, Phillip Carey, Martin Milner, Bill Campbell, Scott Forbes

Let's see, John Wayne is an officer aboard the U.S.S. *Thunderfish*, a submarine operating in the Pacific Theater and Ward Bond is the CO. Wayne is divorced from nurse Patricia Neal, who happens to be intimately involved with carrier pilot Phil Carey, who is Bond's younger brother. Needless to say, the love triangle and fraternal and military loyalty problems make for an overly complicated plot. Fortunately, the Japanese Navy takes care of Bond when a decoy ship lures him topside and forces Wayne to dive the sub. Later, Wayne fishes Carey out of the drink when his plane is shot down. Wayne and Neal repeated their soap-opera romance 14 years later in Otto Preminger's *In Harm's Way* and hadn't learned a thing in the interim.

**

## OPERATION PETTICOAT (1959)

Universal   Blake Edwards (Color)

With Cary Grant, Tony Curtis, Joan O'Brien, Dina Merrill, Gene Evans, Richard Sargent, Arthur O'Connell

Director Blake Edwards, creator of the *Pink Panther* series, keeps the laughs coming in this offbeat comedy, aided and abetted by his fun-loving cast. Old smoothie Grant plays the CO of a crippled submarine being hunted by both the U.S. Navy and the Japanese. On hand is Curtis as a scheming officer who leads a wacky raid on an Army supply depot to obtain needed parts and paint for the sub. The vessel later turns bright pink because it's the only color the men were able to steal. Add to this situation a contingent of giggling rescued nurses and you have a cruise from one laugh to another, with the slightly risqué touches that are an Ed-

wards hallmark. The film subsequently was made into a popular TV series.
***

## OPERATION THUNDERBOLT (1978)

Israel   Menachem Golan (Color)
With Klaus Kinski, Assaf Dayan, Yehoran Gron, Gila Almagor

A good, tingly re-creation of the famous 1976 Israeli commando raid on the Entebbe airport in Uganda that rescued passengers hijacked by terrorists. The events leading to the daring assault are occasionally confusing, but they detail some of the logistics not available to American filmmakers. Klaus Kinski, Europe's leading movie weirdo, probably will get on your nerves as the shrieking head kidnapper. The U.S. versions, made for television, include *Raid on Entebbe* and *Victory at Entebbe*.
**

## OSS (1946)

Paramount   Irving Pichel (Black & white)
With Alan Ladd, Geraldine Fitzgerald, Patric Knowles, Don Beddoe

American espionage agents Ladd and Fitzgerald parachute into occupied France with the requisite secret weapons shortly before D-Day. The film is dated but still involving, and Ladd fans will enjoy seeing the two-fister bash and batter his way through nasty Nazis. Many of the background plot details are correct, but the true story still was classified in 1946. OSS buffs will find this version tame after seeing Cagney's similar *13 Rue Madeleine*, made the same year.
**

## THE OUTSIDER (1961)

Universal-International   Delbert Mann (Black & white)
With Tony Curtis, James Franciscus, Gregory Walcott, Bruce Bennett, Vivian Nathan

A sad footnote to the famous Marine Corps siege of Iwo Jima, this respectful biography traces the demise of Ira Hayes, an American Indian, who became a symbol of the bloody battle. Hayes's problems began when he helped raise the flag on Mount Suribachi in a photograph that became world-famous and subsequently was duplicated as a memorial sculpture in Washington, D.C., and elsewhere. The pressures of celebrity and life in a white society eventually drove him into alcoholism and an early death from exposure. Tony Curtis is very good as Hayes and brings an uncharacteristic sympathy to his slide from lionized hero (which Hayes never believed he was) to drunken outcast. Along the way Stewart Stern's script makes some telling points about the country's shabby treatment of its native Americans.
**1/2

## OVERLORD (1975)

Great Britain   Stuart Cooper (Black & white)
With Brian Stirner, Davyd Harries, Nicholas Ball, Julie Neesam

D-Day is effectively recaptured here with a clever blending of old documentary footage and acted scenes. The story has to do with a young Englishman called to duty just before the invasion of France in 1944. It's the ritual of military training that holds one's interest, however, especially the landing

OVERLORD: Davyd Harries (left) and Brian Stirner star in a film that effectively combines archival film with staged shots to tell the story of D-Day.

on Normandy itself, which has an enthralling cinematic power. Director Cooper, an American, was one of *The Dirty Dozen*.

***

### PASSAGE TO MARSEILLES (1944)

Warner Bros.   Michael Curtiz (Black & white)

With Humphrey Bogart, Sydney Greenstreet, Claude Rains, Peter Lorre, Michele Morgan, Helmut Dantine, Philip Dorn

Lightning failed to strike twice for director Curtiz and the stars of *Casablanca*. Bogart and company supply a few thrills as convicts escaping from Devil's Island to join the Free French, but the flashbacks within flashbacks are more than confusing. Best scene: the German Luftwaffe attacking a Vichy cargo vessel.

**

### PATHS OF GLORY (1957)

United Artists   Stanley Kubrick (Black & white)

With Kirk Douglas, Ralph Meeker, Adolphe Menjou, George Macready, Wayne Morris, Richard Anderson, Timothy Carey

During the brutal Battle of Verdun in 1916, more than 89,000 French soldiers were slaughtered because the Army had based its tactics on the outmoded *l'offensive à l'outrance*, or the offensive to the utmost. Trained for suicidal charges into massive artillery and machine-gun fire, the brave troops fought valiantly until the inevitable occurred: They broke under fire. To the French high command their refusal to face certain death spelled mutiny, so it randomly picked three enlisted men to set an example by being executed at the hands of a kangaroo court. The court-martial was, of course, a cover for the incompetence of the corrupt commanders.

Kubrick stacks his ideological deck somewhat by portraying the French Army as fighting its own war of class differences. His generals all seem to be decadents living in palatial splendor as they play at war with disposable chess pieces. Their pawns are the enlisted men, who suffer in unspeakably squalid, muddy trenches. But Kubrick, in his first important work, covers these flaws with awesome scenes of war and skillful editing, or what the French call *mise en scène*. It's impossible to forget the long dollying shots through the claustrophobic trenches, with the officers safely viewing the battle through binoculars as a spectator sport. And the Ant Hill assault is so marvelously realized that one feels the fright and confusion of an impossible maneuver.

PATHS OF GLORY: Kirk Douglas (center) is superb as a colonel who understands why the troops are reluctant to fight.

Shot in Germany for only $900,000 (a third of which went to Kirk Douglas as the defense attorney), the film's authenticity impressed even Winston Churchill, who was First Lord of the Admiralty during World War I. American military bases initially banned *Paths of Glory*, and it is still unseen in France, where the military establishment considers it a slanderous insult to national honor.

****

## PATTON (1970)
**Also titled** *Patton—Lust for Glory*

20th Century-Fox   Franklin Schaffner (Color)

With George C. Scott, Karl Malden, Edward Binns, Michael Bates, Lawrence Dobkin, Frank Lattimore, James Edwards, John Doucette, Siegfried Rauch, Karl Michael Vogler, Tim Considine

General George S. Patton no doubt would have applauded this four-star biography, which tells the story from his subjective point of view. George C. Scott is magnificent as the controversial centurion, whose dynamism seems better suited to ancient Rome than a modern battlefield. Unlike his equally brilliant but somewhat dull counterparts, Patton is seen as a gutsy disciplinarian whose fanatical dedication to victory eventually gets him relieved of his command.

The film begins with Patton giving a rousing patriotic monologue in front of an American flag spread across the entire wide screen. The first half deals with his wartime campaigns in North Africa and Sicily. There is a bitter

PATTON: George C. Scott is Patton. Scott refused to accept the Academy Award for best actor that he won for his bravado performance. Here he observes the action from the hatch of a tank named for the general.

rivalry between Patton's tank corps and that of German General Rommel, who is defeated at El Guettar. In Sicily Patton is relieved of his command for slapping a shell-shocked soldier but later redeems himself during the liberation of France and with his dramatic relief of Bastogne during the Battle of the Bulge.

Scott, in the performance of his distinguished career, captures the very essence of Patton's tough, blunt style and even duplicates the general's mannerisms and speech patterns. Malden, as General Omar Bradley, is also first-rate in a low-key performance that nicely counterpoints that of the volatile Scott. Francis Ford Coppola's script doesn't embellish his hero's military exploits but searches instead for the key to Patton's complicated personality. The battle scenes are models of their kind, especially the recreation of Patton's first contact with Rommel's Afrika Korps (staged with the help of Spanish infantry and armor). The immense firefight, with all its color, noise and hundreds of soldiers, provides one of the cinema's most exciting combat scenes.

*Patton* took a lion's share of Oscars for 1970. These include best picture, best director, best actor (Scott), best screeplay (Coppola), best art direction (Urie McClearly, Gil Parrondo, Antonio Mateos and Pierre-Louis Thevenet), best sound (Douglas Williams and Don Bassman) and best film editing (Hugh S. Fowler).

****

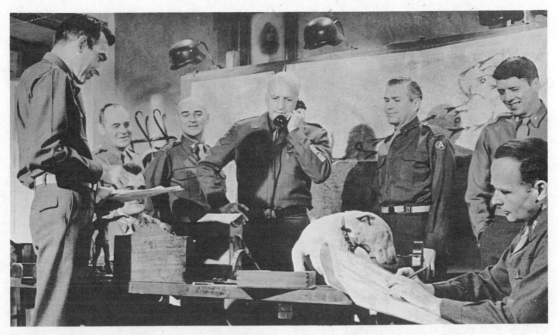

PATTON: George C. Scott holds a staff meeting. Patton's bull terrier, Willie, also is in attendance.

## THE PERFECT FURLOUGH (1959)

Universal-International  Blake Edwards (Color)

With Tony Curtis, Janet Leigh, Linda Cristal, Elaine Stritch, Keenan Wynn, Troy Donohue, King Donovan

Husband and wife (back then), Curtis and Leigh stretch this one-joke comedy way past its 15-minute limit. While stationed in the Arctic, Curtis is a soldier who wins a dream furlough, which he's supposed to enjoy on behalf of his buddies. Leigh plays his military escort who, not surprisingly, falls for the libidinous Curtis. Best is Linda Cristal as a movie star whose publicity stunt fails to go as planned.

*1/2

## THE PIGEON THAT TOOK ROME (1962)

Paramount  Melville Shavelson (Black & white)

With Charlton Heston, Elsa Martinelli, Brian Donlevy, Harry Guardino, Baccaloni

Heston playing comedy is like trying to get one of the great stone faces of Mount Rushmore to smile. Cast as a tough Army officer sent into Nazi-occupied Rome on an intelligence mission, he finds that the lowly carrier pigeon is able to transmit messages every bit as well as modern technology. Martinelli is gorgeous as his love interest, even if she—like the film's other stock Italian characters—is given to too many voluble words and gestures.

*1/2

## PLATOON (1986)

Orion Pictures  Oliver Stone (Color)

With Tom Berenger, Willem Dafoe, Charlie Sheen, Forest Whitaker, Francesco Quinn, John C. McGinley, Richard Edson, Kevin Dillon, Reggie Johnson, Keith David, Dale Dye, Oliver Stone

The best of Oliver Stone's movies to date, *Platoon* is surely one of the most profound and disturbing films ever made about the American experience in Vietnam. The focus of the action is a single combat infantry platoon, fighting in the lush jungle near the Cambodian border in 1967. Through extraordinary camera work, an eye for detail and a tight script, Stone captures the sights, sounds and ironies of this tragic war with force and eery authenticity.

This is a movie that works on several levels. The narrator of the story, Chris Taylor, has left college and volunteered for frontline duty. *Platoon* tells the story of his loss of innocence, as he learns his grisly trade and is stripped of his illusions about war, and the men who fight it. Stone himself served with a unit like this in Vietnam, and there can be little doubt that Taylor, played beautifully by Charlie Sheen, functions as a kind of spokesman for Stone's personal vision of what the war was all about. Taylor is far more articulate than the other platoon members, the majority of whom come from poor backgrounds (as they did in the war itself) and who are in every sense of the word ordinary grunts. Taylor's personal journey comes into view through Stone's brilliant, documentary-like, but nonetheless tension-filled depiction of this small group of infantrymen, whose survival is challenged not only by the North Vietnamese Army, but also by exhausting heat, disease, a completely foreign culture, a war with unclear objectives and poor leadership. Of course,

soldiers in all wars face many of these things; but the genius of the film lies in its capturing and conveying so accurately the *particular* experience of Americans fighting in Vietnam—drugs, futility and all. Through Barnes (Tom Berenger) and Elias (Willem Dafoe), *Platoon* highlights the divisions that co-existed in Vietnam and "back in the world" by pitting the conservative "lifers" and "juicers" against the more liberal draftees and "heads," with the blacks fighting alongside even as they question their position in the war. Berenger, as the over-the-edge, homicidal sergeant and Dafoe, as his rival with an altogether different, more sane vision of the war are absolutely brilliant.

****

## PLAY DIRTY (1968)

Great Britain    André de Toth (Color)
With Michael Caine, Nigel Davenport, Nigel Green, Harry Andrews, Daniel Pilon, Bernard Archard

Another *Dirty Dozen* clone, elaborated with clichés borrowed from other World War II movies. Again, a group of ex-cons "volunteers" for a mission no one in his right mind would accept. Led by cocky officer Michael Caine, the squad makes its violent way across 400 miles of open desert in jeeps armed only with machine guns, for a raid on an Afrika Korps fuel dump.

There are no good guys here. Not the Germans or the British, who will do anything to accomplish their goals, or unfriendly Arabs, who are shot down in cold blood. And especially not the ex-cons, who loot the bodies of English and German soldiers alike, kill unarmed medics for an ambulance and attempt to rape a captured German nurse. The battle scenes are well staged, but *Play Dirty* plays as it says, and it's a bitter pill to swallow.

*1/2

## PORK CHOP HILL (1959)

United Artists Lewis Milestone (Black & white)
With Gregory Peck, Harry Guardino, Rip Torn, George Peppard, George Shibata, Woody Strode, James Edwards, Robert Blake

Perhaps the best film made about the Korean War, this stirring saga was directed by the great Lewis Milestone, who helmed *All Quiet on the Western Front* (1930), the World War I classic, and *A Walk in the Sun* (1945), which ranks among the top movies of World War II. The time is the last days of the war, with company commander Peck determined to hold Pork Chop Hill, a position critical in determining the final truce line at the peace talks in Panmunjom. After a bloody assault his unit takes the hill, only to be faced by a Chinese counterattack. The men hold on—just barely—until reinforcements arrive.

James R. Webb's telling script is based on fact. Milestone stages it with his usual panache and scrupulous attention to military detail, and the performers follow suit. Among the realistic combat scenes is an attack at night with grenades raining down on Peck and company, and the men making a final thrilling stand against enemy flamethrowers. This one would make a great double bill with Anthony Mann's *Men in War*.

****

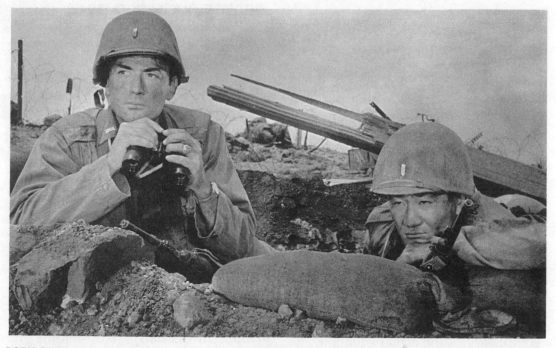

PORK CHOP HILL: Gregory Peck (left) searching for the enemy. The film is one of the best about Korea.

## PRIDE OF THE MARINES (1945)
**Also titled** *Forever in Love*

Warner Bros. Delmer Daves (Black & white)

With John Garfield, Eleanor Parker, Dane Clark, John Ridgely, Rosemary de Camp, Ann Doran, Warren Douglas

The title refers to real-life Marine Al Schmid, who was blinded by a grenade on Guadalcanal after taking out more than 200 Japanese. Tough guy Garfield turns in a remarkably sensitive performance as the maimed veteran, who must face the hardest battle of all. The replay of Schmid's one-man stand with grenades and a .30-caliber water-cooled Browning is thrilling, but it's his homecoming and the problems of readjustment that make this a memorable film. Parker, as the girl back home, sheds her glamor image and delivers a touching performance.
**1/2

## PRISONER OF WAR (1954)

MGM   Andrew Marton (Black & white)

With Ronald Reagan, Steve Forrest, Dewey Martin, Oscar Homolka, Paul Stewart, Robert Horton, Henry Morgan, Stephen Bekassy

Reagan plays an undercover agent who gets himself imprisoned in a Korean POW camp to learn how Americans are being treated by the enemy. Needless to say, it's rough going, what with brainwashing and GI turncoats on all sides, including one who is a Communist intelligence operative. Released just as the United States was preparing dossiers on Korean War collaborators (of which there were quite a few), this film trivializes the complexity of the actual situation.
*

## PRIVATE BENJAMIN (1980)

Warner Bros.   Howard Zieff (Color)

With Goldie Hawn, Eileen Brennan, Albert Brooks

This oh, so trendy service comedy features a self-described "JAP" (a Jewish-American Princess) who enlists in the "New Action Army" after a chain of unfortunate accidents. The role of Private Benjamin is tailored to the talents of Hawn, who makes the story work with her excellent comedy timing and rubber face. Brennan, as her CO, almost steals the show with her atypical portrayal of a frustrated officer trying to make a soldier out of a pampered young woman. The humor is cruel at times, however, and the jokes aren't as funny as those of similar service comedies of the 1940s.
**1/2

## PRIVATE BUCKAROO (1942)

Universal   Eddie Cline (Black & white)

With Harry James and his Orchestra, the Andrews Sisters, Joe E. Lewis

Bandleader James and the boys are drafted during World War II, so they get to work putting together a really big show for the boys. The basic-training story line is awful, but James and the Andrews sisters don't miss a beat and their boogie-woogie still rates a hubba-hubba.
**

## THE PRIVATE NAVY OF SERGEANT O'FARRELL (1968)

United Artists   Frank Tashlin (Color)

With Bob Hope, Jeffrey Hunter, Phyllis Diller, Gina Lollobrigida

Hope, in his early sixties, joins the Army for another bungling go-around, this time in the Pacific. Dated even back in 1968, and the alleged jokes are excruciatingly unfunny. Bob and Phyllis deserved better.

1/2*

## A PRIVATE'S AFFAIR (1959)

20th Century-Fox   Raoul Walsh (Color)

With Sal Mineo, Christine Carere, Barry Coe, Barbara Eden, Terry Moore, Jim Backus, Gary Crosby, Jesse Royce Landis

Fox put its young contract players on parade for this forgettable service musical, and only a few made the grade. The story, geared to what Hollywood took to be the "youth market," has draftee Mineo and three buddies harmonizing for yet another big military show. Best is Landis as a lady general married to Private Backus. Famed action director Walsh probably figured—quite correctly—that his 44th film wouldn't reflect on his impressive body of work.

*

## THE PROUD AND THE PROFANE (1956)

Paramount   George Seaton (Black & white)

With William Holden, Deborah Kerr, Thelma Ritter, William Redfield, Dewey Martin

Kerr plays the proud (a prissy war widow) and Holden is the profane (a brutish Marine colonel). When they fall in love against the backdrop of the Pacific war, Roman Catholic Kerr suffers a lot, and Holden spouts lines like, "My pleasure is physical; my men call me the Beast." As one critic pointed out, "There's an awful lot of plot (and a lot of awful plot)." The film's source is Lucy Herndon Crockett's soap-operish novel *The Magnificent Bastards*.

*1/2

## PT-109 (1963)

Warner Bros.   Lewis Milestone, Leslie Martinson (Color)

With Cliff Robertson, Ty Hardin, Robert Culp, James Gregory, Robert Blake

PT-109: Starred Cliff Robertson (on gangplank) as a young John F. Kennedy in the Solomon Islands during World War II. Ty Hardin (gangplank, bottom) played his executive officer.

Warner apparently was so awed by its subject that it forgot that war movies are supposed to be exciting and vividly realized. *PT-109* was, of course, skipper John F. Kennedy's vessel when he was a Navy lieutenant during World War II. (The patrol boat was rammed by a Japanese destroyer in Guadalcanal's "slot.") Although at 38 Cliff Robertson was too old to play the 26-year-old Kennedy, he nevertheless delivers a credible performance. The dull supporting cast is from Warner's television stable, however, and the sets are obviously on the studio's back lot. For the record, Milestone, uncredited, directed the bulk of the movie. At the time, Robertson was selected to play the president amid a publicity hullabaloo that had the FBI investigating all candidates to make certain their backgrounds were "clean" enough to play Kennedy.

**

### THE PURPLE HEART (1944)

20th Century-Fox   Lewis Milestone (Black & white)

With Dana Andrews, Richard Conte, Farley Granger, Kevin O'Shea, Sam Levene, Donald Barry, Richard Loo, Peter Chong, Benson Fong

General Doolittle's daring air raid on Japan in 1942 was dramatized in *Destination Tokyo* (1943) and *Thirty Seconds over Tokyo* (1944). But this patriotic homage imagines what happened to the pilots taken prisoner there. After crash-landing in China, pilots Andrews, Conte and Granger are handed over to the Japanese by Chinese quislings for a mock trial, torture and execution in Tokyo.

Led by Andrews, the men ably defend their actions after being accused of war crimes, with the Axis and neutral press in attendance. Despite brutal beatings and threats of worse to come, they steadfastly refuse to reveal where their strike was launched from. The racism is thick and heavy, but in fact the real-life airmen were manhandled and three were executed (another died of malnutrition). Darryl Zanuck wrote the febrile script (under the pseudonym Melville Crossman), which, for all its provocative power, seems exceedingly caustic today. But in its time the film carried the ring of truth and expressed the country's righteous anger. At the end of the trial, Andrews, as a sort of national collective hero, says in no uncertain terms, "This is your war . . . you wanted it . . . you asked for it. And now you're going to get it—and it won't be finished until your dirty little empire is wiped off the face of the earth."

***

### PURPLE HEARTS (1984)

Warner Bros.   Sidney J. Furie (Color)

With Ken Wahl, Cheryl Ladd, James Whitmore, Jr.

There are two movies competing for attention here. One is a vapid love story starring Ken Wahl and Cheryl Ladd as, respectively, a Navy doctor and a nurse who meet at a base hospital in Vietnam. Both players are attractive, but their television-size talents are all too apparent on the big screen. Fortunately for the viewer, the love story is interrupted by Wahl's frequent calls to the battlefield—which brings us to film number two. The combat scene, staged by director Sidney J. Furie (of *The Boys in Company C*), are so exciting that one numbly endures the Wahl-Ladd grapplings in the hope of more. The brief, intense firefights typical of the complicated Vietnam War have rarely been more vividly realized, especially in a battle similar to that at Khe San, when Wahl finds himself trapped at an outpost being overrun by North Vietnamese regulars.

**1/2

## PURSUIT OF THE GRAF SPEE (1956)
**Also titled** *The Battle of the River Plate*
Great Britain   Michael Powell (Color)
With John Gregson, Anthony Quayle, Peter Finch, Bernard Lee, Ian Hunter

A slow-moving but well-detailed reconstruction of a much-needed British victory during the early days of World War II. Finch plays the commander of the *Graf Spee*, a German pocket battleship caught in neutral Uruguay's Montevideo Harbor in 1939. The final scuttling of the vessel off the coast of South America resulted from a clever British ploy that is almost stranger than fiction.

**1/2

## THE QUIET AMERICAN (1958)
United Artists   Joseph Mankiewicz (Black & white)
With Audie Murphy, Michael Redgrave, Giorgia Moll, Claude Dauphin, Bruce Cabot, Richard Loo

Audie Murphy is miscast as Graham Greene's meddling American, although he seems boyish and innocent enough to fall victim to the film's worldly Europeans. Arriving in Saigon with plans to help end the French Indochina War, Murphy botches the mission and gets himself murdered instead. Only Michael Redgrave, as the duplicitous narrator/journalist, comes close to suggesting the author's hard-nosed political ironies. Writer/director Mankiewicz also has savaged the novel by switching from a critique of American näiveté to uncompromising anticommunism. The result is yet another one-sided, distorted look at a complicated situation that has yet to be fully understood.

**

## THE RACK (1956)
MGM   Arnold Laven (Black & white)
With Paul Newman, Anne Francis, Wendell Corey, Edmond O'Brien, Lee Marvin, Cloris Leachman, Walter Pidgeon

Originally seen on live television, Rod Serling's intelligent script transferred nicely to the big screen (and back again via videocassette). Newman, in a star-making role, is an Army captain who broke under pressure in a Korean POW camp and now is being tried at home for treason. Serling took his sympathetic cue from the many American POWs who recently had been used for propaganda purposes by the Communists (most recanted later). Newman's crack-up, it is made clear, is the result of brainwashing, fear and loneliness and should not be construed as a treasonable act. That brave men aren't made of steel is convincingly conveyed in Newman's timeless performance.

**1/2

## RAIDERS OF THE LOST ARK (1981)

Paramount   Steven Spielberg (Color)
With Harrison Ford, Karen Allen, Paul Freeman, Ronald Lacey, John Rhys-Davies, Wolf Kahler, Denholm Eliott

Fantasy wizards George Lucas and Steven Spielberg collaborated on this eye-popping, breathtaking pastiche of movie cliff-hangers of the 1930s and 1940s. Fans of Hollywood's old Saturday matinee serials, the pair outdid their models with fast-paced chases, impossible stunts, hair-raising special effects and a terrific send-up of "Nazi spy" movies of the pre-war years. Harrison Ford, stepping comfortably into the brogans of stars like Errol Flynn and Clark Gable, plays the fearless Indiana Jones, an archaeologist on the trail of the Ark of the Covenant. According to the Old Testament prophecy, this biblical relic will be found only during the Second Coming of the Messiah—which is why Jones must keep it out of the hands of Nazi agents and, ultimately, Hitler's.

The film has a witty Art Deco design of the period and some wonderfully realistic spoofs of cliché action scenes. Jones, for example, manages to overcome every impossible obstacle, including the machine-gunning of a

RAIDERS OF THE LOST ARK: In this film, Harrison Ford fights off scores of German soldiers as well as a Nazi submarine.

bar and hand-to-hand combat with a hulking Aryan Nazi. There even is a showdown with a German U-boat. One of movieland's all-time box-office champs, the film inspired an okay sequel, *Indiana Jones and the Temple of Doom.*

An irresistible tale of derring-do, perfect for kids of all ages.

****

### RAID ON ROMMEL (1971)

Universal   Henry Hathaway (Color)

With Richard Burton, John Colicos, Clinton Greyn, Wolfgang Preiss

Hard-drinking star Richard Burton reportedly fell off the wagon while filming this clumsy farrago in Mexico. And the great action director Henry Hathaway seems to have wandered off course. The worn-out plot has supercommando Burton leading British POWs on a raid on a German fuel dump and slipping in and out of enemy lines almost as easily as Rommel himself. Battle scenes are the only excitement here, and these are lifted from *Tobruk*, a clinker made by the same studio only four years before. For a superior version of the Tobruk campaign—and a younger, more vigorous Burton—stay with *The Desert Rats* (1953).

*1/2

### RAMBO: FIRST BLOOD PART II (1985)

Tri Star   George P. Cosmatos (Color)

With Sylvester Stallone, Richard Crenna, Charles Napier, Steven Berkoff, Julia Nickson, Andy Wood

Stallone's second go-around as Rambo, the disgruntled veteran of *First Blood*,

RAMBO: FIRST BLOOD PART II: A Russian Spetnaz (Special Forces) adviser, Steven Berkoff (left), tortures Sylvester Stallone. As villains, the Russians and Vietnamese are throwbacks to World War II stereotypes of Germans and Japanese.

has him lashing into his former Vietnamese enemies rather than the American citizenry. The exciting smash 'n slash plot has Rambo parachuting into the Vietnam jungle to photograph a campsite possibly incarcerating American MIAs (Missing in Action). He's soon spotted, however. Even though he has lost most of his firepower on the jump, he makes do nicely with a bow and arrow and his massive survival knife. Fortunately, a lovely Vietnamese woman steps forward to help him liberate the prisoners.

A phenomenal money-maker, *Rambo* proved to be as controversial as it was popular. President Reagan joked about sending him to rescue skyjacked hostages, while the Soviet press berated the film's aggressive military stance. Sociologists were bewildered by the public's mass acceptance of this

RAMBO: FIRST BLOOD PART II: As Rambo, Sylvester Stallone (left) helps a POW (Andy Wood) escape from the Vietnamese.

borderline psychotic, especially after Rambo posters, dolls and headbands became big sellers. But the success of the film has much to do with the romanticization of the Vietnam veteran, who had been stereotyped for years as a guilt-ridden, drug-addicted baby-killer.

As a war movie *Rambo* is outrageously unrealistic: Bows used for silent sentry removal had largely been replaced by silenced small arms by 1965; exploding arrowheads would weight too much to be accurate and could never produce such large secondary explosions; and firing a Light Antitank Weapon (LAW) inside a helicopter certainly would have incinerated the craft in the backblast. Moreover, it's highly unlikely that Vietnamese regulars, perhaps the best jungle fighters in the world, would have Soviet advisers.

As this generation's fantasy war hero, Rambo combines John Wayne's patriotic machismo with Superman's extraterrestrial powers. Like his cinematic forebears, his antics are harmless fun—unless they are taken seriously.

***1/2

### REACH FOR THE SKY (1956)
Great Britain   Lewis Gilbert (Black & white)
With Kenneth More, Muriel Pavlos, Alexander Knox, Nigel Green

On the face of it, RAF commander Douglas Bader would seem to be just another World War II flying ace. But when you consider that he had lost both legs in an accident several years before, his true-life story takes on a certain fascination. In addition to his aerial heroics, Bader somehow managed to escape from a German POW camp several times. Kenneth More does full justice to the brave handicapped flier, and director Gilbert avoids the usual treacly sentiments.

**1/2

## THE REAL GLORY (1939)

United Artists   Henry Hathaway (Black & white)

With Gary Cooper, David Niven, Andrea Leeds, Broderick Crawford

United States Army advisers Cooper, Niven and Crawford arrive in the Philippines just after the Spanish-American War to put down a Moslem uprising. The trio is assigned to train the constabulary of a small hamlet that is deathly afraid of the Moros, nationalist guerrillas, who have raped and pillaged the countryside. (The movement was known as the Moro Insurrection.) Faced by the canny Americans, the guerrillas send in waves of religious fanatics on a "holy war" mission, some of whom get past the rifle barrage to their assassination targets.

Although cast as a military adventure in the *Gunga Din* mold, the film has much in common with events that took place 26 years later in South Vietnam. For one thing, the basis of the conflict is the "Philippinization" of the islands. For another, the booby traps set in the jungle to protect the Moro hideout, and the Americans' use of a fortified hamlet as a base, are reminis-

cent of the situation in Vietnam. Overall, it's an exciting version of a forgotten conflict with a stirring combat finale.

***

## THE RED BADGE OF COURAGE (1951)

MGM   John Huston (Black & white)

With Audie Murphy, Bill Mauldin, Douglas Dick, Royal Dano, Andy Devine, John Dierkes, Arthur Hunnicutt

John Huston's script and direction capture the subjective mood of Stephen Crane's classic Civil War novel, but he failed to capture an audience. Previews showed the viewers couldn't comprehend the plot, so the studio recut it into more commercial form and added an unnecessary narration spoken by James Whitemore. For his part, Huston denounced the tampered-with film and says he still can't bear to view it. What remains is impressive, however, with World War II hero Audie Murphy giving the performance of his career as a young Yankee soldier who learns the measure of his own courage and endurance under fire. There are no phony heroics here, only a group of very human soldiers who somehow manage to overcome their instinctive reaction of fear and occasional cowdice.

***1/2

## RED BALL EXPRESS (1952)

Universal-International   Budd Boetticher (Black & white)

With Jeff Chandler, Alan Nichol, Sidney Poitier, Hugh O'Brian, Jack Kelly

"Red Ball Express" was the nickname

RED BALL EXPRESS: Sidney Poitier (left) hits Hugh O'Brian over a racial slur.

of the supply column of trucks that kept Patton's Third Army driving through France and into Germany. The unit was made up mostly of black GIs who drove their ammo- and gasoline-loaded trucks at breakneck speed to keep up with Patton. This was the first film to show blacks fighting as a unit, and it gave Poitier his first big break. But the story's idealized "we are all in this together" version of integrated harmony has a hollow ring. Although it has a commendable idea, the film breaks down about halfway through and fails to measure up as either history or entertainment.

**

### RED DAWN (1984)

United Artists   John Milius (Color)

With Patrick Swayne, C. Thomas Howell, Lea Thompson, Charlie Sheen, Darren Dalton, Ben Johnson, Harry Dean Stanton, Ron O'Neal, William Smith, Powers Boothe

There are enough weapons in this bizarre military movie to fight another war in Vietnam (among these are some convincing mock-ups of Mi-24 Hind attack helicopters, RPG-7 rocket launchers and T-72 tanks). Typically, macho-minded director Milius—who cowrote the script for *Apocalypse Now*—supplies plenty of synthetic bellicosity and pain to tell his story of a Cuban-Soviet invasion of the United States. That teenage guerrillas would take arms against the invaders is more than a little farfetched, although the action scenes are realistic and exciting. Best are the initial Soviet air assault of a small Colorado town; a series of attacks by the guerrillas; and a helicopter pursuit of the youngsters, who are on horseback.

On the negative side, Milius delivers the anti-Soviet dialogue with a pair of brass knuckles and a stomach-wrenching amount of gore. Moreover, the young actors are no match for veterans Johnson, Stanton and O'Neal. Technical credits are first-rate, however, and you'll probably be swept along by Milius's expert technique.

***

RED DAWN: Russians and Cubans take over part of the United States.

## RETREAT, HELL! (1952)

Warner Bros.   Joseph H. Lewis (Black & white)
With Frank Lovejoy, Richard Carlson, Anita Louise, Russ Tamblyn

As they were in previous wars, the U.S. Marines are depicted as being supertough, resolute and the ultimate fighting machine — even when surrounded by Communist Chinese during the Korean War. Frank Lovejoy is fine in several flashy battles as an infantry CO who can fight with the best of them. The film's only drawback is the obligatory rhetoric about "why we are in Korea," which is understandable since we still were fighting there when the movie was made.

Producer Milton Sperling, who also wrote the screenplay, had served in the Marines during World War II and was in charge of the photographic unit that made the documentaries *Tarawa* and *To the Shores of Iwo Jima*. Before joining the Corps in 1943 he made the submarine movie *Crash Dive*. His military background and movie experience are used to good advantage here.

\*\*\*

## REUNION IN FRANCE (1942)
**Also titled** *Mademoiselle France*

MGM   Jules Dassin (Black & white)
With John Wayne, Joan Crawford, Philip Dorn, Reginald Owen, Albert Basserman, John Carradine, Henry Daniell, Moroni Olsen, Ann Ayers, J. Edward Bromberg

Crawford plays a Paris *couturiere* hiding downed airman John Wayne in her workroom while she fences with Nazi admirer Philip Dorn. Although the plot is unreal, the tedium is occasionally relieved by director Dassin's gift for cinematic suspense and by Crawford's nasty barbs ("A severe wound, I hope," she snaps to an injured German officer). Woman's-picture favorite Crawford wears her usual glamorous wardrobe, which prompted a critic from the *New York Herald Tribune* to note that "dressing like a refugee is certainly not in her contract."

*1/2

## RUN SILENT, RUN DEEP (1958)

United Artists   Robert Wise (Black & white)

With Clark Gable, Burt Lancaster, Jack Warden, Brad Dexter, Don Rickles, Nick Cravat

Director Wise attempts to insert some food for thought into this underwater mission, but it's little more than a routine World War II outing, held together by its charismatic stars. Gable and Lancaster play a sub commander and his lieutenant, respectively, who are at war with each other over how to run the ship during a trip to Tokyo Bay. Gable seems distracted at times, however, and Lancaster grits his teeth once too often. But director Wise, who filmed *Destination Gobi, The Desert Rats* and, later, *The Sand Pebbles*, has a keen eye for nerve-racking details of men under stress in cramped quarters. *Time* magazine's comment was, "ran noisy, ran shallow."

**1/2

## SABOTEUR (1942)

Universal   Alfred Hitchcock (Black & white)

With Robert Cummings, Priscilla Lane, Otto Kruger, Alan Baxter, Clem Bevans, Alma Kruger, Norman Lloyd

Hitchcock isn't quite up to full power in

RUN SILENT, RUN DEEP: Burt Lancaster and crew.

this wartime espionage thriller, but even at half speed he could outrace most directors. The plot reiterates Hitchcock's favorite theme of a man unjustly accused of a crime who must clear his name. Mistaken for the saboteur who set fire to a California aircraft factory, Robert Cummings journeys cross-country with unwilling accomplice Priscilla Lane to unmask a ring of German fifth columnists in New York.

Among the film's flaws—acknowledged by Hitchcock—are too many plot angles and the casting (forced on him by the studio) of second-string stars. Set in 1941, before the United States entered the war, *Saboteur* attempted to expose the country's strongly entrenched pro-Nazi element. This point was lost somewhat when popular character actor Harry Carey turned down the role of a German agent because of his image. Instead of discerning evil in a likable, benign face, we are given the usual unsympathetic villain. The film is thrilling nevertheless and contains some of Hitchcock's most memorable scenes: a trip through the Nevada desert by a traveling freak show, a shoot-out in front of the immense movie screen of Radio City Music Hall, the sinking of a military ship during its launching (actually, a shot of the *Normandie*, a French ship that mysteriously caught fire in New York Harbor earlier that year) and a breathtaking confrontation between hero and villain on the face of the Statue of Liberty. The latter scene is similar to the ending of Hitchcock's later *North by Northwest*, which has a final chase over the massive stone heads carved out of Mount Rushmore.
***1/2

### THE SAD SACK (1957)

Paramount   George Marshall (Black & white)
With Jerry Lewis, David Wayne, Phyllis Kirk, Peter Lorre, Gene Evans, Joe Mantell, Liliane Montevecchi

One of Jerry's funnier outings, this fast-paced comedy has him back in the peacetime Army. Still a misfit, he tangles with sinister Arab Peter Lorre in North Africa while under the tutelage of kind lady major Phyllis Kirk. The character, a classic Army moron, is based on a popular cartoon character of the same title, created by George Baker.
**1/2

### SAHARA (1943)

Columbia   Zoltan Korda (Black & white)
With Humphrey Bogart, Bruce Bennett, Lloyd Bridges, Rex Ingram, J. Carrol Naish, Dan Duryea, Richard Nugent, Kurt Krueger, Louis T. Mercier

Bogart, no longer the cynical, laid-back cafe owner of *Casablanca* the year before, unleashes his squint-eyed, snarling fury against Rommel's Afrika Korps. As a dedicated American tank sergeant cut off from friendly troops, he assembles his own Army from leftover British, Australian, Free French, Italian and Sudanese soldiers. With the help of the film's other star, an M-3 tank nicknamed *Lulubelle*, the 13 men outwit the Nazis at a desert oasis by holding off a 500-man German battalion. As a result, Montgomery's Eighth Army wins the pivotal North African Battle of El Alamein.

SAHARA: Humphrey Bogart stars as the tough sergeant who leads an international unit in desert fighting.

Everyone involved gets an opportunity to express his reason for fighting, and afterward the bullets and shells fly by the hundreds. Bogart gives an outstanding pivotal performance, and Bennett, Ingram and Naish are right there beside him. The film is based on a Soviet movie titled *The Thirteen* and later was remade as a Western, *Last of the Comanches* (1953).

A quintessential World War II desert movie that shouldn't be missed.
****

### SALVADOR (1986)

Hemdale   Oliver Stone (Color)
With James Woods, James Belushi, Michael Murphy, John Savage

This independent film marked Stone's directorial debut. It's the half truth/half fiction story of a sleazy

SAHARA: Humphrey Bogart (second from left) and Lloyd Bridges (far right) with other Allied soldiers.

photojournalist, played by Woods, who journeys to El Salvador with his spaced-out DJ friend (Belushi) in the early '80s. The time can't be more specific because Stone collapses the events of several years into a few months; the assassination of Archbishop Romero and the murder of the American nuns are made to look like they happened within weeks of each other. *Salvador* basically tells a story somewhat similar to that of another Central America-set film, *Under Fire*—where a journalist becomes involved in the story he's covering. In *Salvador*, it involves Woods' character trying to spirit his Salvadorian girlfriend to safety. Stone's penchant for striking, unpleasant violence is put to good effect here, his sensible idea being that bloodshed should be disturbing, not exciting; the performances are generally good and the story is engaging. However, like *Under Fire*, its politics—pro-rebel, anti-government—seem over-romanticized.

***

## THE SAND PEBBLES (1966)

20th Century-Fox   Robert Wise (Color)

With Steve McQueen, Richard Attenborough, Candice Bergen, Richard Crenna, Simon Oakland, Mako

Overlong and stagey at times, this ex-

THE SAND PEBBLES: Mako is about to be tortured by Chinese revolutionaries.

THE SAND PEBBLES: Candice Bergen, as an American teacher with a Chinese mission, evades capture by Chinese rebels with sailors Gavin Macleod (left) and Joe Turkel.

pensive would-be epic actually benefits from those usually inane cuts made for television showings. McQueen is very good in a low-key performance as an American sailor (which brought him his only Oscar nomination) who arrives in 1926 China aboard the U.S.S. *San Pablo*. The Navy's mission is to put down the insurrection of several warlords, mostly by making its presence felt during cruises on the Yangtze River.

McQueen, withdrawn and stubborn, questions the morality of each sailor having a Chinese coolie to serve him; he wants to do his own dirty work, which makes the others dislike him. His one on-board friend is Attenborough, who makes the fatal mistake of falling in love with a Chinese girl about to be sold into prostitution. Meanwhile, McQueen's love interest, missionary Candice Bergen, questions the very idea of the American presence in Asia. Although this situation was supposed to parallel the then-current Vietnam War, it's tenuous at best and never clarified.

**1/2

## SANDS OF IWO JIMA (1949)

Republic   Alan Dwan (Black & white)

With John Wayne, John Agar, Forrest Tucker, Adele Mara, Wally Cassell, James Brown, Richard Webb, Arthur Franz, Julie Bishop, Peter Coe, Richard Jaeckel, Martin Milner

A preeminent favorite among war movie buffs, this rip-snorting recap of the famous Marine Corps siege of Iwo Jima (which in Japanese means "sulphur island") is held together by the totally dominating presence of John Wayne. Cast as a squadron leader named Sergeant Stryker, Wayne is a tough taskmaster whose men initially hate him. Only when they face the horror of the Tarawa landing do they begin to understand that his harsh military training was for their benefit. For his part, Wayne undergoes a change of character when, during a leave, he meets a bargirl and her baby son (who reminds him of his own estranged boy). There is a happy ending of sorts, before the sad one, with raw recruit John Agar and old hand Forrest Tucker coming to love and admire a man they formerly despised. The payoff is the famed Marine Corps victory on Iwo Jima, with the actors reenacting the celebrated flag-raising on Mount Suribachi. (The invasion cost the lives of more than 5,000 Marines and Seabees and 20,000 Japanese.)

Aside from Wayne, the actors aren't very memorable; all they do is take his orders and fire when ready. Wayne simply blots out everyone else in his first Oscar-nominated role. The use of actual combat footage is highly effective and gives a documentary scope rarely matched in other war movies. These are slowed down, however, by too many scenes involving Wayne's personality clash with his squad. But Wayne's picture-perfect Marine grunt and the realistic battle scenes prop up the mediocre story. Viewers are compelled to "saddle up" every time the film is aired.

***1/2

## SAYONARA (1957)

Warner Bros.  Joshua Logan (Color)

With Marlon Brando, Red Buttons, Ricardo Montalban, Miiko Taka, Miyoshi Umeki, James Garner, Patricia Owens, Kent Smith, Martha Scott

A huge success in its time, this expensive soap opera seems mighty tame today, even though it nobly attempts to redress the American and Japanese racism of the war years. Director Logan opts for a sentimental treatment of James Michener's more thought-provoking novel about the postwar occupation of Japan. Brando, sporting an embarrassing southern accent, is a redneck Air Force pilot having a love affair with a beautiful Japanese showgirl (Miiko Taka). Initially a racist, he advises Red Buttons not to marry "slant-eyed runt" Miyoshi Umeki until he falls in love with a Japanese girl—and Japan—himself. Buttons and Umeki who won supporting-actor Oscars, are touching as lovers.

**1/2

## THE SEA CHASE (1955)

Warner Bros.  John Farrow (Color)

With John Wayne, Lana Turner, David Farrar, Lyle Bettger, Tab Hunter, James Arness, Richard Davalos, Paul Fix, John Qualen

An oddball bit of casting if there ever was one, this routine melodrama has all-American John Wayne as a German officer (albeit a good one) attempting to take his freighter from Australia to South America. The time is 1939, so there are plenty of British vessels around determined to capture or sink Wayne and company. Among the passengers are Lana Turner, looking very much like the hard-as-nails femme fatale she plays, and seaman Lyle Bettger, who lusts after her. This one may stretch your capacity for disbelief to the limit.

**

## SEA OF SAND (1958)
**Also titled** *Desert Patrol*

Great Britain   Guy Green (Black & white)
With Richard Attenborough, John Gregson, Michael Craig, Barry Foster, Dermot Walsh

Compared to the ersatz glow of the usual Hollywood war epic, this small British gem shines with the hardness and clarity of a diamond. Filmed where the story happened, in Libya, the film is dedicated to the British Long Range Desert Group, a brave volunteers-only unit trained in intelligence and sabotage. The film's characters are portrayed as spirited rebels of the type the LRDG attracted, who, despite internal squabbles, kept nipping away at Rommel's flanks and rear. The young Richard Attenborough—since turned director—is especially good as a working-class sergeant who refuses to wear his beret at the correct angle or to address officers formally, and who fills his canteen with brandy for the long haul across the desert. (The brandy comes in handy when Attenborough spits it into a German sentry's eyes to disarm him.)

The film uses real LRDG equipment, including machine-gun-mounted trucks. Shot on immense rippling sand dunes, the combat scenes resemble navy battles on the high seas, with the vehicles firing close-range broadsides at each other. The commandos' bracing lack of military pomp and circumstance may help explain the unit's amazing—and disproportionate—influence on the North African campaign.
***1/2

## THE SEARCH (1948)

MGM   Fred Zinnemann (Black & white)

With Montgomery Clift, Aline MacMahon, Wendell Corey, Ivan Jendl

Former boy stage actor Montgomery Clift made an impressive debut in this touching drama, filmed on location in Austria. Its sensitively handled subject is the psychological dilemma of displaced children in Europe immediately following World War II. The opener has a group of children escaping from an UNRAA van because they think they are being taken to a gas chamber. American GI Clift discovers and befriends one of them, who, initially speechless, overcomes his fear and learns how to play baseball. Eventually the boy is reunited with his Czechoslovakian mother—and taken away from Clift—in one of the cinema's most sincerely heartfelt scenes. Child actor Ivan Jendl won an Oscar (in a special "juvenile" category) for his impressive work, as did the script by Paul Jarrico, Richard Schweitzer and David Wechsler.
***

## THE SEA WOLVES (1981)

Paramount   Andrew V. MacLaglen (Color)
With Roger Moore, Gregory Peck, David Niven, Trevor Howard

This peculiar comedy/drama has a group of over-the-hill British soldiers, retired to India, organizing an unlikely commando unit to destroy a Nazi spy station anchored in Goa, a nearby Portuguese colony. Although the aging cast is likable and delivers professional performances, the story is forced and slow-moving. There's a meaningless spy subplot that gives Moore a chance to act like James Bond.
**

## THE SECRET OF SANTA VITTORIA (1969)

United Artists   Stanley Kramer (Color)
With Anthony Quinn, Anna Magnani, Hardy Kruger, Virna Lisi, Sergio Franchi

Stanley Kramer, who did a credible job with the mammoth comedy *It's a Mad, Mad, Mad, Mad World* (1963), is all thumbs this time around, even though he had Robert Crichton's excellent novel to work from. The plot device, which deflates early on, has a group of villagers desperately working to keep a million bottles of wine out of the hands of retreating Germans in wartime Italy. Quinn does one of his worst ethnic imitations as a bellowing, gesticulating Italian peasant. Worth watching, however, is Anna Magnani as his dominating wife and Hardy Kruger as a *simpático* Wehrmacht officer.

\*\*

## THE SECRET WAR OF HARRY FRIGG (1968)

**Also titled** *The Private War of Harry Frigg*

Universal   Jack Smight (Color)
With Paul Newman, Sylva Koscina, John Williams, Andrew Duggan, Tom Bosley, Vito Scotti, Charles D. Gray, James Gregory

For all his talent, Paul Newman is no comedy actor, at least not on the evidence displayed here. Cast as Harry Frigg, a Pfc. who also is an escape artist, Newman poses as a captured general to infiltrate a POW compound in a villa owned by the lovely Ms. Koscina. The object of the mission is to liberate the real generals, but Newman likes the place so much he decides, at least temporarily, to stay on. It's a good plot idea, but one whose possibilities overreached the capabilities of cast and crew.

\*1/2

## SEE HERE, PRIVATE HARGROVE (1943)

MGM   Wesley Ruggles (Black & white)
With Robert Walker, Donna Reed, Keenan Wynn, Robert Benchley, Ray Collins, Chill Wills

Still an amusing farce despite scores of similar service comedies, this slick Metro product succeeds largely on the "aw, shucks" charm of leading man Robert Walker. As the real-life Marion Hargrove, who wrote a best seller based on his military experience, Walker is every draftee who ever had to undergo the rigors and humiliation of basic training. Also good is Chill Wills as a befuddled training sergeant trying to make fighting men from inept recruits. Basic training hasn't changed all that much in over 40 years, and the humor in *See Here, Private Hargrove* is almost as topical now as it was then. Walker also starred in a forgettable sequel, *What Next, Corporal Hargrove?* (1945), which had him entangled with various beauties in liberated France.

\*\*\*

## SERGEANT DEADHEAD (1965)

AIP   Norman Taurog (Color)
With Frankie Avalon, Caesar Romero, Fred Clark, Deborah Walley, Buster Keaton

Remove the word "sergeant" and you'd have an apt title for this tissue-paper comedy. The plot has teen favorite Frankie Avalon (before he became a "golden oldie") as a shy Pfc. who turns into a ladies' man and disrupts a missile base. It's very much in the *Beach Party* mold but not as good as. The great Buster Keaton is wasted in a minor role.

1/2*

## SERGEANT RYKER (1967)

Universal   Buzz Kulik (Color)

With Lee Marvin, Bradford Dillman, Vera Miles, Peter Graves, Lloyd Nolan

Occasionally intriguing, this small-scale courtroom drama of the Korean War plays better on the home screen than it did in theaters—which isn't surprising, since it was culled from episodes of a TV series that never was, titled *Court-Martial*. Lee Marvin plays the title role, a sergeant accused of collaborating with the Communist Chinese. He knows he is innocent, but the colonel who sent him over enemy lines is now dead. Ordinary but entertaining enough if there's nothing better on.

**

## SERGEANT YORK (1941)

Warner Bros.   Howard Hawks (Black & white)

With Gary Cooper, Walter Brennan, Joan Leslie, Stanley Ridges, George Tobias, Margaret Wycherly, David Bruce, Dickie Moore, Ward Bond

Warner based this key war movie on the diary of Alvin York, who was then America's most famous living war hero (he died in 1964). A poor Tennessee farmer whose parents were deeply religious, York was a pacifist drafted

SERGEANT YORK: Gary Cooper demonstrates his sharpshooting ability as a civilian. Cooper won a best actor Oscar for his performance.

into the Army during World War I. Although reluctant to fight, he nevertheless won the Congressional Medal of Honor for killing more than 25 Germans and capturing 132 more single-handedly in the Argonne on October 8, 1918.

When Warner decided to make the film York insisted that Gary Cooper play him—a wise casting choice that won the actor his first Oscar. The role is a perfect showcase for the naïve and idealistic charms of Cooper, who always was at his best as an idealized American Everyman. The linchpin that holds the film together, he's totally convincing in the first half of the film, which deals with York's changeover from antiwar hillbilly to stone-hard combat soldier. The subsequent battle scenes, although accurately portrayed, are a bit stagey and reduce York's heroic deeds to just another Hollywood glamorization of war. York liked the film, however, and commented that Cooper was "very natural" in the part.

As much a tribute to a vanishing American life-style (that of the rural farmer) as it is a war movie, *Sergeant York* takes an inspiring look at a patriotic American who rallied to action when needed despite not condoning the war itself. Cooper played a similar role in William Wyler's *Friendly Persuasion* (1956), which cast him as a Quaker roused to action during the Civil War.

\*\*\*

## SEVEN DAYS IN MAY (1964)

Paramount   John Frankenheimer (Black & white)

With Burt Lancaster, Kirk Douglas, Fredric March, Edmond O'Brien, Ava Gardner, Martin Balsam, George Macready, John Houseman

Director Frankenheimer and scriptwriter Rod Serling did a fine job in bringing Fletcher Knebel's political thriller to the screen. Lancaster is chillingly believable as chairman of the Joint Chiefs of Staff who plots a military takeover of the United States because the president (March) is a pacifist. Kirk Douglas is the military assistant who blows the whistle on Lancaster. Also giving keen performances are O'Brien as a dipsomaniac senator and Gardner in a small but pivotal role. The intrigue, suspense and political maneuvering are skillfully woven into a subtext of military responsibility and survival in a nuclear age.

Stimulating fare indeed.

\*\*\*

## THE SEVENTH CROSS (1944)

MGM   Fred Zinnemann (Black & white)

With Spencer Tracy, Agnes Moorehead, Signe Hasso, Hume Cronyn, Jessica Tandy, Felix Bressart, George Zucco, George Macready

In a year glutted with escape-from-Nazis chase movies, this sterling effort stands out, thanks to Zinnemann's spare direction and a high-powered performance by Tracy. The plot, told with a minimum of dialogue, has Tracy as a German escaping with fellow prisoners from a Nazi concentration camp, circa 1936. All the others are captured, but with the help of friends and the local underground he eventually reaches the border and freedom. The story is somewhat contrived, but the excitement never flags.

\*\*\*

### THE SEVENTH DAWN (1963)

United Artists   Lewis Gilbert (Color)

With William Holden, Capucine, Susannah York, Tetsuro Tamba, Michael Goodliffe, Maurice Denham, Allan Cuthbertson

Holden, battling a cliché script as well as Malayan terrorists, is eventually defeated by the former. The plot has to do with the 12-year "emergency" situation (which began in the early 1950s) between British soldiers and Chinese Communist guerrillas. Although Holden is disturbed when he finds that his best friend is a terrorist, most of his attention is focused on Capucine and York, the other two angles of the eternal triangle.

(Yawn!)

*

### SINCE YOU WENT AWAY (1944)

Selznick/International   John Cromwell (Black & white)

With Claudette Colbert, Jennifer Jones, Joseph Cotten, Shirley Temple, Lionel Barrymore, Agnes Moorehead, Monty Woolley, Guy Madison, Robert Walker, Keenan Wynn, Nazimova, Hattie McDaniel, Craig Stevens, Albert Basserman

Have a box of Kleenex handy when you tune in this World War II "home front" tearjerker. A seminal film of that era, it represents Hollywood's expertise at its most polished, even though it's essentially a movieland confidence trick. A summation of a family and milieu that never were, the film takes place in a comfortable Norman Rockwell house, described in the prologue as "an unconquerable fortress, the American home, 1943." Inside are mother Claudette Colbert, who has taken a job in a defense plant after her husband was reported missing in action. Adolescent daughter Jennifer Jones has fallen in love with the soldier-nephew of Monty Woolley, a crusty old boarder they have taken in to ease the household economy. Taking care of the hygienically clean house is maid Hattie McDaniel, who had previously played a slave in *Gone with the Wind*. Everyone in the film is wholesome, kind, patient and generous to a fault, especially to those less fortunate than themselves (which means almost everybody else).

For all its falseness, however, *Since You Went Away* undoubtedly gave millions of women brief consolation with its emotionalism. Even today, over a distance of more than 40 years, the movie remains a poignant reminder of the mass emotion engendered by young men going off to war and the feeling of a comfortable and secure world being threatened by distant violence.

Producer David O. Selznick wrote the script based on the book by Margaret Buell Wilder and provided a bit of off-screen drama himself. During filming, star Jennifer Jones decided to divorce costar Robert Walker and marry Selznick. Her decision caused the actress to be unable to perform the requisite love scenes with Walker, which are the only stilted parts of the movie.

***1/2

### SINK THE BISMARCK! (1960)

Great Britain   Lewis Gilbert (Black & white)

With Kenneth More, Dana Wynter, Laurence Naismith, Karel Stepanek, Carl Mohner, Michael Hordern, Geoffrey Keen, Maurice Denham

The sinking of the *Bismarck*, Hitler's pride and joy, gave British morale a shot in the arm during the early days of

World War II. Director Gilbert accurately re-creates the chase and cornering of the pocket battleship, but in doing so he dwells on too many minute details. After a while the successive shots, splashes and shell impacts become boring, and the battle becomes difficult to follow. As intended, the actors seem insignificant next to the lumbering gray warships. Dyed-in-the-wool military buffs probably will enjoy it, though.

**1/2

## 633 SQUADRON (1964)

Great Britain   Walter Grauman (Color)
With Cliff Robertson, George Chakiris, Harry Andrews, Maria Perschy, Donald Houston, Michael Goodliffe

There's lots of action and a superfluous love story in this colorful tale of a Mosquito aircraft attack on a German munitions factory in Norway. Despite untoward complications, Robertson, Chakiris and company literally rise to the occasion and get the job done. The plot is nothing more than a war movie fantasy, but it works—on its own well-worn terms.

**

## SKI TROOP ATTACK (1960)

AIP   Roger Corman (Color)
With Michael Forrest, Frank Wolff, Roger Corman

Roger Corman, king of the B-movies, wrote, produced and directed this low-budget programmer. There are a few good ski battles between German troops and Americans caught behind enemy lines in the Huertgen Forest. But at a running time of only 62 minutes, there isn't time enough for the story to develop. Corman played his first and only film role in this one, as the leader of the German ski troop (the original skier had broken his leg). Filming took place in Deadwood, South Dakota, with the fighting spirit supplied by two local high-school teams vying for screen time.

**

## SOLDIER IN THE RAIN (1963)

Allied Artists   Ralph Nelson (Black & white)
With Steve McQueen, Jackie Gleason, Tuesday Weld, Tom Poston, Tony Bill, Ed Nelson

The inspired casting of Gleason as a scheming master sergeant and McQueen as his dim-witted GI worshiper nearly saves this offbeat tale of peacetime Army life. Gleason handles the dramatic scenes with heart-tugging perfection, and McQueen is surprisingly comic. But far from being a definitive tale of good ole boys in uniform, the film scores only a near-miss. The supporting players, especially Weld, seem insipid in comparison to the stars.

**1/2

## A SOLDIER'S STORY (1984)

Columbia   Norman Jewison (Color)
With Howard Rollins, Adolph Caesar, Denzel Washington, Patti Labelle

Framed as an absorbing murder mystery, this study in military racism takes place at a segregated military base in the South during World War II. The pivot is the murder of a brutal master sergeant (Caesar), who has been shot after a night of heavy drinking. Through a series of flashbacks, it's quickly established that several GIs in his all-black unit had strong motives to do him in. Also under suspicion is a white officer who had a recent altercation with the abrasive noncom, not to mention some local townspeople.

As the black captain sent by Washington, D.C. to investigate the murder, Rollins effectively captures the repressed anger such a character would feel in dealing with racists. Caesar also delivers a first-rate performance as the gruff-voiced martinent of a sergeant (he was nominated for an Oscar). The period costumes and the sets of the small military post and the adjoining town seem like the real thing and create an evocative atmosphere for this masterful whodunit.

***1/2

### SOME CAME RUNNING (1958)
MGM   Vincente Minnelli (Color)
With Frank Sinatra, Dean Martin, Shirley MacLaine, Martha Hyer, Arthur Kennedy, Leora Dana, Nancy Gates

James Jones's autobiographical novel about a disillusioned soldier returning home after the war plays almost like a soap opera in this glamorized Hollywood revision. Sinatra is good as the aspiring writer/veteran, but Shirley MacLaine steals the show as a small-town party girl with the proverbial heart of gold.

**

### SOME KIND OF HERO (1982)
Paramount   Michael Pressman (Color)
With Richard Pryor, Margot Kidder, Olivia Cole, Lynne Moody, Ray Sharkey

Imprisoned by the Viet Cong for several years, Eddie Keller (Pryor) lives

SOME KIND OF HERO: Richard Pryor (left) and Ray Sharkey share a laugh while being held captive in North Vietnam.

to regret his signing of an antiwar document in an attempt to save the life of a cellmate (Sharkey). Repatriated, Keller comes home to the States and finds his loyalty in question as a result of the document. And that's only the beginning of his problems. His wife has squandered all his accumulated back pay and is living with a man their daughter calls "Daddy." In addition, his mother is physically and mentally incapacitated because of a stroke.

Pryor plays his dramatic part with all the mad humor his fans have come to expect of him. He screams, grimaces and cries in what is perhaps his finest screen performance. Kidder, cast as a kindly prostitute, sees Pryor as an unfortunate victim of circumstance and gives her all to help him. Sharkey's brief appearance serves as a perfect foil to Pryor's clown, and their unhappy situation manages to be funny against a backdrop of a horrible POW camp. But the contrived happy ending undermines all that went before.

\*\*\*

## SO PROUDLY WE HAIL (1943)

Paramount   Mark Sandrich (Black & white)

With Claudette Colbert, Paulette Goddard, Veronica Lake, George Reeves, Barbara Britton, Walter Abel, Sonny Tufts, Mary Servoss

A huge success back in '43, this stereotyped tale of the distaff side of the war depicts the fall of Bataan, which was then fresh in the minds of moviegoers. The sacrifices made by military nurses on the peninsula as the Japanese advanced were well documented by the press, notably by *Life* magazine, which provided the most in-depth pictorial coverage of World War II. The Oscar-nominated script by Allan Scott reportedly is based on firsthand accounts of what the nurses went through. The deglamorized star actresses are convincing, with the exception of Lake, whose tight-lipped delivery seems to indicate a mouthful of braces. It's Lake who gets to be the bravest heroine, however, when she stages a one-woman suicide grenade attack on the Japanese. Goddard won an Oscar nomination for best supporting actress, even though she is star-billed.

Also effective are George Reeves as Goddard's love interest, and debuting Sonny Tufts as a happy-go-lucky GI. At the time, Reeves, later to become TV's *Superman*, was being groomed as a major star by Paramount. But he was drafted before he could make his mark. *So Proudly We Hail* still can rouse emotions, even though, in the words of contemporary British critic Richard Winnington, there is "nothing left unsaid and nothing said."

\*\*1/2

## SOUTH PACIFIC (1958)

20th Century-Fox   Joshua Logan (Color)

With Mitzi Gaynor, Rossano Brazzi, Ray Walston, France Nuyen, John Kerr, Juanita Hall

Rodgers and Hammerstein's *South Pacific*, based a book by James Michener, became a runaway success when it opened on Broadway in 1949. In addition to the musical's wonderful songs, the World War II plot summed up the feelings of a generation of Americans who had been through the conflict. The much-heralded (and expensive) movie version is something of a comedown, however, with Mitzi Gaynor lacking the charm and charisma of Broadway star Mary Martin in the key role of Nellie Forbush, an outspoken Navy nurse stationed on a Pacific island. (Doris Day wanted the role and would have been better in it.) And costar Brazzi, as the French planter Forbush falls in love with, seems ill at ease as he mouths lyrics to the superb voice of opera singer Giorgio Tozzi.

Unfortunately for the home viewer, the movie was shot in the super-wide screen process of Todd-AO, which means that significant portions of the frame are missing when the film is shown on television. There are still those wonderful songs to listen to again, however: "There is Nothing Like a Dame," "Younger Than Springtime," "Some Enchanted Evening" and "I'm in Love with a Wonderful Guy."

\*\*\*

## SPITFIRE (1942)
**Also titled** *The First of the Few*

Great Britain Leslie Howard (Black & white)

With Leslie Howard, David Niven, Rosamund John, Roland Culver

An inside look at the invention of the Spitfire fighter, the plane credited with being a major factor in winning the Battle of Britain. Actor/director Howard stars as R.J. Mitchell, who developed the plane because he saw World War II coming. (Howard died shortly after the film's completion when his plane was shot down by Germans on a flight to London.) Niven plays Wing Commander Crisp, the speedy fighter's chief test pilot. Howard's sensitive performance and taut direction make this a better-than-average movie biography.

\*\*1/2

## STAGE DOOR CANTEEN (1943)

United Artists   Frank Borzage (Black & white)

With Judith Anderson, Tallulah Bankhead, Edgar Bergen, Ray Bolger, Katharine Cornell, Helen Hayes, Ed Wynn, Ethel Merman, Paul Muni, George Raft, Ethel Waters and others

An all-star cast congregates for this look at the American Theatre Wing's Stage Door Canteen for servicemen in New York during World War II. There's a plot buried somewhere among all the vintage cameos about GIs and canteen workers falling in love, but don't look

for it. Just sit back and enjoy the legendary stage performers, some of whom have rarely been seen on film.

\*\*1/2

## STAR WARS
**The Trilogy:** *Star Wars* (1977), *The Empire Strikes Back* (1981) and *Return of the Jedi* (1984)

20 Century-Fox George Lucas, Irvin Kershner, Richard Marquand (Color)

With Mark Hamill, Harrison Ford, Carrie Fisher, Alec Guinness, Billy Dee Williams, Anthony Daniels, Peter Mayhew, Ian McDiarmid, David Prowse, James Earl Jones, Frank Oz, Kenny Baker

These three films have, together, made roughly one billion dollars at the box office. The overall story pits Rebels against an Evil Empire in a battle for control of the galaxy. The Rebel hero is Luke Skywalker (Hamill) who, under the tutelage of aging Jedi knight Obi-Wan Kenobi (Guinness), has tapped into the Universe's mystic wellspring of power, the Force. The Evil Empire is personified by the black-robed, Jedi-turned-bad, Darth Vader (body of David Prowse, voice of James Earl Jones), who, in fact, turns out to be . . . I won't give it away. Suffice it to say that, at the end of the third film, the forces of good have triumphed and evil has learned a big lesson. These films, incredibly expensive to produce, have set the standards against which all other space war films will be measured. There are infantry-like battles, guerrilla skirmishes, and amazing space-fighter dog fights (the ones in the first film are said to be closely modeled on the biplane dogfights in William Wellman's *Wings* [1928]). These films are almost beyond criticism now, having joined the ranks of such other cultural icons as *Gone with the Wind* and *The Wizard of Oz*.

****

## THE STEEL HELMET (1951)

Lippert    Samuel Fuller (Black & white)
With Gene Evans, Robert Hutton, James Edwards, Steve Brodie, Richard Loo

A cult favorite from the redoubtable Sam Fuller, who also wrote the script and produced the film. Made for the incredibly low sum of $104,000, *The Steel Helmet* is essentially a "lost patrol" melodrama enhanced by its offbeat leading character—a grizzled, middle-aged sergeant named Zack (Evans). A survivor of a POW massacre in North Korea, Zack stays alive by playing dead, even though his helmet has been pierced by a bullet. After he is rescued by a Korean orphan, he joins with other American soldiers cut off from their units. The only officer at hand is disliked by Zack because of his lack of combat experience. There also is a black soldier (Edwards) to supply the usual military cross section, although in Fuller's hands the character is more than the usual melting-pot allusion.

The dazzling action sequences, particularly when Zack zeroes in on an enemy sniper by tracking his line of fire, are exceptional. In fact, several of them were later used by the Army's Infantry School. While Fuller doesn't glamorize war, he displays a patriotic streak that strongly supports America's involvement in Korea. One wonders what Fuller would have done with a larger budget and the full cooperation of the military.
***1/2

## THE STORY OF DR. WASSELL (1944)

Paramount    Cecil B. DeMille (Color)
With Gary Cooper, Laraine Day, Signe Hasso, Dennis O'Keefe, Stanley Ridges

DeMille based his only war movie on

THE STORY OF DR. WASSELL: Gary Cooper offers medical assistance to a shipload of casualties in Cecil B. DeMille's only sound war film.

the real-life Dr. Wassell, a medical missionary who heroically rescued several wounded GIs from the clutches of the Japanese in Java. (The doctor came to DeMille's attention when President Roosevelt mentioned him during one of his radio "fireside chats.") Old showman DeMille couldn't resist hoking up the story, however. Despite a large budget and some top Hollywood talent, all he was able to muster was a lurid spectacular complete with dancing girls and mock heroics. Cooper's fine performance in the title role is all but lost among a multitude of extras and hyped-up special effects.

*1/2

## THE STORY OF G.I. JOE (1945)

United Artists   William Wellman (Black & white)

With Burgess Meredith, Robert Mitchum, Freddie Steele, Wally Cassel, Bill Murphy

Celebrated war correspondent Ernie Pyle was one of the few journalists who reported from the front lines of World War II and not from rear-area headquarters. Wellman's tribute to Pyle is based on his sympathetic war reportage (Pyle favored the "little guy"); the result is a compelling war movie that emphasizes character over action.

Young Mitchum, in his first starring role, captures the essence of a weary combat officer with his cynical demeanor and thousand-yard stare. Meredith also is effective as the middle-aged Pyle, who marches into Italy with a unit of untried men who evolve into a group of battle-hardened veterans. As in his reportage, Pyle's soldiers aren't superheroes, just ordinary "Joes" who would rather be back with their families rather than slogging through the mud and blood of the Italian campaign. The camaraderie among the men is so brilliantly realized that when Mitchum is hit, our reaction is as if we have lost a family member.

Actual combat footage was used for many of the realistic battle sequences. At the time of its release, General Dwight D. Eisenhower called *The Story of G.I. Joe* the greatest war movie he had ever seen.

***1/2

## THE STRANGER (1946)

RKO   Orson Welles (Black & white)

With Orson Welles, Edward G. Robinson, Loretta Young, Philip Merivale, Richard Long

A durable thriller about a Nazi war criminal (Welles) hiding out as a history professor in a small college town in Connecticut. Hot on the trail, and playing a cat-and-mouse game with him, is Robinson as an Allied War Crimes Commission investigator. Young, as Welles' loving wife, never has looked more beautiful. Her nervous breakdown when she learns her husband's true identity is a masterful acting turn. As a director, Welles is enthralled with dark lighting and shadows and gives himself more than enough close-ups. But his villain is one you won't soon forget. His handling of the symbolic clock tower is brilliant.

***

## STRATEGIC AIR COMMAND (1955)

Paramount   Anthony Mann (Color)

With James Stewart, June Allyson, Frank Lovejoy, Barry Sullivan, Alex Nicol, Bruce Bennett, Jay C. Flippen

Stewart and Allyson often were paired during the 1950s as the epitome of the clean-cut, all-American married couple. Their domestic melodramas haven't aged well, however, and this one is no exception. Stewart plays a professional baseball player called up from the Air Force Reserve to pilot a B-47 for the Strategic Air Command (SAC). The film is in reality a love story about the unit's planes, which carry nuclear bombs. The aircraft are lovingly photographed, and the sound track score swells whenever they take off. Made with the full cooperation of SAC, which offered to promote it with marching bands and real planes, the film is little more than a public-relations gambit. Stewart, by the way, is a real-life retired Air Force General who served in World War II.

**

## STRIPES (1981)

Paramount   Ivan Reitman (Color)
With Bill Murray, Warren Oates, John Candy

This standard service comedy, updated by the say-anything, do-anything Hollywood of the 1980s, is from the folks who gave us the far superior *Ghostbusters*. There are a few good belly laughs when the film focuses on the fun and games of basic training, but the latter half, set in Czechoslovakia, is a bust.

**

## SUBMARINE COMMAND (1951)

Paramount   John Farrow (Black & white)
With William Holden, Don Taylor, William Bendix, Nancy Olsen, Moroni Olsen

A slow-moving underwater drama set during the Korean War. Holden plays the sub's commander, a man plagued by self-doubt because he was responsible for an incident that caused the deaths of several previous crew members. Although Holden delivers his usual appealing performance, there is very little action and what there is takes a long time to get going.

**

## SUBMARINE PATROL (1938)

20th Century-Fox   John Ford (Black & white)
With Richard Greene, Nancy Kelly, Preston Foster

There are a few good thrills left in this vintage Navy adventure, thanks to John Ford's direction. The serviceable plot has an antique sub-chaser on the trail of U-boats during World War I. Nancy Kelly is very appealing in her debut screen performance.

**

## THE SULLIVANS (1944)

20th Century-Fox   Lloyd Bacon (Black & white)
With Thomas Mitchell, Anne Baxter, Selena Royle, Edward Ryan, John Campbell, James Cardwell, John Alvin, George Otterman, Jr., Ward Bond

The true story of five brothers, the Sullivans, who died together aboard the cruiser *Juneau*, which was sunk during one of the many battles of the Guadalcanal campaign. The sleeper hit of 1944, the film attracted audiences not with spectacular battles (the sinking is shown only briefly) but with its touching re-creation of prewar America.

Mitchell and Royle play the parents of the brothers whose upbringing in Waterloo, Iowa, is one of love and strong family ties. The minutiae of everyday small-town America may seem a bit idealistic by today's standards, but in 1944 it was a way of life that was still recognizable. The actors playing the sons as youngsters and as young men are fine in their roles, and they make tangible Mitchell's and Royle's feeling of inconsolable loss. The well-knit screenplay by Mary C. McCall, Jr., was nominated for an Oscar.

***1/2

## SWING SHIFT (1984)

Paramount   Jonathan Demme (Color)
With Goldie Hawn, Kurt Russell, Ed Harris, Fred Ward, Christine Lahti

Cast in the mold of morale-building "waiting women" movies of the 1940s, Swing Shift takes a comic look at the official record and tells what allegedly really went on back home. Goldie Hawn plays a recently married woman whose husband (Ed Harris) enlists in the Navy immediately after the Japanese attack on Pearl Harbor. Going to work in a bomber factory, she initially feels insecure about her unfamiliar role, then becomes as self-confident as the men who preceded her on the assembly line.

Lonely, she has an affair with a draft-dodging 4-F trumpet player (Kurt Russell) who also works in the plant, while still professing her love for her husband (who is due to return home). Although then in her late thirties, Hawn is effective as a young innocent who goes through a rapid maturation process, and Christine Lahti, nominated for an Oscar, is even better as her worldly girlfriend. Russell overplays his smarmy musician, however, and his performance is at odds with the humorous tone of the film.

**1/2

## TAKE THE HIGH GROUND (1954)

MGM   Richard Brooks (Color)
With Richard Widmark, Karl Malden, Russ Tamblyn, Carleton Carpenter, Elaine Stewart, Steve Forrest

The only high ground here is at Fort Bliss, Texas, where a group of young conscripts is getting into shape for Korea. Putting them through the paces is Richard Widmark as a drill sergeant whose bark is worse than his bite. The military exercises have been seen in countless war movies and are overly familiar. Since the film ends with the troops graduating and going off to war, the effect is of watching spring training without seeing a baseball game. It plays like summer camp with rifles.

**

## TASK FORCE (1949)

Warner Bros.   Delmer Daves (Black & white)
With Gary Cooper, Walter Brennan, Jane Wyatt, Julie London, Wayne Morris, Bruce Bennett

Cooper takes a back seat to several aircraft carriers in this pseudo-history of naval aviation. A series of flashbacks, some in Technicolor, recall Admiral Cooper's efforts to convince his superiors of the need for these floating behemoths. The sea-air connection works quite well, despite a sometimes strident pro-Navy message.

**1/2

## THEY WHO DARE (1954)

Great Britain   Lewis Milestone (Color)
With Dirk Bogarde, Akim Tamiroff, Denholm Elliott, Gerard Oury, Eric Pohlmann

Bogarde, then England's most trustworthy leading man, helps win the war by blowing up several airstrips on the German-held island of Rhodes. The commandos, comprised of British soldiers and Greek guerrillas, are convincing, and the action frequently is exciting. Milestone's brisk direction nearly covers the fact that the plot is just a rehash of dozens of special-operations war movies.

**1/2

## THINGS TO COME (1936)

Great Britain   William Cameron Menzies
   (Black & white)

With Ralph Richardson, Raymond Massey, Cedric Hardwicke, Edward Chapman, Margaretta Scott, Sophie Stewart, Derrick de Marney

Science-fiction luminary H. G. Wells offered a cure for the ills of the Depression-bound thirties in this prophetic image of the future. Scripted by Wells from his book *The Shape of Things to Come*, the film concerns a medical doctor named John Cabal (Massey) who becomes involved in a global war. The conflict continues for decades, destroying the world's great cities and returning humanity to barbarism. Finally, after a four-year effort, Cabal and a consortium of scientists establish order in 1970 with a pacifying gas. The film then cuts to the year 2036 and a magnificent Art Deco city of the future. Cabal's grandson (Massey again), also a fighter against reactionary forces, is about to launch a manned projectile to the moon, much to the dismay of a group of humanists who feel threatened by technology. But progress can't be halted by a mere mob,

and the film ends with man reaching out to space—and the future.

Audiences didn't like this expensive movie (which cost $1 million when the average salary was $25 per week), and those who came laughed at the ridiculous notion of bombers coming over from continental Europe to devastate Britain. Wells, of course, had accurately predicted the Battle of Britain, which would begin barely three years later. The robelike costumes, by the way, provided George Lucas with the inspiration for those of his *Star Wars* series.

***

## 13 RUE MADELEINE (1947)

20th Century-Fox   Henry Hathaway (Black & white)

With James Cagney, Richard Conte, Annabella, Karl Malden, Walter Abel, Frank Latimore, Blanche Yurka, Melville Cooper, Sam Jaffe

Made in the documentary style of the *March of Time* news series (and by the same producer, Louis de Rochemont), this prickly thriller was inspired by the exploits of America's wartime intelligence agency, the OSS. Cagney plays a U.S. spymaster who parachutes into occupied France to locate a Nazi rocket base. Although the espionage techniques are somewhat dated now, the film pushes the pedal to the floor in Cagney's hand-to-hand combat scenes with the Nazis. His final capture is particularly well handled. The film's title refers to the address of Gestapo headquarters in the English Channel port of Le Havre, France.

***

## THIRTY SECONDS OVER TOKYO (1944)

MGM   Mervyn LeRoy (Black & white)

With Spencer Tracy, Van Johnson, Robert Walker, Phyllis Thaxter, Robert Mitchum, Scott McKay, Don DeFore, Tim Murdock

Star power and a famous air strike made this detailed chronicle one of the big hits of the war years. Tracy guest-stars as General Doolittle, who staged the first American air raid on Japan, in April 1942. Although the strike didn't do much damage, it alarmed the Japanese, who had believed their islands to be invulnerable to attack. In addition, the successful raid lifted American morale when it needed it most. Johnson plays pilot Ted Lawson—on whose book the script is based—who shows us how the attack was prepared, executed (from the aircraft carrier *Hornet*) and how it culminated (the pilots landed in China).

Despite the period flag-waving, the film works remarkably well, and the action scenes are first-rate. Director LeRoy intercut footage of the actual launch with cleverly faked scenes to stunning effect. Robert Surtees and Harold Rosson won Oscars for cinematography, and A. Arnold Gillespie, Donald Jahraus and Warren Newcombe shared an Academy Award for special effects. The film is over two hours in length, but every second is worthwhile viewing.

Two other films of note concerning Doolittle's daring raid are *Destination Tokyo* (1943) and *The Purple Heart* (1944).

***1/2

## 36 HOURS (1964)

MGM   George Seaton (Black & white)

With James Garner, Rod Taylor, Eva Marie Saint, John Banner, Werner Peters

A spy melodrama with a difference. Garner plays an American intelligence officer who is kidnapped while on a mission to neutral Portugal in 1944. Drugged, he wakes up in what appears to be an American hospital and is led to believe he has been suffering from amnesia and that the war ended years ago. It's all a fiendish plot, of course, hatched by the devilish Nazis to get Garner to divulge the location and date of the Allied invasion of France. Taylor is the almost-convincing Stateside doctor whose Teutonic temperament eventually gives him away. The hoax is entertaining enough, but the elaborate story shifts into low gear about halfway through and becomes just another spy melodrama.

**1/2

## THIS IS THE ARMY (1943)

Warner Bros.   Michael Curtiz (Color)

With George Murphy, Joan Leslie, George Tobias, Alan Hale, Charles Butterworth, Dolores Costello, Una Merkel, Stanley Ridges, Rosemary de Camp, Ruth Donnelly, Frances Langford, Gertrude Niesen, Kate Smith, Ronald Reagan, Joe Louis and others

Prolific forties director Curtiz does a workmanlike job of transferring Broadway's wartime Army musical to the screen. The music and lyrics are by Irving Berlin, who gets to sing his World War I showstopper "Oh, How I Hate to Get Up in the Morning," dressed as a doughboy. Many of the male cast members were actually serving in the

U.S. Army, including Lieutenant Ronald Reagan and Sergeant Joe Louis, then heavyweight boxing champion of the world. The film's considerable profits went to Army relief. Everyone involved gives the numbers their all, and it's still an entertaining period musical.

**1/2

## THREE COMRADES (1938)
MGM   Frank Borzage (Black & white)
With Robert Taylor, Franchot Tone, Margaret Sullavan, Robert Young, Lionel Atwill, Guy Kibbee, Monty Woolley

Erich Maria Remarque's follow-up to *All Quiet on the Western Front* is treated respectfully by MGM's polished assembly line. Taylor, Tone and Young, looking remarkably fit and youthful, play three disillusioned German veterans of World War I. As members of their country's "lost generation" of the 1920s, the men are neurotic and become upset by the stirrings of fascism in Germany. All three fall in love with the same girl—the vivacious Margaret Sullavan, who is dying of tuberculosis. The allusions to the Nazis are apparent, although Hollywood's censors prevented the film from being an all-out attack on Hitler (scenes of Germany's treatment of the Jews were cut, as was another showing the burning of books). The coscriptwriter was famed novelist F. Scott Fitzgerald, who received his only screen credit for this one. Audiences shunned *Three Comrades* at the time, presumably because of its downbeat characters, but it remains a highly evocative study of an unhappy time and place in history.
***

## TILL THE END OF TIME (1946)
RKO   Edward Dmytryk (Black & white)
With Guy Madison, Robert Mitchum, Dorothy McGuire, Bill Williams

This story of veterans returning home after World War II has been described as a blue-collar version of *The Best Years of Our Lives*. Ex-Marine Guy Madison has seen quite a bit of action, and when he joins his family and friends again, he has trouble readjusting. Mitchum plays a friend from the Corps who comes to visit Madison, but he, too, seems at loose ends. Dmytryk puts his fresh young cast to good use, and his message—that coming home isn't easy—still is a valid one. Surprisingly realistic for its time, the film was one of the first to cut through the wartime rhetoric of a "perfect" America.
***

## TILL WE MEET AGAIN (1944)
Paramount   Frank Borzage (Black & white)
With Ray Milland, Barbara Britton, Walter Slezak, Mona Freeman, Lucille Watson, Konstantin Shayne

Downed Air Force pilot Ray Milland escapes from Nazi-occupied France with the help of lovely nun Barbara Britton. The distinguished cast fights a losing battle with a tattered script. Soap opera fans might like the film's "timeless" angle of a forbidden love that can *never* be fulfilled (she has given herself to God).

*1/2

## TIME LIMIT (1957)

United Artists   Karl Malden (Black & white)
With Richard Widmark, Richard Basehart, June Lockhart, Delores Michaels, Martin Balsam, Rip Torn

Popular character actor Karl Malden could have had a second career, judging from this taut, well-reasoned drama—his only directorial outing. Set at the end of the Korean War, the plot concerns GI turncoats who embraced communism while being held in North Korean POW camps. Basehart plays the accused, an American captain being court-martialed, and Widmark is his accuser. As in *Rashomon*, the story is seen through several points of view, shown in gripping flashbacks of POW life. The truth, when it finally arrives, is truly surprising. A commendable first effort which would make a good double bill with *The Rack*, an earlier film tackling the same subject.

***

## A TIME TO LOVE AND A TIME TO DIE (1958)

Universal-International   Douglas Sirk (Color)
With John Gavin, Lilo Pulver, Keenan Wynn, Jock Mahoney, Thayer David, Agnes Windeck

Overlong at 153 minutes, this pretentious adaptation of Erich Maria Remarque's World War II novel has a few effective moments early on. Debuting actor John Gavin is adequate as a German enlisted man who falls in love (with imported German actress Pulver) while on leave, and then departs for his death on the Russian Front. Most of the film is pretty sudsy, and the ending, in which we are supposed to sympathize with Gavin's German and hate his Russian killer, doesn't quite come off. Remarque, who wrote the timeless World War I novel *All Quiet on the Western Front*, plays a sympathetic professor.

**

## TO BE OR NOT TO BE (1942)

United Artists   Ernst Lubitsch (Black & white)
With Jack Benny, Carole Lombard, Robert Stack, Felix Bressart, Lionel Atwill, Sig Rumann, Stanley Ridges, Tom Dugan

Black comedy was still far in the future back in '42, which is probably why this brilliant farce was criticized by some as being in bad taste. Seen today, out of its time, it's funnier than ever. Director Lubitsch somehow managed to find humor in the despair of Germany's ruthless occupation of Poland by deriding its Nazi conquerors.

Jack Benny and Carole Lombard are superb as the leaders of a local theatrical troup who manage to outwit the Nazis before making their escape to free territory. Benny is hilarious imagining he is being cuckolded by wife Lombard, who matches his wit step for step. A singularly untalented Hamlet, he finally exhibits real ability when he impersonates Adolf Hitler. Also memorable is Sig Rumann as an egotistical Gestapo officer who is flattered when he learns of his clandestine nickname: "So they call me Concentration Camp Willie," he repeats, chuckling with delight. The movie was a fitting send-off for bright comedienne Lombard, who was killed in a plane crash during a war bond drive shortly before the film was released.

****

## TO BE OR NOT TO BE (1983)

Orion   Mel Brooks, Alan Johnson (Color)
With Mel Brooks, Anne Bancroft, Charles Durning

Leave it to movie buff Mel Brooks to come up with a remake almost as funny as the original (see previous listing). Brooks actually has the edge on Jack Benny, although real-life spouse Bancroft lacks the animated delicacy of Carole Lombard. Engagingly manic, Brooks hews closely to the original script and seems to be enjoying every moment, especially when *Sweet Georgia Brown* is sung in Polish. Roly-poly Durning, playing Rumann's concentration camp commander, got a best supporting actor nomination. Brooks's codirector, Alan Johnson, choreographed the famous "Springtime for Hitler" number in *The Producers* (1968).
**1/2

## TOBRUK (1967)

Universal   Arthur Hiller (Color)
With Rock Hudson, George Peppard, Nigel Green, Jack Watson, Liam Redmond, Guy Stockwell, Leo Gordon

True, there *was* a British raid on the German-held North African port of Tobruk. And the British commandos *were* culled from the Long Range Desert Group (LRDG) and the Special Air Service (SAS). Moreover, the land-and-sea operation failed miserably. That's about all this movie gets right before digressing into a tired let's-win-the-war-for-God-and-king routine. Rock Hudson has never seemed more aptly named, and Peppard and Stockwell are hilariously miscast as German Jews. The only fresh bit is the opener, when

German frogmen capture Hudson and he learns they are Jews who had imigrated to Palestine and joined the little-known British Special Identification Group (SIG). The flamboyant battle scenes, nominated for an Oscar (they lost to the special effects animals of *Dr. Doolittle*), later turned up in Universal's *Raid on Rommel* (1971).
**

## TO HAVE AND HAVE NOT (1945)

Warner Bros.   Howard Hawks (Black & white)
With Humphrey Bogart, Lauren Bacall, Walter Brennan, Marcel Dalio, Sheldon Leonard, Hoagy Carmichael

Fishing boat captain Bogart, working out of the Vichy French island of Martinique in the Caribbean, gets involved with the French Resistance. The plot is warmed-over *Casablanca* but there's plenty of intrigue and a good romance, although you might have expected more from the combination of talents: Hemingway wrote the short story, William Faulkner coscripted and Hawks directed. Bogart and 19-year-old Bacall met on this one and were married soon after. The film has a certain nostalgic appeal, and who can resist Bacall's famous mating call ("If you need anything, just whistle")?
**1/2

## TO HELL AND BACK (1955)

Universal-International   Jesse Hibbs (Color)
With Audie Murphy, Susan Kohner, Marshall Thompson, Charles Drake, Paul Picerni, Jack Kelly, David Janssen

Audie Murphy, a war hero turned actor, plays himself in this frequently exciting recap of his military career, based on his 1949 memoirs. A veritable one-man army, Murphy won the Congressional Medal of Honor for killing almost 50 Germans with a .50-caliber machine gun from atop a burning tank. (Not even Stallone's fictional heroes can match that incredible, single action body count.) With a total of 24 decorations, the boyishly handsome Murphy used his fame to launch a postwar movie career that took him far from his impoverished upbringing as the son of a cotton sharecropper.

Murphy is surprisingly modest as well as likable for an actor given the rare honor of a movie autobiography. In the film, as in the book, Murphy credits his buddies for his extraordinary military success. He handles rifles, carbines, Thompsons, rifle grenades and the .50-caliber professionally (he knocks out a cluster of German machine-gun nests and shoots down four Germans from the hip with an M-1). There also is a classic housecleaning scene with automatic fire and grenades. Although the GIs on pass scenes are disappointing, the battlefront action is especially exciting, since we know Murphy is not merely acting but reliving his experiences.

Murphy's life story following the war also could make a compelling movie. Never quite recovered from the stress of World War II, he suffered from insomnia and nightmares and slept with a loaded Colt .45 automatic under his pillow. His taste for action apparently had become so ingrained that he arranged to go on drug busts with the Los Angeles Police Department. In 1970, after his movie career had faded

and he had gone bankrupt, he was wrongfully accused of attempted murder in a barroom brawl. Murphy died in a small-plane crash in 1971 on a business trip that he hoped would reverse his fortunes.

***

## TOKYO JOE (1949)

Columbia   Stuart Heisler (Black & white)
With Humphrey Bogart, Florence Marly, Sessue Hayakawa, Alexander Knox, Lora Lee Michel

Bogart should have opted out of this mess when he had the chance. The middle-aged lisper seems out of place as a smuggler who returns to occupied Japan to get back his ex-wife and their cute seven-year-old daughter. There also is a blackmailer on hand, compounded by a lot of threadbare plot angles.

*1/2

## TOP GUN (1986)

Paramount Tony Scott (Color)
With Tom Cruise, Kelly McGillis, Tom Skerrit, Val Kilmer, Anthony Edwards, James Tolkan

This movie-as-recruitment-poster was the top-grossing film of 1986. It's the story of young, hot-shot Navy pilot Cruise (his character's name is Maverick), who's selected to go to "Top Gun"—a training center for the best Navy fighter pilots. Once at school, he cannot, of course, play by the rules; his rival is an ace pilot (Val Kilmer) who does. Cruise ends up falling in love with their rather beautiful female astrophysics instructor (Kelly McGillis), plays volleyball shirtless at sunset to titillate the teeny-boppers, and even gets into a firefight with the

Soviets over the Indian Ocean. The flying scenes are occasionally exciting, but most often confusing. In the theater the brain-numbing roar of jet wash was only surpassed by the persistent, total, body-numbing rock score (which included several Top Ten hits). One of the most cliche-ridden war movies of all time, and the most financially successful.

**

## TORA! TORA! TORA! (1970)

20th Century-Fox  Richard O. Fleischer, Ray Kellogg, Toshio Masuda, Kinji Fukasaka (Color)

With Martin Balsam, Jason Robards, Jr., Joseph Cotten, James Whitmore, E. G. Marshall, Soh Yamamura, Edward Andrews, Leon Ames, Takahiro Tamura

Fox, hoping to repeat the whopping success of its *The Longest Day*, pulled out the stops for this elaborate pageant of the Japanese attack on Pearl Harbor. Although exceptionally well made, the film was released at the peak of the anti-Vietnam War movement and died at the box office. Budgeted at an immense $25 million (double that amount in today's dollars), it nearly ruined the studio financially and brought about the firing of chief Darryl Zanuck. As a result, Hollywood shied away from war movies for several years.

As with many films of the later postwar years, *Tora! Tora! Tora!* has no heroes or villains. The old antagonisms have relaxed into a mutual respect for military abilities and personal sacrifices. There really are three movies in one here, each of which will delight the dyed-in-the-wool military buff. Richard Fleischer handled the prewar American scenes while Toshio Masuda and Kinji Fukasaka handled similar chores in Japan. Ray Kellogg staged the stunning attack at Pearl Harbor, which won Oscars for special-effects wizards A. D. Flowers and L. B. Abbott. The expository plot is heavy going for those who aren't interested in such things. But for those who are, the script is essentially accurate, with both the United States and Japanese diplomats bumbling their countries into the "day of infamy." Moreover, we are told that even the U.S. Navy showed incompetence when it failed to heed warnings of the Japanese threat to Pearl Harbor.

Fox, recovering something of its huge investment, later rented out the magnificent attack scenes for *Midway* and *The Final Countdown* and used them in its own TV miniseries *Pearl*. It's always worth a viewing, especially for that "you are there" bang-up ending.

***

## TORPEDO RUN (1958)

MGM  Joseph Pevney (Color)

With Glenn Ford, Ernest Borgnine, Dean Jones, Diane Brewster

The personal popularity of Glenn Ford turned this routine submarine story into a 1950's hit despite its out-of-fuel pace. Its premise still is intriguing, however, with submarine commander Ford (and first mate Borgnine) being ordered to sink a merchant ship on which Ford's family is sailing. Turns out that the nasty Japs were using the vessel to screen their aircraft carrier.

Ford pursues it with a vengeance and finally sinks the carrier in Tokyo Bay.
**

## TOWN WITHOUT PITY (1961)

United Artists   Gottfried Reinhardt (Black & white)

With Kirk Douglas, E. G. Marshall, Christine Kaufmann, Robert Blake, Richard Jaeckel, Barbara Rutting

Army Major Douglas defends four American soldiers accused of rape in postwar Germany. To get them off, Douglas discredits the girl in a brutal courtroom scene. (This valid plot device became commonplace in similar films of the postfeminist seventies and eighties.) Shot on location, the film has an authentic feel, but director Reinhardt dilutes the drama with his heavy-handed messages about fair play and love thy neighbor. Best is the lovely Christine Kaufmann as a victimized victim.
**

## THE TRAIN (1964)

United Artists   John Frankenheimer (Black & white)

With Burt Lancaster, Paul Scofield, Michel Simon, Jeanne Moreau, Albert Remy, Wolfgang Preiss

A train is steaming its way through the French countryside on its way to Germany. On board are priceless paintings looted from the galleries of Paris and destined for Hitler's art museum. Playing a key part in the plot to retain France's cultural heritage is railway engineer Burt Lancaster, working with the Resistance. His mission is to stop but not to destroy the train and its irreplaceable cargo. Opposing his

formidable efforts is Paul Scofield as the German officer in charge, who is just as determined to get the paintings to Germany.

Director Frankenheimer underlines the clash of wills with some thrilling action sequences staged aboard the scene-stealing locomotive. The performances are superior, and the story unfolds in a straightforward, documentary-style manner. The film's only real fault is that is wasn't shot in color, which would have allowed us to appreciate the paintings and the exquisite French countryside.
***1/2

## TWELVE O'CLOCK HIGH (1949)

20th Century-Fox   Henry King (Black & white)

With Gregory Peck, Dean Jagger, Hugh Marlowe, Gary Merrill, Millard Mitchell, Robert Arthur

A superior drama about a B-17 bomber command in the early days of World War II. Peck assumes command of the group after officer Merrill is relieved of command because of slackening morale. Peck's job is to rebuild the bomber crews' faltering confidence, which he proceeds to do while almost cracking up under the strain. For their part, the airmen have to fly daylight bombing attacks on Germany without fighter escorts, while trying to outmaneuver enemy fighters and clouds of flak from antiaircraft guns.

The performances by all concerned are first-rate; Jagger got a best supporting actor Oscar for his portrayal of a ground officer who backs Peck when others detest him. The sound-stage set, simulating an Army Air Corps base in

Great Britain, looks like what it is, but the combat scenes are the real thing, shot during World War II. This is a film by and for adults that becomes more enjoyable as time passes.

****

## THE 25th HOUR (1967)

France/Yugoslavia   Henri Verneuil (Color)
With Anthony Quinn, Virna Lisi, Michael Redgrave, Alexander Knox

A harrowing tale of a Romanian peasant (Quinn) caught up in the holocaust of World War II. Initially a sympathetic character, the dim-witted peasant eventually becomes a concentration camp guard without really knowing what he is doing or why. He eventually becomes aware of the meaning of the war, although it doesn't help him much. Director Verneuil's intention obviously was to show the effects of the war on a well-meaning Everyman in central Europe. The film never quite rises to its aspirations, however, although it's engrossing as an offbeat adventure.

**1/2

## TWILIGHT'S LAST GLEAMING (1977)

Allied Artists   Robert Aldrich (Color)
With Burt Lancaster, Richard Widmark, Charles Durning, Paul Winfield, Richard Jaeckel, Burt Young, Roscoe Lee Browne

Director Aldrich has made some powerful war movies (*The Dirty Dozen*, *Attack!*). This one's not quite up to his usual high standards, however, and it's often confusing. Aldrich frames his anti-Vietnam War statement as a farfetched tale of political and military intrigue. Lancaster plays a cashiered Air Force general who takes over a guided-missile silo so he can blackmail the president. The plot concerns a secret document that has to do with Vietnam. If released to the public, it would have enormous (and unexplained) impact, which is why Lancaster and his fellow missile hijackers are ready to start World War III.

The split-screen technique adds to the suspense (although less so on the small screen), and the performances keep the ball rolling. Lancaster, Widmark (as a general) and Durning (as the president) should hold your interest.

***

## TWO WOMEN (1962)

Italy/France   Vittorio de Sica (Black & white)
With Sophia Loren, Jean-Paul Belmondo, Raf Vallone, Eleanora Brown

Loren gives one of her most powerful performances as a wartime Italian mother who, with her teenage daughter, is gang-raped by Allied soldiers. The daughter's life is nearly ruined, but with the help of her strong-willed mama she survives the tragedy.

Loren received her only best actress Oscar for the role, which fell to her when Anna Magnani decided she wasn't old enough to play the mother (Loren was slated for the daughter). In the novel by Alberto Moravia, the rapists are identified as brutal American GIs. Here they have been changed to lusty Morrocans, apparently to make the film more palatable to the American market. A deeply affecting film, directed with sensitivity by de Sica.

***1/2

### UNCOMMON VALOR (1983)

Paramount   Ted Kotcheff (Color)
With Gene Hackman, Fred Ward, Reb Brown, Harold Sylvester, Tim Thomerson, Patrick Swayze, Robert Stack, Tex Cobb

The sleeper hit of the 1983 Christmas season, *Uncommon Valor* signaled that the military was on the rebound. Gene Hackman plays a Marine colonel whose MIA son is captured in Vietnam in the film's prologue. (A large recon patrol abandons five men after losing two of three helicopters to heavy small-arms fire.) After a decade of sleuthing in the back alleys of Bangkok, Hackman locates his son's POW camp. With the backing of wealthy businessman Robert Stack—whose son also is an MIA—he assembles a rescue team from his son's old unit.

Among the film's reworked cliches is the unit's cross section of American types—1980s-style. There's Blaster (Reb Brown), a suntanned surfer and an expert in demolition; Wilkes (Fred Ward), an ex-tunnel rat who's an expert in silent killing; Charts (Tim Thomerson), a prematurely gray, crop-dusting pilot on the verge of burnout; and Major Johnson (Harold Sylvester), a successful hospital administrator reluctant to return to battle. Finally, there's Sailor (Tex Cobb), a borderline psychopath who fits the stereotype of the Vietnam veteran.

After a gung-ho training session in the Texas desert, the group flies to Bangkok and travels to the "Golden

UNCOMMON VALOR: Armed with a potpourri of weapons, a POW rescue team trains for its mission. From left to right, Randall "Tex" Cobb with a German MG-42 machine gun, Patrick Swayze with a BAR and Fred Ward, Reb Brown, Gene Hackman, Tim Thomerson and Harold Sylvester with M-16s.

Triangle"—the point at which Laos, Burma and Thailand converge. The mission nearly is scrubbed, however, when the CIA confiscates their high-tech weaponry. But no matter. The men look up an old drug contact and buy bargain-basement Thompson sub-machine guns, M-1 rifles and an antiquated 57mm recoilless rifle. Although the film's final half hour is rife with action and heroics, it's doubtful that so few men could inflict so much damage with such ancient weapons.

Technically, however, *Uncommon Valor* is perfect. For once, the men look as if they know what they are doing, especially Hackman, who had served in the Marine Corps during the late 1940s. (The actors were trained by Vietnam veteran and weapons expert Chuck Taylor, who receives screen credit.) The training sequences, helicopter scenes and explosive special effects blend together for an exciting war movie.

\*\*\*\*

## UNDER FIRE (1983)

Orion Roger Spottiswoode (Color)
With Nick Nolte, Gene Hackman, Joanna Cassidy, Jean-Louis Trintignant, Ed Harris, Richard Masur, Rene Enriques

This was the first major American film to look at the situation in Central America. The time is 1979, and the three stars are journalists, in Nicaragua to cover the rise of the Sandinistas and the fall of the Somoza regime. We follow Nolte, a cynical "war-junkie" photographer, as his sacred professional objectivity erodes in the face of brutal injustice, leading him to eventually help the Sandinistas by committing the ultimate photojournalist sin—falsifying a photograph. In a subsequent run-in with police, Hackman (another fine performance as usual) is killed. Nolte and Cassidy run, barely elude capture and are just saved as Somoza is overthrown and the Sandinistas march triumphantly into Managua. The film is at its best with the three journalists and their professional-code-versus-moral-responsibility anguish. The war action is harrowing and the film conveys well a sense of the bewildering confusion endemic to the region.

\*\*1/2

## UP FROM THE BEACH (1965)

20th Century-Fox  Robert Parrish (Black & white)
With Cliff Robertson, Broderick Crawford, Irina Demick, Francoise Rosay, Red Buttons, Marius Goring

The beach is Normandy, where an American squad led by Robertson liberates a small French town the day after the Allied landing. Still to be freed, however, are several French civilians held hostage by SS troopers in a farmhouse. It's Robertson's job to resolve the situation. A good premise, but how is it possible to fall in love in the midst of history's greatest and most difficult invasion?

\*\*

## UP FRONT (1951)

Universal-International  Alexander Hall (Black & white)
With David Wayne, Tom Ewell

Wayne and Ewell do a pretty good imitation of Bill Mauldin's Willie and Joe, the leading characters of a comic strip made popular in the Armed Forces newspaper *Stars & Stripes*. There are a few funny bits, but the World War II plot (on the Italian front) fails to live up to Mauldin's sense of humor or reality. Mauldin's pen-and-ink characters were funny in themselves, due to the illustrator's knowing caricatures of fighting ex-civilians.

**

## UP IN ARMS (1944)

RKO    Elliott Nugent (Color)
With Danny Kaye, Dinah Shore, Dana Andrews, Lyle Talbot, Elisha Cook, Jr., Vera Ellen

Comedian Danny Kaye, playing a hypochondriac draftee, made his film debut in this splashy musical, produced by Sam Goldwyn. A big hit in its time, the film launched Kaye on a brilliant movie career and boasts an early appearance of top recording and radio star (back then) Dinah Shore. Enjoyable as a period piece, although Kaye's mugging may grate on your nerves.

**

## UP PERISCOPE (1959)

Warner Bros.    Gordon Douglas (Color)
With James Garner, Edmond O'Brien, Carleton Carpenter, Alan Hale, Jr.

A formula submarine film with Garner, fresh from his TV *Maverick* success, being given little to do while being groomed for stardom. The action scenes are adequate, but they've been done before and done better. Wait for *Run Silent*, *Run Deep* or *Destination Tokyo*.

*1/2

## THE VICTORS (1963)

Columbia    Carl Foreman (Black & white)
With George Peppard, George Hamilton, Eli Wallach, Vincent Edwards, Mervyn Johns, Melina Mercouri, Romy Schneider, Jeanne Moreau, Senta Berger, Albert Finney

More a series of brief vignettes than an integrated film this epic antiwar movie follows a squad of American soldiers through World War II Europe. There are several excellent action scenes counterbalanced by some mediocre performances. Foreman does make war look unattractive and, by film's end, you will have seen Allied war crimes, profiteering, and racism behind the lines. Apparently there were no good guys in the war. But the romantic liaisons, for once, are believable. Mercouri, Schneider, Moreau and Berger are appealing as women of the world who will do anything to survive.

A good try on Foreman's part, but he has put too much into the story without weaving together the big picture he was aiming for.

**1/2

## VICTORY (1981)

Paramount    John Huston (Color)
With Michael Caine, Sylvester Stallone, Pele, Max Von Sydow

Another banal attempt to elicit humor from World War II German POW camps. Stallone, who trimmed down

VICTORY: Max Von Sydow plays a Nazi officer with good intentions. After World War II, some films made Germans and Japanese humane characters.

to 159 pounds from his *Rocky* weight of 200 to look like an underfed prisoner, is as unbelievable in the role as he is uninteresting. Caine seems to have telephoned in his part, and director Huston apparently was interested only in staging an elaborate soccer game between the German captors and the POWs (professional soccer players actually staged the match). Famed ex-soccer star Pele gets the most applause onscreen because of a slow-motion cartwheel kick that is instantly replayed in slow motion. Unfortunately for Stallone and company, you can't build a movie from a soccer goal and a lovable slob.
*

## VON RYAN'S EXPRESS (1965)

20th Century-Fox   Mark Robson (Color)
With Frank Sinatra, Trevor Howard, Sergio Fantoni, Edward Mulhare, Brad Dexter

A mass break from an Italian POW camp during World War II provides the action for this fast-paced movie. Sinatra does a credible job as an American Air Force colonel named Von Ryan who finds himself in command of a group of mostly British POWs. For once, he doesn't hog the screen and instead allows the supporting cast to turn in some well-drawn performances of their own. Howard is especially effective as his gruff second-in-command.

After their escape, the men hijack a German freight train, and the chase is on. Pursued by everything the Nazis can muster, they manage to hold their own and make their way to safety. Best scene has the POWs returning fire with Schmeisser submachine guns, liberated from the train, while being strafed by enemy planes. If *Von Ryan's Express* has a fault, it's because it makes war look like good, clean fun.
**1/2

## THE WACKIEST SHIP IN THE ARMY (1960)

Columbia   Richard Murphy (Color)
With Jack Lemmon, Ricky Nelson, John Lund, Chips Rafferty, Tom Tully

Director Murphy skillfully blends comedy and drama in this engaging fantasy. Sailing expert Lemmon is drafted into manning a useless old boat and commanding a group of useless sailors to spy in Japanese waters during World War II. The jokes come naturally, and the humor never is forced. Lemmon is at his comic best, and even teen idol Ricky Nelson isn't bad. The photography, by the way, is stunning. **1/2

## WAKE ISLAND (1942)
Paramount   John Farrow (Black & white)
With Brian Donlevy, Robert Preston, Macdonald Carey, Albert Dekker, William Bendix, Mikhail Rasumny, Walter Abel

The first World War II movie to show an American military unit in action, *Wake Island* was released to great acclaim only nine months after the island's fall. For once, Hollywood didn't need to embellish the truth. Before the war, Wake had been a refueling stop for Pan American's Clipper flights to the Orient. Later it also became an important U.S. outpost facing the Japanese Pacific island garrisons in the Gilberts and Marshalls.

The Navy began constructing an airfield on the island early in 1941, with less than 500 Marines as protection, along with more than 1,000 civilian construction workers. The Japanese were on to the installation, however, and two hours after bombing Pearl Harbor, they attacked Wake from the air. The Americans on Wake fought back valiantly and managed to hold out for two weeks before the island fortress fell.

The film uses the standard ingredients that have come to define the war movie: a friendly rivalry between two Marines (Preston and Bendix); a reluctant civilian hero (Dekker); and a ramrod-straight commanding officer (Donlevy). The Japanese, as usual, are unspeakaby vicious and pull heavily on the trigger whenever they shoot Americans. There also is the mandatory flag-waving of the era, although this doesn't get in the way of the action.

*Wake Island* set a high standard for the many war movies that followed, but few have matched its winning synthesis of compelling performances, fast-paced story, good camerawork and thrilling combat scenes. After more than 40 years of changing political realities, the film holds up well and never misfires. ****

## WAKE ME WHEN IT'S OVER (1960)
20th Century-Fox   Mervyn LeRoy (Color)
With Dick Shawn, Ernie Kovacs, Margo Moore, Don Knotts, Jack Warden

Shawn has his moments as a Bilko-like veteran called back into the Army by mistake, but the great TV comedian Kovacs doesn't get enough good lines. The comedy goes a bit overboard when Shawn and Kovacs (as his CO) build a luxury hotel from Army surplus on a Pacific island liberated from the Japanese. There are a lot of moaners among the one-liners, and the film is aptly named. **

## A WALK IN THE SUN (1946)
20th Century-Fox   Lewis Milestone (Black & white)
With Dana Andrews, Richard Conte, Sterling Holloway, George Tyne, John Ireland, Herbert Rudley, Richard Benedict, Norman Lloyd, Lloyd Bridges, Huntz Hall

One of the most memorable of war movies, *A Walk in the Sun* concentrates on the effects of combat on a small unit of veteran soldiers during a fateful morning in 1943. Their objective is a German stronghold during the invasion of Salerno, Italy, which has a telling impact on each of them. Robert Rossen's script is faithful to Harry Brown's authentic-sounding novel, and director Milestone stresses the human rather than the technical side of combat.

None of the soldiers is a hero in the usual sense: Some break under the strain of battle, others courageously charge machine-gun fire, and still others become casualties before they reach their objectives. By the film's end, the viewer has experienced the men's fears, exhaustion and hunger, all of which are as much a part of battle as bullets. Despite its emphasis on character, the film has two exquisitely choreographed fighting sequences: the platoon's ambush of a German half-track with small arms and grenades; and a frontal assault on a farmhouse, shot from behind Nazi machine-gun positions. Andrews and Conte are standouts in the large cast, with Ireland, Tyne and Bridges also making outstanding contributions.

****

## WAR HUNT (1962)

United Artists  R. Denis Sanders (Black & white)

With John Saxon, Robert Redford, Charles Aidman, Sidney Pollack, Tommy Matsuda

This unpleasant film deals with a subject few are comfortable with—men who love war. Saxon is properly grim as the sadistic soldier who enjoys killing enemy in Korea. Redford, making his movie debut, isn't remarkable, but he's competent as a soldier who becomes aware of Saxon's psychological problems. Not your typical war movie but original enough to make it worth viewing.

**1/2

## THE WAR LOVER (1962)

Columbia   Philip Leacock (Black & white)

With Steve McQueen, Robert Wagner, Shirley Anne Field, Michael Crawford

McQueen delivers an exceptional performance as a hotshot B-17 bomber pilot who loves his job. His physical reaction when the bombs drop on their targets is almost orgasmic. The men who fly with him are a bit put off by this strange habit, but they tolerate it because they consider him a lucky charm as well as a good pilot. But on the ground they find him a cocky, grandstanding bore. Wagner plays his copilot, the one who dislikes him most because of the way he treats his girl (Field) and his crew. The plot is only so-so, but when *The War Lover* takes to the air, it really soars. Some of the exciting footage was shot during World War II, including a German fighter attack on the B-17s as they attempt to fly through a hail of defensive fire.

**1/2

## WATCH ON THE RHINE (1943)

Warner Bros.   Herman Shumlin (Black & white)

With Bette Davis, Paul Lukas, Geraldine Fitzgerald, Lucile Watson, George Coulouris, Henry Daniell, Kurt Katch

Based on a successful Broadway play by Lillian Hellman (and scripted by her

WATCH ON THE RHINE: Paul Lukas comforts Bette Davis. Lukas won a best actor Oscar for his portrayal of an expatriate German.

lover Dashiell Hammett), this dated polemic is still worth a look, especially for the Academy Award-winning performance of Paul Lukas. Cast as a dissident German living in prewar America, Lukas must decide whether to retire in safety or to return home and fight the Nazi menace. Also good are his villainous visitors: slimy Kurt Katch, marble-eyed Henry Daniell and the slickly duplicitous George Coulouris, who plot Nazi atrocities at Lukas's table. Nominal star Bette Davis, as Lukas's wife, is excessively mannered, however, and the direction by stage director/producer Herman Shumlin is ponderous and slow. The exchange of ideas, although interesting, soon becomes a bore.
**1/2

## WHAT DID YOU DO IN THE WAR, DADDY? (1966)

United Artists   Blake Edwards (Color)
With James Coburn, Dick Shawn, Harry Morgan, Aldo Ray, Sergio Fantoni, Giovanna Ralli, Leon Askin, Carroll O'Connor

An uneven slapstick comedy that tries to make you believe the Italian campaign was one of World War II's greatest parties. There are a few humorous situations before the jokes begin to wear thin. Someone must have thought it was a cute idea.
*1/2

## WHAT NEXT, CORPORAL HARGROVE? (1945)

MGM   Richard Thorpe (Black & white)
With Robert Walker, Keenan Wynn, Cameron Mitchell, Chill Wills

Robert Walker makes corporal and takes his comedy act to France in this sequel to *See Here, Private Hargrove*. It doesn't come close to the earlier film for laughs and winning charm, although Walker has more women to flirt with than he had in basic training.
*1/2

## WHAT PRICE GLORY? (1952)

20th Century-Fox   John Ford (Color)
With James Cagney, Dan Dailey, Corinne Calvet, James Gleason, William Demarest, Robert Wagner

Cagney and Dailey are the rival Marines in this remake of Raoul Walsh's 1926 silent classic. As Flagg and Quirt, the two gyrenes compete with each other throughout the film. Their drinking, loving and fighting bouts are high-water marks in the annals of macho movie characterizations. But even with these exceptional guys, it's still the original *What Price Glory?* that scores a knockout punch.

**

## WHERE EAGLES DARE (1969)

MGM    Brian G. Hutton (Color)

With Richard Burton, Clint Eastwood, Patrick Wymark, Robert Beatty, Mary Ure, Donald Houston

Burton handles most of the dialogue in this rousing, twisty war adventure, while Eastwood takes care of most of the action. The pair are members of a special operations team parachuting into Germany wearing Wehrmacht uniforms. As it happens, Burton and Eastwood soon are on their own, since their intelligence unit in England was infiltrated by Nazi moles. With the help of two local women agents they ferret out the spy back at headquarters before blasting their way out of an impregnable castle and making an exciting escape via cable car, school bus and airplane. The plot has almost nothing to do with reality, and in its way it's a send-up of all those behind-the-lines commando movies. (The script was adapted from the novel by war fantasist Alistair MacLean.)

Burton delivers his usual professional performance, and Eastwood seems to be rehearsing his Dirty Harry persona as a superwarrior who kills bad guys without emotion. At one point he picks up a pair of Schmeisser submachine guns and fires not one but both at the pursuing Germans. And from the hip yet! Despite its somewhat satiric content, the film is a thrilling action trip, with a bonus surprise ending.

***1/2

## WHO'LL STOP THE RAIN (1979)

United Artists    Karol Reisz (Color)

With Nick Nolte, Tuesday Weld, Michael Moriarty, Anthony Zerbe

Ex-Marine Nolte becomes a merchant mariner and smuggles heroin from Vietnam into America for friend Moriarty. But the deal goes bad, and Nolte finds himself on the run with the smack and Moriarty's wife (Weld). Although their pursuers are nasty characters, Nolte often is just as ruthless. The film's source is the novel *Dog Soldiers*.

*1/2

## THE WILD BLUE YONDER (1952)

**Also titled** *Thunder Across the Pacific; Bombs Over Japan*

Republic    Allan Dwan (Black & white)

With Wendell Corey, Vera Hruba Ralston, Forrest Tucker, Phil Harris, Walter Brennan

B-movie nonsense about B-29 raids against Japan late in World War II. Not bad if you can concentrate on the sleek, silvery bombers in flight and blank out the bland performances on the ground. It plays like an old-fashioned recruiting poster.

*1/2

## THE WILD GEESE (1978)

Allied Artists    Andrew V. McLaglen (Color)

With Richard Burton, Roger Moore, Richard Harris, Hardy Kruger, Stewart Granger, Frank Finlay

Mercenaries have been around for centuries, but not until the 1960s did they begin to enjoy a certain media appeal. This was the result of the actions of hired soldiers in the Congo and, later, in Nigeria. Burton plays one of these hard-drinking pros, hired to rescue a former African premier from imprisonment by his desposer. Financer of the job is the head (Granger) of a multinational conglomerate that wants mining rights to the country, agreed to by the jailed politician. Recruiting old friend Harris and saving Moore from a London mob hit, Burton then enlists other like volunteers for the mission.

The training takes place in a neighboring African country, and subsequently they jump in the target area in HALO (high-altitude, low-opening) parachutes. After rescuing the desposed leader, they are double-crossed by the corporation, which has found another way to get the mineral rights. Naturally, it doesn't want to pay them and, naturally, the mercs are determined to get what's coming to them. The action gets pretty heavy, with the mercs handling modern assault rifles, submachine guns and rocket launchers in textbook style. Unnamed, the other side is assumed to be the bad guys because they have Cuban and East German advisers.

As with most mercenary war movies set in Africa, the action is more akin to a cowboy movie, with the soldiers of fortune playing the role of the cavalry rescuing settlers from marauding Indians. There are lots of gasoline-simulated grenade and rocket explosions that toss enemy troops into the air like cartoon figures. Burton, Moore and Harris make a great team and really seem to be enjoying their roles, as does the good supporting cast. Even if it glorifies men of dubious morals, *The Wild Geese* is a thrilling war movie.

***1/2

## WING AND A PRAYER (1944)

20th Century-Fox   Henry Hathaway (Black & white)

With Dana Andrews, Charles Bickford, Don Ameche, Cedric Hardwicke, Richard Jaeckel

The title of this run-of-the-mill tale of aircraft carrier pilots during World War II refers to a popular description of their landing maneuvers when returning from battle: "Coming in on a wing and a prayer." Among the good action scenes is a thrilling attempt to recover an aircraft on a moonless night under a security blackout. But what can you say about a film in which a pilot sings "Deep in the Heart of Texas" while keeping the beat with his machine gun? Stanley Kubrick later played a similar scene for black comedy in *Dr. Strangelove*.

**

## WINGED VICTORY (1944)

20th Century-Fox   George Cukor (Black & white)

With Lon McCallister, Jeanne Crain, Edmond O'Brien, Jane Ball, Mark Daniels, Don Taylor, Judy Holliday

Based on Moss Hart's patriotic Broadway play, this tribute to the U.S. Army Air Corps features a cast of real-life airmen (except for the girls). Among those emoting and/or performing with the Army Air Corps Chorus are Karl Malden, Red Buttons, Gary Merrill, Barry Nelson and Lee J. Cobb. The routine plot has the uniformed characters training for active duty. The actors are enthusiastic, but it's a waste of manpower because there isn't much of a story.

**

## A YANK IN THE RAF (1941)

20th Century-Fox   Henry King (Black & white)
With Tyrone Power, Betty Grable, John Sutton, Reginald Gardiner

Producer Darryl F. Zanuck pulled out all the stops when he decided to drum up support for the British war effort. He assembled his top box-office stars, Tyrone Power and Betty Grable, added plenty of soaring air battles, seasoned the mix with a bit of swing music and came up with *A Yank in the RAF*.

Power plays an adventurer who becomes embroiled in the war after he ferries a bomber from Canada to England. His inspiration proves to be old girlfriend Grable, whom he spots emerging from a taxi (actually, its Grable's famous legs he sees first). Deciding to enlist in the RAF to win back her love, he coincidentally finds himself assigned to a squadron with a bloke competing for her affections. Power's first mission has him tossing pamphlets out of a bomber door over Berlin without a safety belt. Of course he scores a direct hit when he drops the leaflets by the bundle on a searchlight, all the while singing "I've Been Working on the Railroad."

The real heroics finally begin when one Brit dives into a searchlight to save his mates. Next, Power and his rival (Sutton) crash-land in Holland and make an unbelievable escape. After arriving in Britain, Power—until then a bomber pilot—seemingly overnight becomes a top-notch fighter pilot before being shot down over Dunkirk. Given up for dead, he appears—to Grable's and the audience's relief—among the walking wounded evacuees saved there. (An earlier script had Power losing his life, but at the request of the British, he was saved to avert misgivings on the part of Americans that their boys were dying for a foreign cause.)

Zanuck, who made no bones about his full support of the Allied cause, was called a warmonger for making the picture, a charge he didn't deny, especially since the picture proved to be one of the year's most popular releases.

\*\*\*

## A YANK ON THE BURMA ROAD (1942)

**Also titled** *China Caravan*

MGM   George B. Seitz (Black & white)
With Laraine Day, Barry Nelson, Stuart Crawford, Keye Luke

Released barely seven weeks after Pearl Harbor, *A Yank on the Burma Road* was America's first wartime war movie. The plot has a mercenary truck driver (Nelson) meeting up with a gorgeous damsel in distress (Day) stranded in China. Nelson's Yank is a standard cynic who becomes a fighter for democracy when he realizes the full extent of the threat. Add Crawford, and Day becomes the hypotenuse of the requisite love triangle. Add Chinese guerrillas who need American know-how to defeat the Japanese and you have one mess of a movie.

\*1/2

## YANKS (1979)

Columbia   John Schlesinger (Color)
With Richard Gere, Vanessa Redgrave, William Devane, Lisa Eichorn

Love blossoms between American GIs stationed in England and some local, rosy-cheeked beauties. *Yanks* does

right by the accurately re-created 1940s sets, costumes and slang, but the story doesn't live up to its surroundings. Redgrave, playing a married woman having an affair with Devane, is at her glowing best. But Gere acts as if World War II is simply a great way to meet girls; somehow he doesn't fit the persona of the soldier he plays. At more than two hours, *Yanks* is yards too long and boring from beginning to end.
*1/2

## THE YEAR OF LIVING DANGEROUS-LY (1983)

UA/MGM   Peter Weir (Color)
With Mel Gibson, Linda Hunt, Sigourney Weaver

The year is 1965 and the place is Indonesia, where a civil war is being brutally put down by the military. Dangerously involved in the country's political machinations is Australian journalist Mel Gibson, whose lover (Sigourney Weaver), employed by the British embassy, has given him critical inside information. Gibson meanwhile has an inside track to the rebels via his pint-sized cameraman (Linda Hunt, who won a supporting actress Oscar, playing a man). The color photography is stunning and there's an authentic hothouse ambience, but the film comes to an unsatisfying conclusion. Unless you're conversant with Indonesian politics, you may be confused.

**1/2

## THE YOUNG LIONS (1958)

20th Century-Fox   Edward Dmytryk (Black & white)
With Marlon Brando, Montgomery Clift, Dean Martin, Mai Britt, Barbara Rush, Maximilian Schell

THE YEAR OF LIVING DANGEROUSLY: Mel Gibson plays an Australian journalist covering the 1965 Indonesian Civil War.

This ponderous adaptation of Irwin Shaw's popular war novel is worthwhile whenever Brando is onscreen. Playing a blond Nazi officer who has difficulty accepting his orders let alone following them, Brando more than suggests the futility and disillusionment experienced by many Germans. Clift has a few good moments as a Jewish soldier pitted against some violent anti-Semites (a character not unlike his Prewitt of *From Here to Eternity*), but Martin is out of his depth as a man of the world drafted into the Army. There's not much action after Brando's ambush of a British patrol in North Africa, but the few combat scenes that follow are well staged and exciting.

A great outing for fans of Brando (who had Shaw's brutalized Nazi changed into a sensitive soul), but otherwise it's a tepid brew.
**

## ZULU (1963)
MGM   Cy Endfield (Color)
With Stanley Baker, Jack Hawkins, Ulla Jacobsson, James Booth, Nigel Green, Patrick Magee, Michael Caine

In 1879 British troops battled the Zulu tribe for control of Natal, a cornerstone of modern South Africa. This spectacular colonial war movie depicts one of the battles fought at an isolated church mission on a mountain called Roarke's Drift. One hundred British troops held off more than 4,000 African warriors in this amazing military stand, which won 11 of the soldiers the Victoria Cross, Britain's highest decoration for bravery.

The film pits *impis*, Zulu regiments of 1,000 men each, in ferocious combat against the red-jacketed infantrymen. The sight of the horde closing in on the mission is truly epic, and when the action switches to brutal hand-to-hand combat, *Zulu* becomes an inspirational study in heroism on both sides. The repeated charges bring one crescendo after another, giving the audience barely a chance to relax before another stirring scene appears. There are no large secondary explosions, only rapid fire from antique, single-shot Martini lever-actuated rifles. The use of the descendants of the actual combatants as extras gives the film a heightened sense of reality, and they duplicate the intricate maneuvers of their ancestors with skillful ease.

Baker, who also coproduced, commands the detachment—and the picture—with an authoritative performance. And Caine, in his debut role, is prissily effective as the effete second in command. Green's superefficient sergeant-major also is well acted. The war isn't of particular interest to most Americans, but the film is an unforgettable motion-picture experience.
****

## ZULU DAWN (1979)
Great Britain   Cy Endfield (Color)
With Burt Lancaster, Peter O'Toole, Simon Ward

Endfield, who directed *Zulu*, subsequently made this sequel about the massacre of 1,500 soldiers by the Zulu tribe at the Battle of Isandhlwana in Natal (now South Africa). Though

Endfield re-creates the battle with real Zulus and splendid results, the performances aren't on a par with his earlier film. See it for the action only, and don't be surprised when Lancaster and O'Toole, top-billed, turn up in cameo roles. A double bill with *Zulu*, might make this one look better than it is.

**1/2

# BIBLIOGRAPHY

Baxter, John. *Sixty Years of Hollywood*. South Brunswick, N.J., and New York: A. S. Barnes and Company, 1973.

Bonds, Ray (ed.). *The Encylopedia of Land Warfare in the 20th Century*. New York: Thomas Y. Crowell Company, 1976.

Brown, Jay A., and the Editors of *Consumer Guide*. *Rating the Movies*. New York: Beekman House, 1982.

Butler, Ivan. *The War Film*. South Brunswick, N.J., and New York: A. S. Barnes and Company, 1974.

Cowie, Peter (ed.). *A Concise History of the Cinema*, Volume 2: *Since 1940*. New York: A. S. Barnes and Company, 1971.

Gregg, John. *1943: The Victory That Never Was*. New York: Hill and Wang, 1980.

Griffith, Richard, and Arthur Mayer. *The Movies*. New York: Simon & Schuster, 1970.

Knightley, Phillip. *The First Casualty*. New York: Harcourt Brace Jovanovich, 1975.

Ladd, James. *Commandos and Rangers*. New York: St. Martin's Press, 1978.

Manvell, Roger. *Films and the Second World War*. New York: Dell Publishing Company, 1974.

Morella, Joe, Edward Z. Epstein and John Griggs. *The Films of World War II*. Secaucus, N.J.: The Citadel Press, 1973.

Morris, Eric, Christopher Chant, Curt Johnson and H. P. Willmot. *Weapons and Warfare of the 20th Century*. Secaucus, N.J.: Derbibooks, 1975.

Pickard, Roy. *The Award Movies*. New York: Schocken Books, 1981.

Ricci, Mark, Boris Zmijewsky and Steve Zmijewsky. *The Films of John Wayne*. New York: The Citadel Press, 1970.

Sklar, Robert. *Movie-Made America: A Cultural History of American Movies*. New York: Vintage Books, 1975.

Smith, John M., and Tim Cawkwell. *The World Encyclopedia of the Film*. New York: Galahad Books, 1972.

Smith, Julian. *Looking Away: Hollywood and Vietnam*. New York: Charles Scribner's Sons, 1975.

Wagner, Ray. *American Combat Planes*. Garden City, N.Y.: Doubleday & Company, 1968.

Wheeler, Richard. *A Special Valor*. New York: Harper & Row, 1983.

White, David Manning, and Richard Averson. *The Celluloid Weapon: Social Comment in the American Film.* Boston: Beacon Press, 1972.

Winterbotham, F.W. *The Ultra Secret.* New York: Harper & Row, 1974.

Young, Peter. *The World Almanac Book of World War II.* Englewood Cliffs, N.J.: Prentice-Hall, 1981.

# INDEX